Mothers without Citizenship

Mothers without Citizenship

Asian Immigrant Families and the Consequences of Welfare Reform

Lynn Fujiwara

University of Minnesota Press

Minneapolis

London

Published by the University of Minnesota Press
111 Third Avenue South, Suite 290
Minneapolis, MN 55401-2520
http://www.upress.umn.edu

Library of Congress Cataloging-in-Publication Data

Fujiwara, Lynn, 1964–
Mothers without citizenship : Asian immigrant families and
the consequences of welfare reform / Lynn Fujiwara.
p.   cm.
Includes bibliographical references and index.
ISBN: 978-0-8166-5076-7 (pb : alk. paper)
1. Women immigrants—Services for—United States.   2. Asian American
women—Services for—United States.   3. Children of immigrants—
Services for—United States.   4. Public welfare—United States.
I. Title.
JV6602.F85   2008
362.83'9—dc22
2007039512

For Steve, Kyra, Joanna, and Martin

Contents

Acknowledgments

This book would not have been possible without the many mentors, colleagues, friends, and family members who have supported me along the way. First and foremost, I must thank the many community organizers, organization directors, staff, volunteers, and immigrants who allowed me to work beside them throughout my ethnographic research. I especially extend my gratitude to the many immigrants who spoke to me and shared parts of their lives during very traumatic times; their courage and determination is inspirational. My time at the University of California–Santa Cruz allowed me to seek answers to troubling social disparities with creativity and without conventional constraints. I am deeply indebted to a wonderful team of mentors who pushed me to challenge my own assumptions and ask hard questions: Dana Takagi, Patricia Zavella, Herman Gray, and Gwendolyn Mink. Dana Takagi and Patricia Zavella have ceaselessly shared their wisdom, support, and friendship as I turned an unruly research project into this book.

I am grateful to the Sociology Department at the University of California–Santa Cruz and to the Women's and Gender Studies Program at the University of Oregon; both have been amazing homes in which to ground myself in a very ungrounding profession. I also extend gratitude to the Asian American Studies Center at the University of California, Los Angeles (UCLA), where I received the Institute of American Cultures Postdoctoral Fellowship, and to Don Nakanishi, Paul Ong, Shirley Hune, and Dennis Arugelles for providing the time, space, and intellectual engagement for me to rework major portions of the manuscript. At the University of Oregon, the support and resources of the College of Arts and Sciences, the Wayne Morse Center for Law and Politics, and the Center for the Study of Women and Society have been crucial to the completion of this book. Thanks to Nancy Raymond, my book midwife, whose editing suggestions and insightful reading of the manuscript have been enriching far beyond this immediate project; to Jason Weidemann of the University of Minnesota Press, whose excitement and support for this book definitely kept me going through its final stages; and to Adam Brunner for his assistance with so many details. I also thank Richard Morrison, whose early interest gave me the steam to push the manuscript in the direction I envisaged.

I have many wonderful senior mentors who have become anchors against my fierce tendency to want to change everything immediately: Joan Acker, Linda Fuller, Margaret Hallock, Greg McLauchlan, Sandra Morgen, Robert O'Brien, Peggy Pascoe, Barbara Pope, Jiannben Shiao, Lynn Stephen, and Mia Tuan. Through the past six years, I could never have managed all the demands the profession puts on junior faculty without my Women's and Gender Studies colleagues. Thanks to Sabena Stark, who was always there to mind the details of my work; to Elizabeth Reis and Judith Raiskin for often carrying more than their share of the load, when childbirth and book birth became overwhelming; and to Julie Novkov, who more than anyone was instrumental in helping me bring this book to fruition, as her willingness to jump in and give concrete feedback and guidance came at a critical time when I really questioned whether I could complete the manuscript. More recently, Monica Guy and Julia Schewanick have made day-to-day functions miraculously easier. I have had the opportunity to work with many wonderful students, who have taught me as much as I have taught them. In particular, I thank Khanh Le, who has shared a deep commitment to social change, along with an admirable earnestness, commitment, and passion that comes from his own family history of survival.

While at the University of Oregon, I have been fortunate to have a community that is not only politically and intellectually stimulating but also deeply caring and supportive. Although some people have come and gone, the intellectual work could not happen without such a community. I extend thanks to Jayna Brown, Anthony Foy, Sangita Gopal, Michael Hames-García, Daniel HoSang, Adria Imada, Lamia Karim, Brian Klopotek, Enrique Lima, Ernesto Martinez, Norma Martinez-HoSang, Dayo Mitchell, Priscilla Ovalle,

Irmary Reyes-Santos, Analisa Taylor, Tania Trianas, Cynthia Tolentino, and David Vazquez.

Through the years I have also been extremely fortunate to have committed friends who have helped me through my lowest times and celebrated my successes. I could not have done what I have without the support of Martin Summers, Karl Mundt, Shari Huhndorf, Ellen Scott, Jocelyn Hollander, Tammy ko Robinson, and Deborah Vargas. I also owe deep gratitude to Jane Vogel for her wisdom and insights as she led me through my journey and helped me to find the self-confidence to see my passions through.

I thank Chang Morozumi, who watched over my family so I could do my postdoctoral fellowship at UCLA and has been a constant source of support and encouragement. Thanks also to Greg, Toni, and Jenni Morozumi and to Rhonda Romero, Pete Perry, Greg Tolman, Eddie Kochiyama, and Pamela Wu for all the years of family support and encouragement; the Morozumis are an amazing family, and I am honored to be a member. Yuri Kochiyama's endless human rights activism has been a constant inspiration to do more. Thanks to my brothers, Mitchell and Mark Fujiwara, who always believed in their little sister's abilities, and to their families; to my sister, Melissa Fujiwara, and to Aaron Hollenbaugh, who gave me a home in Los Angeles and whose support and care have been unmatched as we share the journey; and to my parents, Yetsuko Sakamoto and Thomas Fujiwara, who were incarcerated as children in Manzanar, California, and Amache, Colorado, and taught me from an early age to look injustice squarely in the eye. I grew up with my parents' childhood stories of guard towers and rifles, block after block of thin-walled shacks, the fear of stealing the delicious peaches on the other side of the barbed-wire fence, freezing cold winters, horrible canned food, long vaccination lines, backed-up latrines, and the loss of a beloved brand-new bike to the neighbor kid when it came time to move to the Santa Anita Race Track. My parents' childhood trauma speaks of a nationalism that branded them enemies of the state when they were children, and embedded in me a need to speak up to that injustice that reappears in new forms and contexts time and time again. I thank my parents for teaching me not only the reality of betrayal but also the need to embrace life, to love one's family, and to live fully.

I must give my deepest appreciation to my children and partner, who have endured every moment of this book with me: to Kyra, for giving me a renewed faith in the goodness of people; to Joanna, for teaching me the importance of asserting myself; to Martin, for bringing peace and serenity into our home; and to my partner, Steve, who has stood by me unconditionally, with unwavering confidence and love, and has supported me through the many ups and downs of a project that speaks to the injustices we remain committed to fight together.

Introduction
Sanctioning Immigrants
"Ending Welfare as We Know It"

Once the President signs this bill the real crisis will begin . . .
The counties will have virtually no ability to raise the tax revenues,
but they'll still have to care for these people. It's a real disaster in
the making.

> —Frank Mecca, executive director of California Welfare
> Directors Association, *Washington Post,* August 2, 1996

Struggles over immigration have typically been shaped by nativist concerns over the racial and cultural fabric of the United States as a nation-state. Concerns over immigrants are often couched in terms of scarce resources, workplace competition, cultural unity, and assimilability. Contentious and controversial immigration politics are not new to the United States; in our increasing state of globalization, immigration policy has increasingly concerned citizenship politics that differentiates rights and entitlements on the basis of citizenship status.

Within the United States, contemporary nationalist formations reveal an anti-immigrant sentiment and discourse resonating with a racialized and gendered hostility that reasserts assumptions of white nativist "belonging" and the immigrant as outsider.

Movements over immigration control and the intended racial and ethnic configurations are embedded in the historic fabric of the nation. Politically produced immigration policies determine who may enter, reside, work, and naturalize; these policies continue to shape and reshape the country's racial demography. In the past decade, numerous immigration policies have been enacted that further restrict immigrant rights, entitlement, and who may enter and reside in this country. In the face of expanding neoliberal policies, global economic restructuring, and mass levels of displacement, immigration policies in the United States remain a volatile target for political maneuvering and nativist racism.

The 1994 U.S. elections resulted in a Republican majority in the 104th Congress. This majority rode in on a hostile anti-immigrant campaign that blamed liberal immigration policies for the visible influx of foreigners charged with burdening the American people through social costs. This hostile discourse was legitimized and nationalized, for example, through the Republicans' so-called Contract with America. This "contract" carried, among other things, Newt Gingrich's promise as Speaker of the House to preside over a freewheeling congressional debate about the "cultural meanings of being American."[1] At the same time, the document capitalized on President Clinton's 1992 campaign promise "to end welfare as we know it" by a commitment to overhaul the existing welfare system. The collusion of nativist politics and the crescendoing war on the poor crystallized in sweeping reform movements that shaped the convergence of immigration and welfare law to exclude noncitizens from public resources.

In 1996 (described by immigrant advocates as a particularly bad year for immigrants), President Clinton, in conformity with the Contract with America, signed three major policies into law that drastically transformed the fundamental rights and responsibilities of immigrants in the United States. Welfare and immigration reforms effectively excluded from benefits those legally residing immigrants who had previously received most forms of public assistance on a par with citizens. These anti-immigrant enactments included the Personal Responsibility Work Opportunity Reconciliation Act (Public Law 104–193), or PRWORA; the Illegal Immigration Reform and Immigrant Responsibility Act (Public Law 104–208), or IIRIRA; and the Antiterrorism Effective Death Penalty Act (Public Law 104–132), or Antiterrorism Act.

The Illegal Immigration Reform Act and the Antiterrorism Act both paved the way for more draconian legislation in post-9/11 immigration politics. Welfare usage and immigrant poverty were used to justify barring future immigrants' entrance into the country and access to legal residency and naturalization. This contemporary anti-immigrant movement, which intensified in the 1990s, was rooted within a national racial identity crisis arising with the emerging majority of a nonwhite population in the United States. The racial demographic profiles that speculated a coming nonwhite majority ignited an increasing fear of Latino and Asian immigration.

Less understood are the ways that Asian immigrants were positioned vis-à-vis the anti-immigrant movement of the closing decade of the twentieth century. The growth and visible presence of the Asian American population fed popular constructions of Asian immigrants as unfairly utilizing public benefits instead of relying only on their well-to-do family members—a commonly recognized "model minority" construction. The heterogeneity among Asian Americans and Asian immigrants reveals vast differences among these persons not only in national origin but also in socioeconomic status, educational level, refugee or migratory process of entry, language, religion, cultural practices, and economic situation.

With the passing of the 1996 immigration and welfare reform laws, nearly a half-million elderly, disabled, and blind immigrants were expected to lose their Supplemental Security Income (SSI—cash assistance for the blind, elderly, and disabled). Seventy-two percent of those immigrants expected to lose SSI were women. Nearly one million immigrants did lose their food stamp benefits, resulting in a documented rise in hunger in immigrant families. With the implementation of Temporary Assistance to Needy Families (TANF) (the cash assistance program that replaced Aid to Families with Dependent Children [AFDC]) and of TANF's five-year lifetime limits and welfare-to-work requirements, immigrant families were sanctioned from the rolls at much higher rates than were citizen families. A more detailed examination of the specific welfare provisions in relation to immigrants and citizenship appears in chapter 2, but it is important to note that the citizenship provisions were haphazard, obscure, and brutal, leaving immigrants confused, panicked, and in despair.

As various provisions of PRWORA were implemented, targeted communities faced extreme dilemmas and fear. With the impending loss of benefits, cruel levels of trauma were experienced by frail, elderly, and disabled immigrants fearing for their own survival. Similarly, immigrant mothers and their children (in most cases, U.S.-citizen children) who remained eligible for particular forms of cash assistance were dubbed the "disappeared," because fear and panic in response to the hostile discourse led many immigrants to believe that they were no longer eligible, or that they risked future naturalization or even deportation for utilizing public assistance. The power of the anti-immigrant discourse proved lethal in itself, with immigrants the fastest population to drop off the rolls as welfare reform set into gear.

To challenge these harsh provisions pushing many immigrant families into greater poverty, immigrant rights activists and researchers worked urgently to show how false claims and data manipulation operated through the racist nativist context to gain public support and conservative votes. In the present examination of the welfare and immigration politics that manifested in the 1996 policy overhaul, I focus on the way citizenship was instrumental in shaping immigrant provisions in welfare policy, and on the traumatic impact these political maneuvers had on Asian immigrant communities. What happened to immigrant women and families in the face of welfare cuts remains largely invisible, with little concern evidenced by policymakers and the public. Although Asians are the fastest growing immigrant group in the United States, few of the (primarily foreign-born) Asian American population are seen as experiencing language barriers, economic constraints, racism and discrimination, or domestic violence.[2] The pervasiveness of the "model minority" myth concealed the depth of poverty among some Asian immigrant and refugee groups, and the increasing need for public assistance among Asian immigrants and refugees, thus veiling the obstacles that these individuals and families negotiate as they operate in a system that defines them as outsiders and undeserving of public support.

Mothers without Citizenship is about the racial and gendered politics established through a new nativist racism to target women and children immigrants in poverty. I question why, at a time of increasing global economic expansion, immigrant women and children are perceived as a threat to the nation's stability. A close racial and gendered analysis of Asian immigrants and refugees in the context of welfare reform presents an opportune moment to examine the politics of citizenship in shaping social policy, as well as the particularities of such shaping for a heterogeneous immigrant group. I argue that it is the very context of the global displacement of women—the feminization of migration—that has shaped the racial gendered underpinnings of this current form of foreigner racialization. The construction of Asian immigrant and refugee women as fraudulently abusing the welfare system easily coupled with preexisting notions of a model minority and a transnational elite professional class with no legitimate need for public assistance; my examination uncouples this strategic assumption through a critical exploration of the persistence of poverty among Asian immigrant and refugee communities.

Asian immigrants have been precariously situated within a racial discourse that neglects their role and impact. On the one hand, prevailing cultural narratives of the so-called model minority have been politically employed to legitimize existing systems and impose group or cultural blame to dismantle federally mandated social programs. However, contrary to popular narratives of Asian success and assimilation, the reality is that at the time of the welfare reform movement poverty among Asian Pacific American families rose from 11.9 to 13.5 percent from 1990 to 1994.[3] The 1990 U.S. Census showed that, although 10 percent of all Americans were officially impoverished, 47 percent of Cambodians, 66 percent of Hmong, 67 percent of Laotians, and 34 percent of Vietnamese officially lived in poverty.[4] Thus, public assistance was an integral form of income for keeping these families out of complete destitution. The increasing use of public assistance by more recent Asian immigrant and refugee groups galvanized the anti-immigrant campaign, provoking accusations against Asian immigrants and refugees for welfare dependency and for failure to assimilate to the American way of life and work.

The welfare reform law did away with a sixty-year entitlement program that ensured a safety net from total destitution for poor women with children, and it damaged economic and political conditions for all women. However, the citizenship status of poor Asian immigrant and refugee women differentiated them categorically as undeserving of other public benefits that were basic protections from abject poverty. Given that the majority of immigrants most directly affected by converging provisions in the welfare and immigration laws were women, this is the perspective from which an analysis of the current so-called era of devolution must occur. Asian immigrant and refugee women as subjects within the contemporary American politic represent an invisibility as women, mothers, and caretakers that contradicts a visibility as global migrants, workers, and an exploitable labor pool.

Throughout *Mothers without Citizenship,* I argue that central to the connection between welfare and immigration reform was the issue of accessibility to public benefits by primarily poor immigrant women. I stress, and will demonstrate, that citizenship as a formal demarcation of belonging placed Asian immigrant women outside of entitlement through a particular gendered *foreigner* racialization process that deemed them inassimilable, perpetrators of welfare fraud, and welfare-dependent. A more critical examination of the relationship between Asian immigrants and public assistance reveals a counterintuitive logic. This new thinking defies popular conceptions and monolithic hegemonic assumptions that Asian Americans do not experience poverty, rely on public assistance, or play a critical role in both formations and challenges of social policy.

The cutting of welfare benefits to immigrant women has had a devastating impact on Asian immigrant women and refugees, particularly within the Southeast Asian[5] community where public assistance is inextricably tied to the resettlement process. For Asian immigrant and refugee[6] women who continue to face high poverty rates, language conflicts, domestic violence, and single-parent family struggles, local organizations and advocates stress the uncompromising necessity for continued public support. Thus, the distance between current policy and the actual material conditions confronting Asian immigrant and refugee women affected by policy reforms needs to be exposed and addressed. My research shows how a racialized gendered politics of citizenship worked to further disenfranchise Asian immigrant women and their families, but that these women and their communities consistently fought back to expose the criminality of the U.S. government in denying the means for survival.

To fully interrogate the political moment presented to us in the 1990s, and to examine the multiple levels of complexity that distinguish the new nativist era, we must include Asian immigration in the postindustrial global and gendered context in any meaningful discussion of domestic social policy. This book intervenes in the broader political and academic marginalization and exclusion of Asian immigrants from debates around social policy and domestic politics. It is necessary to reverse the systematic tendency to dismiss Asian American politics from larger discussions surrounding forms and patterns of social inequality in the United States.[7] Thus, I examine the increasing significance of citizenship in the convergence of welfare and immigration reform, and the particularities of these policies in relation to Asian immigrants and refugees.

In the late 1990s nonwhite immigrants in the United States faced a backlash to their growing numbers in forms reminiscent of the anti-immigrant movement one hundred years earlier. Then, as well, numerous immigration laws developed that clearly excluded immigrants deemed undesirable or inassimilable to a white hegemonic formation. The new nativist movement of the nineties was a response to the increasing presence and perceived permanence of a growing racialized foreigner. The attack was strategic, as it targeted immigrants in poverty. The anti-immigrant movement was able to draw on two distinct discursive strategies. First, the immigrant was constructed as not belonging, and therefore not entitled to public resources: this cultural stereotype was charged with siphoning resources away from "hardworking Americans." Second, welfare "reform" presupposed two things: that welfare use led to dependency and that public assistance programs had created a cycle of poverty. Thus, the rationale went, the elimination of public assistance would push recipients into work and self-sufficiency. The nativist racism that dominated the anti-immigrant movement assumed that poverty was the fault of the poor; that child-bearing women depended on the state rather than a spouse; and that immigrant children took resources from citizen children.

MAPPING *MOTHERS WITHOUT CITIZENSHIP*

In this book, I address three major predicaments for Asian American politics, in theories encompassing race, gender, class, and citizenship in race and social policy:

(1) By centering Asian American women in the context of immigration and welfare politics, I challenge simplistic understandings of racial politics based on dichotomous definitions of race as a social category. Inserting Asian American issues into the discourse of immigration and welfare politics is much more complex than merely adding "other" or additional variables to complicate the existing dichotomous models. Recent critical race scholarship examining issues within Asian American politics has moved beyond Black and white binary examinations of race relations to complicate racial politics with terms of *citizenship* and the persistence of *foreigner* racial constructions.[8]

(2) Incorporating Asian Americans into the larger racial/gendered analysis points critically to the inseparable and complex relationships in which racial groups operate and negotiate positions, and are understood within the larger social politic. Policy impacts all marginalized groups, and does so differentially, with some groups remaining more visible than others.

(3) Research that focuses on the state and examines race relations and social policy must move toward a more comprehensive interweaving of social citizenship and legal citizenship. Given the current and expected state of global politics and economic restructuring, poor immigrants of color face differentiated rights based upon their race, class, gender, and country of origin. As noncitizens, Asian immigrants find their political status further complicated by a differentiated noncitizenship that plays out in both cultural and legislative

venues. Both social citizenship and legal citizenship are integral to a more comprehensive understanding of how Asian immigrants were politically positioned and impacted by welfare reform. A look at the formation of social policy in the face of changing racial demographics, in relation to the contemporary formations of *foreigner* racialization, reveals the increasing complexity of race, gender, and citizenship, a complexity that requires integrated examination.

This critical examination interrogates the structural location and political implications of this group so simultaneously invisible and visible, with great impact to the making and consequences of social policy. Given the multiple levels of heterogeneity that constitute Asian America in the United States, approaches toward race and social policy have to encompass the specificities of citizenship status with respect to current racial constructions shaped by broader global geopolitical relations with Asian nations.

CITIZENSHIP AND ENTITLEMENT IN A THEORETICAL SCHEMATIC

To pull together such broad areas as welfare and immigration policy, I draw from and push existing theoretical discussions of citizenship, gender, race, and nation. The broader questions I address are: How does citizenship continue to shape race relations and racial politics in the United States? How do Asian noncitizens (as immigrants and refugees) present a way for us to understand citizenship-making in social policy and public discourse? How are Asian immigrants incorporated into the arguments of anti-immigrant nativist movements, and how do Asian American communities challenge the racial and gendered constructions associated with anti-Asian sentiment?

To develop these questions, I draw throughout from multiple theoretical frameworks and interdisciplinary scholarship. The goal was not so much to dissect all the elements and provisions that shaped existing and differing forms of inequality for poor citizens and noncitizens, nor was it my intent to establish a legal argument for the continuation of welfare eligibility for particular groups of noncitizens. Rather, I looked to the convergence of these two policy formations at the nexus of community impact and response. Welfare reform "ended welfare as we know it" for all poor Americans: my focus on immigrants is not to suggest that only immigrants were demonized and unjustly cut from public benefits. Rather, I assert that welfare reform engaged in a racialization of the undeserving poor, to the detriment of all poor women and families of color.

By focusing on Asian immigrant and refugee women, my research demonstrates how social policies worked as a catalyst for community response and advocacy to assist and protect a marginalized group of people, nearly invisible to the public, facing despair and desperation as the anti-immigrant movement and citizenship politics pushed them further outside the realm of public entitlement and belonging. Given the breadth of work that exists on immigrants and immigration politics, as well as the important body of feminist scholarship that interrogates the welfare state, differential citizenship, and the persistence of poverty among women-headed households, it was necessary to pull these two entities together to construct a framework centering on the significance of citizenship status and immigration politics while integrating the role of social citizenship and the question of rights for all residents in the United States.

As I discuss in greater detail in chapter 2, I draw from a multilayered approach to analyze how the politics of citizenship shaped welfare and immigration reform, and what the specific implications were for Asian immigrant women facing the loss of benefits and/or an increasing inaccessibility to assistance for themselves and their families. An examination of the convergence of immigration and welfare reform entailed a broad conceptual frame that encompassed two concerns, the feminization of globalization and the feminization of poverty. In the following chapter, I establish how a foreigner racialization worked in a time of increasing immigrant hostility through constructions of fiscal blame for increasing economic insecurity. The idea of a foreigner racialization, as established by Lisa Lowe and Angelo Ancheta,[9] is helpful for us to see how immigrant legislation is driven by nativist politics embedded in Orientalist assumptions that Asians are perpetually inassimilable and thus outside the national identity.

I push the conceptualization of foreigner racialization to interrogate complicated notions of citizenship politics that operate through strategic encompassment and differential exclusions across racial, gendered, national-origin, and class lines. In our current state of globalization, with the proliferation of neoliberal projects and trade agreements that increasingly ease the flow of capital, women immigrants have become subjected to xenophobic movements designed to deny their motherhood and reproductive rights by cutting resources for social services for themselves and their children. A focused examination of the experiences of Asian immigrant and refugee women calls into question some existing presumptions, about the nature of belonging and of exclusion, in contemporary theoretical works on citizenship. Obviously, the conditions and experiences of Latina/o exclusion share similarities with those of Asian immigrants; however, my research helps us to see that the specific experiences within Asian immigrant and refugee communities require reconsideration of notions of citizenship and national belonging. Also, the affective dimensions of belonging may be specific not only across but also within different racial groups.

Throughout this book, I draw from a range of theoretical discussions. To analyze the devastating impact of welfare reform on Southeast Asian refugees with a very particular history of trauma, displacement, and war, I consider the relevancy of betrayal and grievance as forms of agency in response to inhumane social policy designed to categorically exclude noncitizens. Embedded in this examination is the political ambiguity surrounding human rights, particularly at the hands of U.S. social policy. At the loss of life-sustaining benefits, distraught refugees utilized testimony to assert grievance toward the U.S. government for taking away the public assistance they had been promised when they assisted the nation in its military efforts in Southeast Asia.

In a more comprehensive examination of naturalization and the process of acquiring citizenship when immigrants faced loss of benefits, I have drawn from theoretical discussions of race and citizenship that recognize the broader politics of exclusion and national identity. To analyze the unprecedented need for citizenship status so as to receive benefits, I move beyond the theoretization of citizenship and race for understanding differential noncitizenship and access to rights; rather, I consider the way citizenship has increasingly become a proxy for race in our increasing globalization, creating a state of differential exclusion of so-called undesirable (poor) immigrants of color. Although contemporary exclusions may not be based solely on country of origin, they clearly target poor working-class immigrants whose migration is usually the result of economic or political displacement. Those most likely to be seen as future burdens on the state, women, become the *hyperexcluded*.

As I examine the politics of motherhood and the devaluation and marginalization of women in poverty, I draw from well-established feminist jurisprudence and sociological scholarship on women, poverty, and the welfare state. The war against the poor, and the move to discipline women into supposed personal responsibility, proved a loss of major rights promised to all residents in the United States. I examine the ways citizenship status as a legal framework further marginalizes women already subjected to a gendered demonization of dependency. Needing help from the state, regardless of historical and social circumstances, was constructed as counter to the ideals of citizenship and belonging. For noncitizen mothers, the racialized gendered constructions of foreign invasion meant being placed even further outside the possibilities of belonging and being considered deserving of assistance. Pulling together critical race feminisms with broader global theories of women's displacement helps to better understand the effects of merging immigration reform and welfare reform in the lives and experiences of Asian immigrant families.

While these particular theoretical concerns work their way through the book, I tie them together under the conceptual notion of a multilayered citizenship that illuminates the multiple forces differentiating across particular bodies and groups through social policy. By centering the experiences of Asian immigrant families, my analysis informs our understanding of how citizenship gets utilized through social policy, and how consequences vary across group positions and locations (specifically, mothers of young children, elderly, disabled, refugees). This policy analysis is unique in that I situate the convergence of welfare and immigration provisions at the level of the community. As a result, I could examine the consequences of citizenship politics as it unfolded. My methodology, too, has incorporated multiple levels of approach and interdisciplinary frameworks.

FEMINIST ACTIVIST METHODOLOGY

Working from a feminist ethnographic approach, I engaged in participatory research in the Bay Area of Northern California from 1996 through 1998. My primary region of research focused on three counties: San Francisco, Alameda, and Santa Clara. Within all of these areas, Asian immigrant organizations were particularly hard-hit with confused and panicked immigrants. I volunteered and participated in immigrant community outreach programs, immigrant welfare workshops and forums, and citizenship drives. Organization sites included the Asian Women's Resource Center in San Francisco, the Asian Law Caucus in San Francisco, the Asian Law Alliance in San Jose, the Northern California Coalition for Immigrant Rights in San Francisco, the CalWORKs Advisory Board of Santa Clara County, the Asian Pacific Islander Force based in Oakland, and the Center for Employment Training and SEIU International Local 250 in San Jose. Each organization or service provider dealt with different demographic communities. However, my focus on immigrant rights groups and Asian immigrant organizations allowed me to see the implications of welfare reform for two broad categories: East Asian (mainly persons from China) and Southeast Asian, including Vietnamese, Cambodian, Laotian, Hmong, and Mien, legal permanent resident constituencies.

I began by visiting and interviewing directors, staff, and volunteers at these organizations and agencies working with immigrant communities. As I gained a clear picture of the organizations and programs with a sizeable Asian immigrant constituency, I volunteered and participated in service programs (such as citizenship drives and teaching citizenship classes), information forums about welfare reform, and community-based organizing of demonstrations and protests.

I conducted approximately thirty interviews with immigrant community organization directors, program coordinators, social service providers, and advocates. The interviews reflect the depth of community-based work involved with issues of poverty, labor, domestic violence, family support, hunger, immigration and citizenship status, and language. Scheduled interviews were tape-recorded and later transcribed, and field notes were recorded and analyzed thematically. In addition to utilizing the fieldwork that centrally informs my examination of Asian immigrants, citizenship, and policy formation, I draw from extensive policy analyses, congressional records and reports, and media text that reflect the political and popular understandings of immigrants and their *place* in the idealized cultural homogeneity of so-called American culture. I examined local and national newspapers (i.e., local Bay Area publications, *San Francisco Chronicle, Los Angeles Times, New York Times*) for articles that focused on immigrants and welfare reform from 1996 through 1998. The newspaper stories were an excellent barometer of popular sentiment and of trends in the congressional debates.

EVOLUTION INTO PARTICIPATORY RESEARCH

I approached my study from a feminist epistemological approach that worked to reduce power differentials between myself as researcher, the community members whom I worked with, and the immigrants I assisted.[10] I had not entered the field with the intention to specifically examine community responses to welfare reform. I had first entered the field to explore the particular ways welfare reform was playing out in Asian immigrant and refugee women's lives. For numerous reasons, particularly language issues and fear, I found that it was too invasive and threatening to interview immigrant women facing cut-offs. At first I made attempts to contact women through organizations that assisted them with their applications for naturalization. According to the programming staff, it was okay for me to contact these women because, having submitted their applications for naturalization, they would be working toward English proficiency. Not only did my attempt at interviews fail miserably, my very effort to contact women ignited a terror that I would regret tremendously. I abandoned my plan to conduct interviews, and instead began to participate in community efforts to assist immigrants facing the confusing and terrifying changes in their public assistance situation. After several months of engagement with the community organizations, I soon was immersed in, and participating in, community service and advocacy efforts. My project grew into more definitely participatory research, where my role as researcher and activist often merged.[11] Participatory research is characterized by the intent to implement social change not from the top down but rather by following the course of action led by community participants.[12]

The data I draw from are important, as they reflect the front lines of communities working with immigrants in two areas: providing direct services and assisting in advocacy efforts toward equal access to public resources for noncitizens. I found myself in meetings with city officials, county task-force groups, and state representatives, representing community organizations and presenting information and data gathered through my research. Through my participatory methods, I was able to conduct an ethnographic examination of community impact and response. Most revealing were the testimonies presented through hearings, forums, and day-to-day contact with those immigrants and refugees most directly impacted by the changes in welfare eligibility requirements. Through such testimony, immigrant rights groups and immigrants themselves voiced their concerns, to show legislators the massive harmfulness of welfare cuts to noncitizens. Organizers documented, compiled, and presented often desperate testimony to persuade Congress to restore lost benefits.

As a volunteer in citizenship drives, I would assist immigrants in filling out applications for naturalization. Through this process, I would participate in the general conversations involving "difficult cases." In my volunteer role, I could see immigrants' day-to-day experiences through the life situations presented by families as they shared their stories within the space of community support. Seen as a team member among a group of knowledgeable volunteers, I was understood by the immigrant as a coassistant, there to help as much as possible. Although the power relation still existed, the relationship was more collaborative and supportive.

As a citizenship course instructor for immigrants in the process of naturalizing, I was able to gain a first-hand account of the complexities the immigrants faced in this attempt. The struggle to learn the answers to the one hundred U.S. civics and history questions in a second language proved challenging and stressful, particularly for those facing welfare cuts. As a citizenship instructor, my role as a teacher within the community organization allowed me to see more intimately the harsh circumstances immigrants were facing with the new welfare and immigration rules, and the immediate importance for them of acquiring citizenship.

The field research project I was fortunate to obtain reflects the very power issues I set out to study. That is, the social conditions that resulted from a hostile anti-immigrant welfare and immigration reform ultimately shaped the methodologies I could use; hence, my methodology was affected by existing power relations. My initial attempt to interview immigrant welfare recipients proved untenable and led to a complete shift in approach; however, such a purely policy and social service analysis would have resulted in a top-down perspective that primarily considered the implementers' frame of reference. Because of the existing terror and fear felt by these women, my methodological options bear the imprint of the power that ultimately shaped my need to examine the convergence of welfare and immigration reform at the community level, from the community point of view. As a result, I was able to examine how social policy affected immigrant women and their families at the community level—I was able to see how the power of the state operated on multiple levels (individuals, families, and community).

Beyond 1998, I continued to research media representations, policy reports, community assistance efforts, and the resurgence of the congressional debate when Temporary Assistance for Needy Families faced its first attempt at reauthorization in 2002. Just celebrating its tenth anniversary, PRWORA has been showered with economic reports seeking to show how successful welfare reform has been by noting the drop in recipients; the biggest indicator that it has been less successful is the level of poverty and hunger that has arisen since the implementation of PRWORA. I continued to examine policy analyses, follow-up reports, and county by county assessments throughout the ten years of the law's existence. Immigrant community organizations were the primary source for research that focused on the impacts to noncitizens. Thus, I continued to follow welfare projects within immigrant organizations and advocacy groups.

In chapter 1, "New Nativism and Welfare Reform: Asian Immigrants as Racialized Foreigners," I discuss the political trajectory of a foreigner racialization that has shaped assumptions of Asian inassimilability. I further elaborate on new nativism as a conceptual framework that pulls together the broader contemporary anti-immigrant movement and the precarious positioning of Asian immigrant women as welfare abusers. Although the discourse of the 1990s anti-immigrant movement was clearly embedded in an anti-Latina/o racial project, Asian immigrants figured centrally in congressional debates of "welfare fraud" that assumed these immigrants did not need such assistance. However, it was the invisibility of Asian immigrants and refugees in dire poverty that discounted the intense impact that would unfold once benefits were lost.

In chapter 2, "Welfare Reform and the Politics of Citizenship," I look specifically at particular provisions from PRWORA and examine the ways citizenship has reshaped welfare policy for immigrants. This endeavor requires a two-fold process, as the immigrant provisions in the welfare reform law are embedded in existing systems of differential citizenship confronting all women in poverty, particularly women of color. The racial politics that surround welfare as a demonized system of "overdependency" and "irresponsibility" is further complicated when we integrate the racialization of the "inassimilable foreigner" and "fraudulent immigrant welfare mother." I consider the significant relationship between legal citizenship and social citizenship as interconnected forces that work through global processes of race and gender migrations. Centering Asian immigrants as political subjects demonstrates the dynamic relationship between the cultural politics of new nativist formations and the social policies that use citizenship to protect national interests from a perceived foreign threat.

Chapters 3 through 6 explore the formations and implications of specific provisions within the welfare and immigration reform laws of 1996. Because these social policies were so sweeping and multilayered, each chapter focuses attention on the particular logic generated from the rationalization to exclude noncitizens, and the implications for Asian immigrants and their respective communities. Chapter 3, "Refugees Betrayed," begins this section with an investigation of the racial and gendered politics of refugees from, primarily, Southeast Asia. In the face of loss of life-sustaining benefits, some refugees resorted to suicide. Community organizations were crucial to the advocacy efforts that reinserted narratives of war, trauma, and dislocation, and obliged the U.S. government to bear responsibility for the poverty and unemployment that persists within these communities. The testimonies, narratives, and voices from Southeast Asian refugees were critical in reestablishing a collective historical memory of the longstanding plight refugees have faced following resettlement in the United States. This focus on Southeast Asian refugees further demonstrates the heterogeneity within the category *Asian immigrant,* a heterogeneity that reflects a welfare story sorely unrecognized and poorly understood.

Chapter 4, "The Rush for Citizenship: Naturalization as a Technocratic Apparatus of Exclusion," examines the formation of citizenship drives in response to the loss of important public benefits suddenly requiring U.S. citizenship status. Through ethnographic research, I participated in citizenship drives revealing the compromised position immigrants in poverty confront when naturalization is seen as the only sure means for survival. Here, the technologies of the state reflect a politics of closure through a system designed to keep particular racialized foreigners out, especially those in poverty. Difficulties in the Asian immigrant community with the naturalization process illuminate the confounding forces of race, nation, gender, and poverty making citizenship status pivotal to survival.

In chapter 5, "On Not Making Ends Meet: Mothers without Citizenship," I examine the effects of Temporary Assistance to Needy Families. The mandatory welfare-to-work requirements and five-year lifetime limit imposed by TANF have led many immigrant families to leave the rolls, as public assistance has become too difficult to obtain. Initially referred to as the "disappeared" by county welfare agents, eligible immigrants, through confusion and fear, simply dropped from TANF during the transition from Aid to Families with Dependent Children. Drawing from exemplary cases of Asian immigrant women who faced this transition, I discuss the complications they must struggle with to fulfill mandatory work requirements and the likelihood that they will end up in dead-end exploitative jobs to sustain their families.

Chapter 6, "The Devaluation of Immigrant Families," examines the implications of welfare cuts to immigrant families, most of whom are mixed-citizenship, with U.S.-citizen children. The documented rise of hunger in immigrant households since welfare reform requires a critical interrogation of social policies that put citizen children in jeopardy of malnutrition because their parents are noncitizens. Given such policies, immigrant mothers have avoided using public health care for themselves and their children even though they remain eligible. As a result, immigrant women and their children are in poorer health than before. New rules in the IIRIRA further discouraged noncitizen women from utilizing means-tested benefits, for fear of not being able to naturalize in the future. These compounding issues raise important questions regarding their citizen children, who often, as a result of their parents' citizenship status, do not receive due benefits.

In the Conclusion, "The Continuing Significance of Racialized Citizenship," I consider the multiple ways that the immigration and welfare reform laws were executed to keep immigrants out. In a broader scope, the two acts have worked in tandem to redefine, on a basis of economic requirements, who may enter the United States; who may naturalize; and who may receive benefits. As a result, immigrant women, the largest proportion of immigrants in poverty, have fewer avenues for support and assistance should they find themselves in need. Although some benefits were restored, immigrant and refugee women have, by and large, been pushed further outside the national politic. Regardless of the persistent need and desire for immigrant women's labor in the United States, the welfare and immigration reform acts of 1996 sent a clear message: if you become poor or destitute, regardless of how it came about (even if through a job injury), do not expect to rely on public benefits.

I conclude with a critical consideration of the unarticulated differentiation between welfare rights and immigrant rights movements. Why did these two entities not merge in a more coherent and organized form? I argue that citizenship plays out in these political formations as well. The "ending of welfare as we know it" connoted a loss of liberty and justice for women in poverty, framed by welfare rights advocates in terms of civil rights, equal access, and an end to discriminatory politics. The loss of benefits for noncitizens evolved into a human rights platform that focused on the loss of equal protection and on general abuses faced by immigrants in an exploitative economy that casts them as unwelcome outsiders. I believe that the limitations of the immigrant rights movement for full restoration of lost benefits demonstrate the shortcomings from having unconnected platforms of immigrant rights and welfare rights efforts that did not effectively integrate social citizenship and legal citizenship as interconnected entities.

I reconsider the broader politics of social location of Asian immigrant and refugee women residing in the United States within the context of global economic restructuring and post-9/11 antiterrorism politics. The examination of the welfare and immigration policy reform movements illustrates the way noncitizen women are faced with vulnerabilities to state technologies as well as to exploitative practices, a situation that reflects a general devaluation of immigrant women's lives and their families' well-being. The convergence of the welfare state with immigration control has resulted in a racialized gendered nativism embedded in the politics of reproduction and white racial hegemony. Although the *reproducing immigrant woman* stereotype has been replaced with the *foreign terrorist,* subsequent welfare and immigration policy amendments have not fully reconsidered the unequal parameters established through citizenship criteria for welfare eligibility. Rather, the ongoing anti-immigrant course continues to refortify the power of citizenship status in further degrading the rights of immigrants in the United States.

1
New Nativism and Welfare Reform
Asian Immigrants as Racialized Foreigners

In the last century and a half, the American "citizen" has been
defined over against the Asian "immigrant," legally, economically,
and culturally.

—Lisa Lowe, *Immigrant Acts*

You get illegal alien children, Third World children, out of the schools
and you will reduce the violence. That is a fact.... You're not dealing
with a lot of shiny face, little kiddies.... You're dealing with Third
World cultures who come in, they shoot, they beat, they stab and they
spread their drugs around in our school system. And we're paying
them to do it.

—Barbara Coe, drafter of California's Proposition 187,
Immigrants Out!

ASIAN IMMIGRANTS AS INASSIMILABLE OUTSIDERS

In the latter decades of the twentieth century, the Asian American population grew exponentially. From 1980 to 1990, the overall Asian Pacific American (APA) population in the United States increased 95.2 percent. By the
year 2000, 12.5 million Asian Pacific Americans resided in the United
States, comprising 4.5 percent of the total U.S. population.[1]

Regional patterns of settlement have always shaped Asian American politics as well as community and individual experiences. California has, from the
start, been at the forefront of contentious state politics in response to Asian
immigration. In the year 2000, 48 percent of Asian Pacific Americans (APAs)
lived in the western states. That year, 13 percent of California's population

consisted of APAs (3.8 million), representing 33.2 percent of San Francisco County's, 28 percent of Santa Clara County's, and 13 percent of Los Angeles County's populations. (Los Angeles County then contained 1,282,466 APAs, the greatest number in any U.S. county.) The primary force behind this vast growth was the dramatic increase in Asian immigration to the United States. Eighty-eight percent of APAs in 2000 either were foreign born or had at least one foreign-born parent.[2]

Asian immigration and citizenship have remained central to the politics that have shaped the history, culture, and political experiences of both Asian immigrants and U.S.-born Asian Americans. Lisa Lowe's statement at the head of this chapter—"In the last century and a half, the American *citizen* has been defined over against the Asian *immigrant,* legally, economically, and culturally"[3]—emphasizes the critical role Asian immigration has played in broader U.S. citizenship politics. Lowe's 1996 *Immigrant Acts* traced the trajectory of Asian American cultural politics through the historical and contemporary patterns of capitalist expansion, colonization, war, and globalization. Drawing from a racial formation perspective, Lowe's examination of the nativist racial politics surrounding Asian immigrants, and the series of immigration laws to emerge in response to such politics, reveals the particular racial constructions and meanings that shape the social policies that determine inclusion, exclusion, and entitlement. Fundamental to her analysis is the central role of citizenship as it interacted with forces of race, gender, economic dislocation, and the U.S. racial state. As a legal apparatus, the racial state negotiates nativist racial desires for cultural homogeneity that conflict with global economic and political forces that have included the need for laborers and professionals from Asia.

As subjects within U.S. terrain, Asian immigrants and Asian Americans have been positioned as *racialized others* through both cultural and legislative formations. *Immigrant Acts* conceptualizes and describes "the contradictions of Asian immigration, which at different moments in the last century and a half of Asian entry into the United States have placed Asians 'within' the U.S. nation-state, its workplaces, and its markets, yet linguistically, culturally, and racially marked Asians as 'foreign' and 'outside' the national polity."[4] Unlike immigrants from Europe, Asian immigrants have been subjected to an *outsider racialization* that has worked instrumentally to exclude them from full and equal participation in the American polity and to deny them equal access to resources.[5] For Asian Americans, the process of outsider racialization formulates them as foreign, un-American, and always a poten-tial threat. Thus a pervasive *foreigner racialization* continues to affect con-temporary Asian American politics in popular culture, everyday life, and social policy. Asian foreignness has been based on Orientalist racializations, in which alleged barbaric cultural practices and exotic rituals, as well as phys-ical traits, would imply racial differences inassimilable to white normativity. Placed as outsider to the American national culture, the Asian is always seen as immigrant, as the "foreigner-within," regardless of citizenship status.[6]

"Racialized foreigner" is entrenched in Asian American identity (even apart from immigrant status), so that the racial formation of Asian Americans does not fall along a black-versus-white, but rather an American-versus-foreigner, axis.[7] Several contemporary examples can illustrate the persist-ence of projection of a racialized foreigner identity onto Asian immigrants and Asian American figures. This outsider racialization can be seen in what otherwise might be considered a trivial event. When U.S. world figure-skating champion Michelle Kwan lost the gold medal to Tara Lipinsky in the 1998 World Olympics in Nagano, Japan, the headline announcing the upset vic-tory on the MSNBC Web site read: "American Beats Out Kwan." Again, at the 2002 Olympics in Salt Lake City, Kwan, although favored to win, lost the gold to Sarah Hughes and the silver to Russian skater Irina Slutskaya; the day after the women's figure skating finals, the *Seattle Times* sports page ran a controversial subhead on its lead story about Hughes's performance: "American Outshines Kwan, Slutskaya in Skating Surprise." Kwan, an American-born Chinese American, was simply positioned as foreign and outside of the imagined white cultural homogeneity of the United States.

The foreigner racialization also emerges in times of shifting geopolitics, usually during U.S.–Asia military or economic crisis. In World War II, all persons, of all ages, of Japanese ancestry on the West Coast were classified as "enemy aliens" and forcibly removed, to be imprisoned through the duration of the war in remote and isolated areas of the interior. More recently, the case of Dr. Wen Ho Lee caught national attention; this sixty-year-old nuclear physicist and employee of Los Alamos National Laboratories was arrested and held in pretrial solitary confinement for ninety days. Lee had come to the United States from Taiwan in 1964, became a naturalized citizen, and earned his doctorate degree from Texas A & M University. Lee was indicted on December 10, 1999, for fifty-nine counts of transferring nuclear secrets to his desktop computer and portable data tapes. Along with the charges went allegations that nuclear secrets were passed to China, but Lee was never formally charged with espionage. He was put in leg-iron shackles in solitary confinement, and denied bail.

The Lee case became the centerpiece of a tangled web of charges that the Clinton administration had been "soft on" Chinese espionage or had even willfully transferred American secrets to Chinese agents in exchange for a few hundred thousand dollars in campaign contributions. As Lee sat awaiting trial, the case, along with related investigations by the Department of Justice, Department of Energy, and the FBI, crumbled for lack of evidence. Released with a plea bargain to one count of mishandling sensitive information, Lee received formal apologies from President Clinton for the mistreatment he endured. After months of interrogative battery, threats, and attempts to get him to sign a confession, Lee was set free on September 13, 2000, by Judge James Parker, who stated that this case "was an embarrassment to the nation."[8]

Foreigner racialization always evokes some form of potential threat to the nation's welfare. The nature of the threat is contextual to the social, economic, and global politics within any given historical moment. By the 1990s, U.S. racial politics included a reemergent, and escalated outsider racialization specifically focused on Latino/a and Asian immigrants as a threat to the nation's economic stability. Most vociferous in states like California and Texas with dramatic increases of immigrants, politicians and anti-immigrant groups employed a nationalist discourse through *nativist racism* to demarcate who "belongs" and who should be entitled to public resources.[9] The shifting racial demographics in California, in particular, heightened the significance of terms like "the emerging majority." Paradoxically, this term ignited venues for community empowerment and multiculturalism, as well as the racial backlash associated with fear of a predicted "white minority." The contradiction between the mainstream's purported embracing of racial multiculturalism and the increasing demonization of racial minorities as the cause of crime, poverty, poor educational systems, drugs, and unfair ethnic preferences led to a full-fledged movement to "clean up" the state.

The so-called immigration problem took the forefront of racial scapegoating, with the claim that immigration was the cause for the nation's economic and social problems. Despite specific constructions of undocumented immigrants as "illegal aliens" from Mexico, and the politicking to further militarize the U.S.–Mexican border, borders were opened to the free flow of *capital* through "free trade" agreements (such as NAFTA, North American Free

Trade Agreement); this of course was in contradiction to the fortification of the border by heightened technology and arms to prevent the crossing of displaced Latina/o workers.[10] In the following section, I focus specifically on the backdrop and context of the immigration growth and welfare reform movements that, together, pushed immigrants outside the boundaries of entitlement.

NEW NATIVISM AND THE IMMIGRANT THREAT TO AMERICAN WHITENESS

The documented increase of Latina/o and Asian immigrants produced regional effects by the early 1990s: Californians grew familiar with a new terminology that referenced the *majority minority* or *emerging majority* to connote the nascent minority status of whites. Predictions in the early 1990s estimated that by the year 2000, nonwhites would outnumber whites in California—the first state, other than Hawai'i, to lack a white majority. A closer look at the anti-immigrant trajectory that influenced passage of the 1996 federal anti-immigrant and welfare "reform" laws highlights the critical role California played in shaping the so-called national immigration problem.

Historically, California has been a center for Asian immigration and settlement. As a result, resentment of Asian immigrant groups has shaped the state's racial politics and nativist movements toward exclusion, denial of citizenship, exploitation, and legitimized violence. The contemporary period, although complicated by changing geopolitical and economic relations with Asia and the increased flux of transnational migration from Asia, manifests redoubled nativist concerns over California's status as a multicultural/multiracial state. The racial demographic shift in California was clearly shaped by the rapid rise in nonwhite immigration following the reopening of immigration in 1965 through the Immigration and Nationality Act, which ended racially discriminatory bars, and the internal growth of Asian and Latina/o communities. From 1981 until 1990, among immigrants entering the United States, 84 percent came from Asia and Latin America (U.S. Census 1990). According to the 1990 census, 40.2 percent of Asian immigrants and 38.7 percent of immigrants from Latin America and the Caribbean settled in California. In 1990, demographics continued to change racial composition: whites consisted of 58 percent of the California population, Latinos 25 percent, and Asian Pacific Islanders 9 percent. By the year 2000, white Californians represented 46.7 percent of the population (an 11.3 percent drop),

Asian pacific Islanders 10.9 percent (36 percent increase), and Latinos 32.4 percent (42.6 percent increase).[11]

In parallel with increasing immigration rates, a growing multiethnic population, and an expected white minority, California experienced in the early nineties one of its deepest and most prolonged recessions.[12] According to the 1995 *California Policy Seminar Brief,* by 1992, California was experiencing the worst economic downturn since the Great Depression: 4.9 million Californians (15.9 percent) lived in poverty, including one out of every four children.[13] The restructuring of industry, outsourcing of manufacturing to third-world countries, and military base closures made California one of the few states in which median household incomes fell (by 2.1 percent) between 1992 and 1994.[14] Health care, secondary education, and housing became less affordable for a wider segment of the population as poverty became more widespread and intense.[15] At the same time, Latina/o and Asian immigrants became, as already noted, more visible as a proportion of the California population. This simultaneity of changing racial demographics and economic anxiety catalyzed the demonization of "illegal aliens."

Blaming immigrants for a state's (in this case, California's) social and economic problems is not a new phenomenon. In fact, patterns of heightened American nativism during periods of economic recession are documented through the nation's history.[16] Critical immigration scholars coined the term *new nativism* to elucidate nativist trends within contemporary patterns of globalization, displacement, and transnational migration. The concept of new nativism reflects the anti-immigrant sentiment and discourse—a racialized hostility—that reinserted assumptions of white nativist entitlement, rights, and belonging. The new nativist impulse perceived a threat from contemporary transnational migrants (immigrants who maintain strong ties to their home countries, sustain transnational families, often travel to and fro, and remain potential sponsors for additional family migrants). This new class of migrants challenges cultural assumptions of what an *American* is supposed to be, intensifying multiculturalism and questioning cultural assimilation.[17]

However, the nativism that mounted in the 1990s contained elements distinct from past nativist movements. The arguments—blaming immigrants for poor economic conditions as well as for crime, poor education, and lack of health care—took on gendered overtones that reflected the increased migration of women following expanded global economic restructuring. According to the *National Council of Research on Women's Issues Quarterly,* by

1993, 80 percent of the world's 44 million refugees were women and their dependent children, and half of the world's 30 million migrant workers were women. In addition, from 1930 to the early 1980s, women consistently outnumbered men as legal immigrants to the United States, a proportion that repeated in 1986, 1987, and 1993.[18] The large-scale migration of women resulted in a "feminization of migration"[19] going beyond family reunification. The increasing levels of migrant women of color posed concerns of "gendered dependency" for nativist interests, who saw this influx as exacerbating the preexisting ailments of poverty, inadequate health care, and reliance on welfare. The heightened visibility of women immigrants materialized in a new nativist construction, one that targeted women and children through anti-immigrant reform movements focusing on reproduction and access to social services.

The new nativism of the 1990s gained momentum through this targeting of undocumented immigrant women and their children, which equated *illegal* status with nonentitlement to American resources. Although politicians (Governor Pete Wilson) and anti-immigration coalition leaders (from the Federation for American Immigration Control [FAIR] and the American Immigration Control Foundation [AICF]) argued that immigrants were unfairly "taking needed jobs from Americans" (a popular portrayal of the male immigrant), the focus on reproduction (that is, on women) highlighted the perceived accessibility of public benefits and the argument for social "reform."[20] The attack on undocumented immigrants used varying racialized and gendered discursive strategies charging undocumented women with abusing an overgenerous welfare system. The media's sensationalized portrayal of the hyperfertile undocumented immigrant woman centered on the Latina migrant and her children.[21]

Such racist arguments that undocumented migrants were degrading the state found success in California's Proposition 187,[22] the "SOS—Save Our State" initiative (approved by 59 percent of California voters) denying undocumented immigrants health care (including reproductive health care), public benefits, and education. Although federal programs (with the exception of emergency health care, immunizations, WIC [nutritional assistance for poor women, infants, and children], and education) have never been available to undocumented immigrants, such immigrants were repeatedly charged with draining the public welfare system. The racialized/gendered images of migrant Latinas crossing the border to have their children and receive medical care through state-funded health care services played on working- and middle-class resentments over perceived misuse of their tax dollars.

The new nativist language of Proposition 187 was critical in constructing undocumented immigrants as a threat to the nation. Otto Santa Ana's critical-discourse analysis of the anti-immigrant movement of the 1990s demonstrates the strategic use of language and metaphor in newspaper text that played on anxieties over the apparent loss of Anglo-American cultural hegemony.[23] The use of metaphors to characterize the intensifying immigration threat was racialized through the imagery of an impending danger of brown bodies as an *inexorable flow,* a characterization more concerned with the cultural impact of immigration than with the initial economic concerns that Proposition 187 pundits declared. In fact, Santa Ana found that nearly 60 percent of the metaphors in the public discourse on immigration were metaphors for dangerous waters, while less than 5 percent were metaphors for burden (economic burden).[24] According to Santa Ana, the real signal that *dangerous waters* expresses is not the assumed issue of budgetary issues but, rather, cultural alarm. The fear is that "the rising brown tide will wash away Anglo-American cultural dominance."[25] The *flood from the South* through the *porous border* threatening *the American home front* established the illegal immigrant as Latina/o.

The construction of immigration as *dangerous waters* resulted in the dehumanization of immigrant workers and their families. Just as the U.S. nation was characterized as *unitary* through the metaphor of *house, body,* or *ship,* so immigrants were denuded of any individuality or humanity, and instead were massed as one huge flood, disease, or invasion to be feared. Santa Ana cites numerous quotes that characterize the *inexorable influx* of immigrants as potentially sinking the *ship,* flooding the *house,* and sickening the *body* with disease and illness. The statement by Barbara Coe quoted at the front of this chapter illustrates the notions of invasion and disease. Targeting Latina/o children and youth as the Third World menace infecting American school children was potent in the broader characterization of the massive flood of immigration as ultimately destroying the structures of the American house. Coe's assertion ("That is a fact. . . . You're not dealing with a lot of shiny face, little kiddies . . . You're dealing with Third World cultures who come in, they shoot, they beat, they stab and they spread their drugs around in our school system"),[26] clearly demarcated immigrant children as a cultural threat to the well-being of American school children.

Coe's notorious statement reflects another important theme that shaped popular assumptions about immigrants and welfare usage. After making racist and degrading assumptions of Third World criminality and destruction to "our" schools, she implies that American tax payers are paying illegal immigrant children to come in and ruin these schools: "and we're paying them to do it."[27] Indeed, the notion of taxpayer burdens took hold in a climate of what Kitty Calavita refers to as *balanced-budget nativism*, spawned in the 1980s and solidified in the anti-immigrant and welfare reform movements of the 1990s.[28] Calavita draws from the argument that a "balanced-budget conservatism"[29] was an ideological response devised to deflect attention away from existing economic transformations that were resulting in a more vulnerable middle class and a greater gap between the working poor and the wealthy, by focusing on fiscal matters of budget deficits and rising taxes as causes of increasing economic insecurity and decline. According to Calavita, "This balanced-budget conservatism serves as a target for the frustration and anger of those facing economic uncertainty, deflects responsibility from the private sector's cost-cutting, and facilitates the austerity measures of the government as it dismantles the safety-net."[30]

Proposition 187, then, became an ideal policy to rally behind in the climate of California's recession, as it identified clear targets of blame for fiscal costs arising from public support programs. Meanwhile, the "deficit-mania" hid neoliberal government policies of increasing privatization, deindustrialization, and outsourcing to global markets and labor pools that resulted in higher unemployment, economic insecurity, and the cheapening of labor in the United States. Rather, social costs were targeted across the board, as the "undeserving" poor were blamed for deficits, large government, and cultural degradation. Those who were not citizens (indeed, not even legal residents) became the ideal target of blame, more undeserving than the traditional undeserving poor.[31] This assumed issue became the major agenda for federal welfare and immigration reform advocates.

Immigrant children were linked with crime and school degradation, immigrant men were accused of taking jobs from Americans, and immigrant women were called a drain on welfare and Medicaid. Despite counterevidence that undocumented immigrants contribute more to national, state, and local economies than they take out in assistance (one study concluded that immigrants contribute $90 billion in taxes while taking only $5 billion in social services),[32] by 1994 a 59 percent majority of California voters believed them to be a drain on the public treasury. Ultimately, the imagery of immigrants as a cultural threat to the nation concentrated on access to public resources, and took hold as hardworking Americans came to blame immigrants for their own economic hardships. The logic in the discourse, that too many in a lifeboat would result in the demise of all, influenced voters to assume that undocumented immigrants were indeed taking the resources they themselves could not obtain. Thus, the lifeboat needed to take care of its own first: the SOS—Save Our State initiative appealed to voters' sense of saving Californians from uncontrolled flood and disease.

With Proposition 187, the construct that welfare was a magnet attracting immigrants to the nation took hold in California, and anti-immigration advocates not only pushed for the restriction of public benefits and a moratorium on immigration altogether, but also the denial of birthright citizenship to those born to undocumented mothers.[33] Governor Pete Wilson's first attempt to implement Proposition 187 proposed to deny undocumented women prenatal health care. However, in November 1995, U.S. District Judge Mariana R. Pfaelzer ruled Proposition 187 unconstitutional, basing her decision on the 1982 Supreme Court decision in Plyler v. Doe, which ruled that the equal protection clause of the Fourteenth Amendment prohibits states from denying undocumented children a free public education.[34] Shortly after the ruling against Proposition 187, the California Coalition for Immigration Reform put an official-looking billboard on the California–Arizona state line at Interstate 10: "WELCOME TO CALIFORNIA. THE ILLEGAL IMMIGRANT STATE. DON'T LET THIS HAPPEN TO YOUR STATE. Call Toll Free (877) NO ILLEGALS." Harking back to the early 1900s, when the country's economic and cultural stability was perceived as threatened by foreign degradation, new nativist racism played off the assumed moral depravity that would follow the loss of a white national cultural identity. Although Proposition 187 was ultimately ruled unconstitutional, and was never officially implemented, the popularized trope of the welfare-abusing "illegal alien" acquired saliency at the national level.

With fundamental concerns over shifting demographics and over a formidable permanence of multiculturalism, the so-called national immigration problem reached beyond the scapegoating of undocumented immigrants to all immigrants, third-world immigrants in particular. Peter Brimelow's 1995 national best seller, *Alien Nation: Common Sense about America's Immigration Disaster,* best reflects the anti-immigrant construction claiming immigrants were a drain on society. Brimelow's fear of an alien nation moved beyond the "invasion" of "illegal aliens" to argue that all immigration in general (including legal immigration) is the crux of the nation's problems. As a simply written polemic on the nation's immigration/race problem, Brimelow's narrative expressed a popular sentiment blaming immigrants from the Third World for increased crime, loss of jobs, failing public schools, welfare dependency, and a weak national identity.

Concerned with the complexion of the United States, Brimelow demanded a complete overhaul of U.S. immigration laws to restore the white majority population to 90 percent.[35] An immigrant himself from Great Britain, Brimelow argued that white homogeneity be re-established, as "the American nation has always had a specific ethnic core. And that core has been white."[36] The recommitment to Western European immigration should coincide with the dismantling of all third world funding, and "all diversion of public funds to promote 'diversity,' 'multiculturalism,' and foreign-language retention must be struck down as subversive of this American ideal."[37] Most threatening of his proposals was his call for the abolition of birthright citizenship for children born to undocumented parents, who would then be ineligible for all publicly funded programs. By 1995 two congressional subcommittees held hearings on proposals to abolish birthright citizenship to children born to undocumented parents in the United States. Representative Brian Bilbray (R–CA) sponsored H.R. 1363, the Citizenship Reform Act of 1995, which "would deny automatic citizenship at birth to children born in the United States to parents who are not citizens or permanent resident aliens." To establish such a law would require the undoing of the Fourteenth Amendment, which established birthright citizenship in 1868, as it states: "All persons born or naturalized in the United States, and subject to the jurisdiction thereof, are citizens of the United States and the state wherein they reside." Although the Citizenship Reform Act was ultimately unsuccessful, the growing sentiment espoused by Brimelow possessed a broad base of supporters anxious to "keep America American" (where American was clearly defined as white).[38]

The fear of an impending third-world-ization of California drove the anti-immigrant movement beyond the Proposition 187 campaign. As the move to dismantle the sixty-year-old entitlement programs keeping women and children from destitution was in full force, the pervasive stereotype of the "welfare queen" (a Black single mother producing more children to acquire more cash assistance) was joined with another racially constructed "welfare cheat." Immigrant women and their children were supposedly coming to this country specifically to obtain welfare benefits. Politicians and anti-immigrant advocates based their arguments to exclude immigrants from public assistance on the idea that welfare, even more than jobs or family reunification, was the magnet attracting immigrants to this country. By 1995 (a pre-election year), immigration and welfare reform had solidified as an intertwined set of issues and of policy proposals. Representative E. Clay Shaw Jr. of Florida argued that public benefits such as Aid to Families with Dependent Children (AFDC), food stamps, and Medicaid should be denied to noncitizens. He argued that the denial of benefits to immigrants would take away the attraction of coming to the United States.[39]

Through such popularly recognized discourse of *citizenship* as the foundation of social, economic, and political entitlement, immigrant reproduction took priority over economic production in the nativist discourse arguing for immigration reform.[40] The arguments that claimed that undocumented Latina/o immigrants were a drain on the welfare system joined with another, considerably different, narrative of immigrants and welfare abuse. In the congressional welfare reform debates, the foreigner racialization discourse included Asian stereotypes, specifically claims of high public assistance use by noncitizens from Southeast Asia, and charges of fraudulent receipt by elderly immigrants from Asia of Supplemental Security Income (SSI, cash assistance for the elderly, the disabled, and the blind living below the poverty level). Welfare reform and immigration reform became interconnected, as, in a massive overhaul, public assistance was specifically revised, provision by provision, with different forms of citizenship requirements than before. The move to deny public benefits to all or most noncitizens, including legal permanent residents, moved beyond the scope of California's "Save our State" initiative.

According to William Wong: "During the Congressional debate about reforming welfare in 1996, a new villainous image emerged to supplement that of the former welfare queen. This image was of an elderly Chinese immigrant undeservedly getting Supplemental Security Income (SSI). This foreign-looking senior citizen should be supported by his or her middle-class children and not by the U.S. Treasury, the image implied."[41] Accordingly, some welfare reform proposals suggested cancellation of SSI benefits for this population. Norm Matloff, a University of California professor of computer science, presented a "comprehensive" testimony to the U.S. Senate Judiciary

Committee on February 6, 1996, claiming that immigrant Chinese senior welfare recipients did not need SSI assistance. Focusing on census data of immigrants who arrived in California between 1980 and 1987, Matloff claimed that the recent increase in public assistance use by Chinese elderly was due to a scam perpetrated by well-to-do, middle-class, naturalized-citizen Chinese children who were undeservedly putting their parents on public assistance and in some cases even profiting from their parents' SSI cash payments.[42] Basing his conclusions on the increase of SSI benefits to recent immigrants from China, and on selective interviews[43] obtained within a two-month period from urban and suburban locations in the San Francisco Bay Area, Matloff concluded that these elderly parents merely waited for their five-year deeming period to end so they could, inevitably, receive cash assistance through SSI.

After citing instances of elderly Chinese SSI recipients enjoying all the comforts of middle-class life, including Caribbean cruises, Matloff's testimony before the Senate Judiciary Committee advocated the banning of SSI to all immigrants until they became naturalized citizens. He argued that "since the deeming period is set for five years, and one can apply for naturalization after residing in the U.S. for five years, the bill's impact on immigrant usage of SSI is very small."[44] Matloff in his testimony also claimed that any bar to public assistance for immigrants would be easily thwarted by the "easiness" of obtaining citizenship, given especially the likelihood of such elderly immigrants' passing the civics exam and English requirement for citizenship.

Drawing from the assumed model-minority stereotype, Matloff's analysis depended upon the assumption that most Chinese elderly recipients were associated with economically successful offspring. In his final arguments, he claimed to have demonstrated that welfare, not family reunification, is the primary attraction for immigrating to the United States. This perception prevailed in the provisions eventually passed by the Senate and later signed into law by President Clinton. By the time the Welfare Reform Bill reached Clinton, the immigrant provisions cutting benefits to noncitizens far surpassed those demanded by earlier arguments to reduce some benefits.

In line with Matloff's argument to exclude immigrants from public benefits, widely recognized immigration scholar and Harvard professor George Borjas was instrumental in coining the notion of the United States as a "welfare magnet" for low-skilled immigrants. (Borjas has been a forceful spokesperson and prolific writer in favor of eliminating public benefits to immigrants.) Along with Matloff, Borjas testified before the U.S. Senate Sub-committee on Immigration. With an abundance of research on immigrant welfare use, Borjas concluded that the shift toward a less skilled immigrant flow leads to a sizable increase in costs associated with welfare use among immigrants.[45] Noting the drastic shifts in immigration percentages arising from the 1965 Immigration Act (from 53 percent European, 25 percent Latin American, and 6 percent Asian in the 1950s, to 11 percent European, 42 percent Latin American, and 42 percent Asian), Borjas argued that recent immigrant groups showed, in addition to this shift in national origins, a drastic decline in marketable skills. Borjas provided economic calculations of labor force earnings and welfare utilization by immigrants; he noted the increase in welfare use from pre-1965 to post-1965 cohorts due to the deskilled nature of recent immigrants. Although providing a somewhat narrow econometric model to make such determinations, Borjas argued that an overly generous welfare state offered disincentives for current immigrants to work. In a 1991 article, Borjas and Stephen J. Trejo argued that immigrants in the United States actually assimilated into overly generous welfare dependency.[46]

Several significant problems with Borjas's findings have been noted by immigration researchers from the nonpartisan Urban Institute. Although Borjas actually found a very small difference between immigrant and native use of cash benefits, he overemphasized the "increase" in immigrant participation as an indicator of immigrant overuse. Borjas also did not recognize that a sizable portion of immigrants utilizing welfare were in fact refugees, elderly, and disabled noncitizens. Borjas also based his conclusions on household data rather than on individual utilization rates; thus, citizen children of immigrant parents were counted as immigrant household utilizers of benefits—which has drastic statistical implications, given the high poverty levels of immigrant households with citizen children. Borjas also included in his studies a broader measure of welfare use, one including cash assistance as well as Medicaid, food stamps, energy assistance, housing assistance, and WIC (the supplemental food program for women, infants, and children), programs that go beyond those typically considered "welfare."[47]

Regardless of the flaws and broad conclusions based on narrow research in the work of both Matloff and Borjas, their testimonies proved influential. The Personal Responsibility Work Opportunity Reconciliation Act (PRWORA), signed by President Clinton on August 22, 1996, included provisions that created qualifications for eligibility based on citizenship status. The 104th

Congress enacted new qualification rules for immigrants, based on principles of self-sufficiency, specifically to disqualify larger categories of immigrants from public assistance.[48] Matloff's investigative research and conclusions were openly documented in Title IV, "Restricting Welfare and Public Benefits for Aliens," of PRWORA, where Congress reported:

> It continues to be the immigration policy of the United States that (A) aliens within the Nation's borders not depend on public resources to meet their needs, but rather rely on their own capabilities and the resources of their families, their sponsors, and private organizations, and (B) the availability of public benefits not constitute an incentive for immigration to the United States. (C) Despite the principle of self–sufficiency, aliens have been applying for and receiving public benefits from Federal, State, and local governments at increasing rates.[49]

Thus, although immigrants utilize public benefits at rates comparable to U.S. citizens, cuts to immigrant communities accounted for 44 percent of the overall estimated federal savings from the Personal Responsibility Act.[50] The elimination of coverage for immigrants saved an estimated $23.7 billion over the first six years, constituting the 44 percent savings of the Act's total $53.4 billion savings package.[51] Demarcating eligibility on citizenship status was a convenient means for an economically motivated legislative agenda. By the time 1996 rolled around, this broad sweeping cut to immigrants had been shaped and legitimized through the anti-immigrant campaign that defined immigrants as outsiders, foreign threats, and leeches on scarce public resources. The construction of an immigrant threat successfully targeted the most vulnerable noncitizen populations: women, children, and the elderly. However, this constructed threat to the nation's well-being was multifaceted. Thus, even while immigrants were losing access and rights to public assistance, they were also seen as potential terrorist threats. It is important to understand how these intersecting constructions merged and reinforced the anti-immigrant hostility that furthered immigrant vulnerability and the fear over their use of public resources.

WELFARE CHEATS OR TERRORISTS: CRIMINALIZING IMMIGRANTS

In the wake of the bombing of the Federal Building in Oklahoma City, the Antiterrorism and Effective Death Penalty Act was signed by Clinton early in April 1996. Although the parties responsible for the bombing of the Federal Building were whites identified with a white militia organization, this antiterrorism law targeted immigrants and noncitizens. The immigrant provisions of the law required that any immigrant who committed a serious crime could face deportation regardless of the age at which he or she had entered the country, the duration of time since the crime was committed, or time served for the sentence. The antiterrorism law eliminated an immigrant's right to apply for a waiver of deportation or to appeal the case in federal court. Once they came to the attention of immigration authorities, immigrants would now be subject to mandatory detention, no matter how many years have passed since they were convicted, or how serious their offense.[52]

Merely one month after passing PRWORA, on September 30, 1996, President Clinton signed the Illegal Immigration Reform and Immigrant Responsibility Act of 1996 (IIRIRA). Aiming to "crack down" on illegal immigration, this immigration reform law broadened legal restrictions on immigration and welfare provisions to immigrants already residing in the country, as well as to those desiring or planning to immigrate.[53] Perhaps the most devastating provision within the IIRIRA was the loss of due process for all noncitizens ever convicted of a "serious crime [definitions of which were broadened in this act]." In the face of the foreigner racialization of the "terrorist threat" and the criminalization of immigrants of color, this law moved beyond the Antiterrorism Act, passed just five months prior, to establish that noncitizens perceived as a threat (specifically, convicted of a felony) be immediately ordered for deportation without trial, regardless of time already served for their crime. Those affected included noncitizens who arrived when they were infants, felons who had committed two misdemeanors (e.g., stealing a loaf of bread on two separate occasions), and those who had served time for a felony in their youth but gone on to establish a family and a stable life. The 1996 laws also took away a judge's ability to oversee the actions of the Immigration and Nationalization Service to ensure that it acted in accordance with the law and not in an arbitrary manner. Therefore there are no review processes, no hearings, no options for immigrants who fall into this category. Since the passing of these laws, thousands of immigrants have been deported each month through this provision alone.

In addition to new deportation rules, the IIRIRA established higher hurdles for immigrants' use of public assistance. The law increased the sponsorship earnings requirements so that sponsors' incomes had to be 125 percent above the poverty level. The binding affidavits of support signed by sponsors were made legally enforceable, so that the sponsor's income would always be calculated into the immigrant's income level and thus prevent eligibility for means-tested public assistance. If the immigrant should receive assistance, the sponsor would then become legally liable and could be sued for any benefits deemed falsely obtained by the immigrant. The public charge provision might label the immigrant ineligible for reentry to the country, as a "potential cost to society," if he/she received any form of cash assistance.

The 1996 welfare and immigration reform legislation led to the further erosion of rights and entitlements for immigrants residing in the United States. Like citizens, immigrants contributed to the public welfare system through paying taxes. Yet the use of citizenship to demarcate eligibility for such services set immigrants further outside of constitutional protections. The hostile climate that marshaled in welfare exclusions (and the loss of rights and guarantees for immigrants generally) resulted in a state of panic, confusion, and betrayal among immigrants from Asia. The unfolding of this story is rarely told and little understood, yet the impact of welfare reform on Asian immigrant women and their families provides a critical exposure of the implications of race and gender politics on social policy.

This analysis of the citizenship politics that shaped the 1996 anti-immigrant reform movement proves salient to understanding the anti-immigrant movement of nearly ten years later. The 1996 policies were critical in the erosion of rights that shaped the formation and implementation of post-9/11 anti-immigrant reforms in the name of national security. The ten-year anniversary of welfare and immigration reform has not revealed less poverty among immigrant communities. In fact, with the resurgent attack on undocumented immigration at the national level, physical, political, and economic insecurity for immigrants worsened beyond what was, in the 1990s, thought the lowest point. In many ways, it was the passage of these groundbreaking immigration and welfare reforms in 1996 that paved the way for the even harsher policies and practices of the first decade of the twenty-first century.

Although, in my concluding chapter, I address the implications of the 1996 policies on the anti-immigration movement in post-9/11 in more detail, here I want to stress the importunate pattern of Asian invisibility. Under the guise of "comprehensive immigration reform," the most hyperbolic strains of the anti-immigrant agenda called for the criminalization and removal of the estimated 11.5 million undocumented immigrants residing in the United States. To codify the idea that "illegals" (primarily migrants from Mexico) were entering the country to take jobs away from Americans, drive wages down, and act in complete disregard to U.S. laws, the Sensenbrenner bill (H.R. 4437), the Border Protection, Anti-Terrorism, and Illegal Immigration Control Act of 2005, was passed by the House of Representatives on December 16, 2005. Most notable was that this legislation made it a felony for a noncitizen to be in the United States without proper documentation, and that apprehended immigrants would be taken into custody by the federal government. As felons, undocumented immigrants would then be subject to deportation or indefinite incarceration, and would subsequently be ineligible for legal entry in the future. This bill also prohibited aid of any kind to undocumented immigrants. Existing law against assisting an undocumented immigrant to remain or enter the United States was expanded to include sanctions against any charity, church, or neighbor who aids that person to remain in the country—for example, by providing food, clothing, or shelter. The Sensenbrenner bill essentially signaled to undocumented immigrants that they were regarded strictly as criminals subject to expedited deportation and/or extended incarceration. Previous law that eroded noncitizens' rights to due process (that is, the IIRIRA of 1996) was to be fortified through broadening the power of local law enforcement officials to enforce federal immigration law.

The passing of the Sensenbrenner bill by the House propelled immigrants, including thousands of undocumented immigrants, and their supporters across the country into the streets, in highly visible protests. Immigrants demonstrated in response to the heightened scapegoating of the undocumented population for the country's waning economic and national security. Angered by the anti-immigrant drive for policies that would essentially push undocumented immigrants into complete hiding and vulnerability, demonstrators brought their mass presence into prominent public view, showing in full display their national origins as well as their connection to America.

With the mass demonstrations of legal and undocumented immigrants visible in the streets of major cities across the country, soon the question arose: where were the Asian immigrants? As of 2004, of the estimated 11.5 million undocumented immigrants in the country, 13 percent (approximately 1.5 million) were from Asia. What was striking, however, was not necessarily the quantitative difference between Asian and Latina/o undocumented immigrants, but rather their vastly different characterization. In an article published in *Z Magazine* in June 2006, prolific activist Betita Martinez stated that undocumented Asian immigrants had not demonstrated to the same degree as Latino immigrants, arguing that this arose primarily from differences of interests. According to Martinez, the undocumented Asian immigrants were primarily concerned with the family reunification provision of immigration reform; because a major difficulty for lawful entry had to do with backlogs of up to twenty years for family reunification visas, Martinez stated, Asian immigrants would not have the same compelling urgency to demonstrate as would other undocumented immigrants.

One unfortunate description of the demonstrations was that Asian immigrants simply were not there, or that their presence was insignificant. Martinez argues that, given the smaller population of illegal Asian immigrants, "it is not surprising to find small numbers of Asian-origin demonstrators supporting the demand for immigrant rights, although some Chinese Americans did come out for the protests in New York and San Francisco. Filipinas/os have higher rates of 'illegals' and are more supportive of the struggle for immigrant rights."[54] It does make logical sense that the sheer demographics and smaller Asian population in the United States would result in fewer persons of Asian origin being at immigrant rights rallies. However, to conclude that the smaller numbers of Asian immigrants and Asian American advocates meant that they were less supportive of immigrant rights denies other factors at play for Asian immigrants. To dismissively say that, in two cities, only a few Chinese showed up erases the presence, coalitions, and investment of thousands of people of Asian origin who did show up, and the hundreds of thousands who were too fearful to go out in public. A scant few newspaper articles mentioned the presence of Asian contingencies, usually through the image of Asian groups beating on Korean drums while chanting "Si se puede" alongside a vast majority of Latina/o demonstrators.[55] Although it remains logical that, due to sheer demographics, there would be far fewer Asian immigrant demonstrators, what remains less understood are the particular levels of fear and stigma that leave undocumented Asian immigrants in hiding.

Asian immigrants tend to arrive legally through temporary visas, but then overstay them to continue working or to live with family members. The geographics of the journey significantly shapes the ability to leave Asia and the ability to enter the country, either through U.S. ports of entry or through Mexico or Canada. For Asian migrants, crossing via the U.S. borders poses numerous challenges and obstacles, given issues of language, foreignness, and lack of connections, of networks, and of resources. Thousands arrive through trafficking, or are smuggled in shipping containers that have occasionally led to deadly situations. Deportation back to Asia can be a final and tragic ending to their lives in the United States.

Within Asian communities in the United States, a stigma has remained attached to undocumented immigrants. Even within their own communities, Asian people live in fear and do not talk about their immigration status openly. According to the former Immigration and Naturalization Services, in the year 2000 the largest group of estimated undocumented immigrants from Asia were Chinese (23 percent), followed by Filipinas/os (17 percent), South Asians (14 percent), and Koreans (11 percent).[56] Within the community of undocumented Filipinos/as, the term *Tago Ng Tago* (commonly referred to as TNT) emerged; the term translates as "always hiding," connoting the intense level of fear and invisibility. Given the fewer numbers of Asian immigrants, undocumented Asian immigrants (and legal permanent residents) have avoided public demonstrations from fear of being recognized or identified. The added stigma and hiding experienced by undocumented Asian immigrants has contributed to situations of extreme employer abuse, exploitation, and violation of labor laws. Thus, other significant reasons resulted in fewer Asian immigrants at these important immigrant rights demonstrations.

The immigration and citizenship politics that emerged in 2005 revealed very similar patterns to the constructions that played out in 1996. The invisibility of the particular circumstances Asian immigrants faced, during the debates over welfare reform, resulted in an unexpected upsurge of suffering, distress, and trauma with the law's passing. As happened with other immigrant groups, the historical legacies of exclusion and violence persisted in the contemporary practices initiated through social policy. The intense and devastating implications that unfolded with the implementation of welfare reform should be a lesson for immigration scholars and activists to consider more comprehensively the multilayers of citizenship and race, so that dominant nativist forces cannot pit groups against each other or project a criminalization of particular groups. Through the course of this book, I provide detailed examinations of, and analyze the particular circumstances and implications for, certain constituencies of Asian immigrant women who were both devastated by welfare reform and instrumental in achieving major restorations through collective action and agency.

Integral throughout my discussions of nativism, race, gender, and the state as they pertain to the convergence of welfare and immigration reform is an examination of the outsider racialization that embroils Asian immigrants.[57] The anti-immigrant movement clearly involved multiple levels of foreigner racialization to rationalize the massive welfare and immigration reform movements that would fundamentally restructure the rights of noncitizens residing in the United States. Less understood and recognized are the critical details of how the anti-immigrant movement constructed Asian immigrants as foreigners who were "unfairly utilizing American resources." Also missing from academic discussions are the modes of resistance developed by Asian American community organizations and immigrant rights coalitions to challenge anti-immigrant provisions that targeted vulnerable groups of noncitizens. The heterogeneity within the Asian American community, and the complex differences due to the high number of noncitizens who arrived as refugees, have further complicated the dynamics between the politics of citizenship and the responsibility of the state. The next chapter examines the way citizenship politics reshaped welfare for noncitizens, and specifically how Asian immigrants and refugees were configured through this process.

2

Welfare Reform and the Politics of Citizenship

> When the Personal Responsibility Act of 1996 transformed welfare,
> it also transformed citizenship. Flouting the ideal of universal citizen-
> ship, the act distinguishes poor single mothers from other citizens and
> subjects them to a separate system of law. Under this system of law,
> poor single mothers forfeit rights the rest of us enjoy as fundamental
> to our citizenship—family rights, reproductive rights, and vocational
> liberty—just because they need welfare.
>
> —Gwendolyn Mink, *Whose Welfare?*

Why does citizenship matter in an examination of welfare? For the first time in welfare history, the 1996 reform law explicitly made citizenship status a criterion of eligibility for public benefits. At a minimum, the economic motivations were implicit in the 40 percent savings made to the welfare budget from immigrant cuts alone. The rationale to exclude immigrants from public assistance came at a time when neoliberal free trade policies were proliferating to advance the movement of capital, and while nativist Americans struggled to fortify U.S. borders in the face of a persistent transnational migration to the U.S. imperial center. The increased visibility of the emerging majority population, largely due to migrants from Mexico, Central and South America, and Asia, including Southeast Asia, necessitated a reinscription of who belonged to the American politic and who remained outsiders. A broader investment to reestablish the citizen subject was embedded in the idea that poor immigrants were taking resources from hardworking citizens.

Given the complexity of welfare reform, an analysis based solely upon legal citizenship status would oversimplify and overlook the ways citizens were also pushed outside the borders of the nation.[1] Welfare recipients, primarily women of color, were often constructed as threats to American families and as enemies of the state—what Jacqui Alexander refers to as the construction of the "internal enemy."[2] Regardless of economic and social conditions perpetuating poverty, women's dependency on the state was likened to degeneracy, pathology, and a breeding of tomorrow's criminals. The concept of *dependency* became antithetical to *personal responsibility*. Thus, any mother who relied on the state for public assistance was thereby not taking *personal responsibility* for her welfare and her children's well-being. Although using welfare is not a crime, citizen welfare recipients have long been subjected to state technologies and disciplining that challenge their fundamental rights.

By bringing together these two strains of citizenship politics in an examination of welfare and immigration reform, it is possible to see how social citizenship and legal citizenship are inextricably tied together and have profound implications for immigrant women of color, who in 1996 were held to a newly defined *immigrant responsibility.*

Addressing conditions of globalization, antiracist and feminist scholarship have expanded the intellectual concept of *citizenship* as a primary element in contemporary global politics.[3] Reformulations of citizenship have further developed conceptual and structural frameworks for belonging, membership, exclusion, justice, and equality.[4] New theories of citizenship have responded to racial and cultural formations within a more fluid transnational marketplace and to a global economic restructuring leading to increased cross-border migrations. The reemergence of citizenship in political discussions, as Stuart Hall and David Held noted in 1990, has been due both to national debates over entitlement and equity and to processes stemming from globalization and the growing pace of international interdependence. Although no single formal definition of citizenship suffices, three primary notions encompass the logic of citizenship: membership; rights and duties in reciprocity; real participation in practice.[5] The terms of citizenship have been shaped both historically and spontaneously, as societies struggle over the meaning and scope of membership to the community in which one lives. The issue around membership—who does and who does not belong—is where the politics of citizenship begins. It is impossible to chart the history of the concept very far without coming up sharply against successive attempts to restrict citizenship to certain groups, and to exclude others. In different historical periods, different groups have propounded, and profited from, this *politics of closure:* property owners, men, white people, educated people, those in particular occupations or with particular skills, adults.[6]

TRANSNATIONALISM AND THE POLITICS OF CITIZENSHIP

We have come to understand the *politics of closure* as the processes by which *differential citizenship* is evoked to exclude some citizen members from full participation in the social polity; the term also covers the more general demarcation that delineates who can belong and acquire inclusion. Citizenship is a multilayered construct at constant play on the local, national, and international political terrain.[7] However, a tendency has emerged to examine citizenship at two disconnected levels. Social citizenship is imbued with political issues encompassing the notions of rights, liberty, and justice for marginalized groups denied equal citizenship due to discriminating factors (race, gender, sexuality, age, class, etc.). British sociologist T. H. Marshall is frequently cited for his influential elaboration of social citizenship as a framework of rights and inclusion in relation to social inequality.[8] Writing in postwar England, Marshall argued that citizenship by definition should guarantee full membership within the community of all of its members. However, factors such as social class impeded the full membership and equal participation of those members of society unable to participate in all facets of civil and political citizenship due to their economic conditions. The inherent conflict between citizenship as a system of equality and social class as a system of inequality results in unequal citizenship. To guarantee full rights to citizenship, Marshall argued for a liberal welfare state that would ensure that every member of society would be able to access and participate in the common life of society.[9] This would mean that all citizens would possess the protections of civil, political, and social rights (which include public education, health care, unemployment insurance, old-age pensions) that lead to equal access to basic human goods (security, prosperity, and freedom).[10] Thus, social citizenship involves concerns of power and marginalization (where all citizens do not have equal access to the rights and guarantees granted by their citizenship status).

The study of legal citizenship has been preoccupied by less theoretical constructions, and is often situated in discussions regarding immigration and political status. Work by Will Kymlicka and Wayne Norman points out the massive proliferation of citizenship theory in light of transnational patterns of international migrations and questions of national belonging. They argue that citizenship is linked to ideas of individual entitlement, on the one hand, and of attachment to a particular community, on the other.[11] For Asian Americans, citizenship has remained central to the politics of immigration, exclusion, inclusion, and community activism. With 68 percent of the Asian American population consisting of foreign-born Asians, the politics of citizenship remain critical in social policies that attempt to differentiate along citizenship lines. Given the continued high rate of immigration from Asia, the politics of citizenship in the era of transnational migrations and displacements requires a reconceptualization of rights and entitlements within national borders.

Citizenship-as-legal-status—that is, as membership in a particular community—and citizenship-as-desirable-activity, where the extent and quality of one's citizenship is a function of one's participation in that community, converge when societies struggle to position cultural newcomers outside social entitlements.[12] Coinciding with the so-called age of migration, in which massive numbers of people are moving across borders, is an age of nationalism in which the politics of cultural difference shape and challenge national policies.[13] The new nativism that shaped the most recent anti-immigrant movement illustrates Benedict Anderson's now widely recognized theorization of *imagined communities*. Official nationalism appears as an anticipatory strategy adopted by dominant groups threatened with marginalization or exclusion from an emerging nationally imagined community.[14] In this case, the threat consisted of the emerging majority of people of color, the increased visibility of immigrants from the global South, a redefining of American multiculturalism, and a challenge to unquestioning whiteness. Where nationalism and racism meet, Anderson argues, "nationalism thinks in terms of historical destinies, while racism dreams of eternal contaminations."[15] Official nationalism, then, which is a conscious self-protective policy, operates through self-preservation, often attacking the emerging imagined communities that threaten its superiority and political interests.

Although transnational movements and formations are not new, the magnitude of transnational movements has, in the current state of globalization, redoubled in scope.[16] Both the magnitude of migration and the formation of transnational communities have elicited questions of national identity, whereby exclusionary projects work to deny immigrant access to basic resources. Christian Joppke offers a helpful conceptualization of a new model of postnational membership, *denizenship,* which marks an inherently vulnerable status for immigrants residing in countries with increasing emphasis on citizenship status. He argues that "immigration has opened up a post-Marshallian view of citizenship, which stresses its externally exclusive dimension, the drawing of boundaries between members and non-members."[17] When the United States was, once, considered a nation of immigrants, the distinction between citizens and immigrants had more to do with political rights than with civil rights. Then, equal protections under the Constitution were granted to all people resident in the nation, but with the increasing power of citizenship for determining rights, immigrants face a deterioration of rights and must live in a second-class status.

Concerned centrally with the racialized processes of transnational politics, immigrant inclusion, and national agendas, *race theorists* emphasize racist structures that shape vulnerabilities for specific immigrant groups. Speaking to Benedict Anderson's conceptualization of the *nation,* David Theo Goldberg argues that both nation and race are historically embedded and remain intersecting signifying discourses.[18] Depending on the historical moment and the political conditions at play, nation and race may have more or less common cause in movements over national interest. Thus, although Joppke positions national interest (as opposed to politically motivated interest groups) as the primary force behind immigration control, Goldberg establishes that national interest is never fully devoid of racial interests.

Stating that transnationalism and the explosion of immigration from the global South have created "new racial conditions," Howard Winant suggests that U.S. white hegemony faces a formidable new problem in the "homeland": the problem of *diaspora.*[19] He argues that U.S. immigration has always been organized by national racialized policies and practices, but that in post-9/11 American immigration policy faces not only a racialized concern, but a patriotic turn under the terrain of national security. Yet, in spite of hegemonic racial conditions that continue to shape the process of inclusion and exclusion of the world's migrants, the broader global demographic transformations have resulted in settled migrant communities that reshape the sociopolitical landscape. The presence of stronger, more established migrant communities from "below" offers possibilities for substantial grassroots responses to racially based immigration policies from "above."[20]

In relation to transnational migration and immigrant communities, the well-known debate over the durability of state sovereignty has been pressed by the prolific work of Saskia Sassen.[21] Although the issue of state sovereignty is far beyond the scope of the present volume, Sassen's conceptualization of the transnationalizing of immigration policy is helpful for understanding contemporary debates in light of current policy formations. In particular, Sassen emphasizes the increasing significance of human rights in national courts.[22] For her, not only have the conditions of globalization resulted in transnational economic processes that must interact with governance of national economies, but also national immigration concerns must be in dialogue with international entities concerned with the political positioning of migrants. There is much disagreement over the strength of the United Nations to protect immigrants and displaced peoples across the globe, but Sassen recognizes that the existing body holds potential for developing a stronger human rights entity to shape immigration policies and practices. Although I do not intend to deliberate legal claims that human rights violations through U.S. social policy may have denied immigrants life-sustaining benefits, I do show (in chapters 3 and 4) the role of human rights discourse from the immigrant communities of resistance (what Winant refers to as from "below") to reshape existing policies of exclusion that left noncitizens desperate for economic survival. These conceptual arguments centering transnationalism, nation, and immigration politics foreground the anti-immigrant movement of the 1990s that reshaped social policy and altered fundamental rights for noncitizens in the United States.

Success in this anti-immigrant project required the denial of U.S. expansionist roles in global economic and political displacement leading to the post-1965 immigration waves, while reimagining poverty and economic dependency in race and gender terms as ideological challenges for full citizenship. The era of welfare and immigration reform established the neoconservative premise that it is every citizen's responsibility to be economically dependent on the market or male spouse rather than on the state. Immigrants in the United States, regardless of what they contributed to the U.S. treasury, were set fundamentally outside the bounds of public entitlements, as non-Americans who needed to learn the ascribed value of economic independence as an assumed responsibility of American citizenship.

This chapter looks specifically at the logic behind the 1996 welfare reform law, the Personal Responsibility Work Opportunity Reconciliation Act

(PRWORA), to examine the way citizenship politics has reshaped welfare policy for immigrants. Citizens and noncitizens in poverty who use public assistance remain disenfranchised and subject to state surveillance and technologies, unlike those whose economic security is not encompassed by the welfare state. To show how social citizenship and legal citizenship are intertwined, I first consider the racialized and gendered citizenship politics that demonized "overdependency" as un-American and made "personal responsibility" an insider-defined proviso for citizenship. I then integrate the added complexities of the racial and gendered politics of legal citizenship that charged poor immigrant women as "inassimilable foreigners" who should be kept outside of the structural confines of citizenship entitlements. The availability of formal citizenship status as a demarcating eligibility factor in social policy further complicates how technologies of the state are able to add another layer of enforcement and discipline in the lives of poor immigrant families. Finally I take up again the theoretical salience of a multilayered citizenship in better understanding the convergence of immigration and welfare entitlement for immigrants in the United States.

DIFFERENTIATED CITIZENSHIP, WOMEN OF COLOR, AND PRWORA

By the time President Clinton vowed "to end welfare as we know it" in the 1994 presidential campaign, the construction of the "welfare queen" was firmly etched into the imaginaries of the majority of Americans. The stereotype of the welfare queen moved beyond a mere racialized and gendered construction, to a *public identity* with moral underpinnings supporting a specific legislative outcome.[23] The public antipathy for all the assumed behaviors of welfare mothers resulted in a *politics of disgust* that fully legitimized the complete dismantling of welfare.[24]

> The welfare mother is a deviant social creature. She is able-bodied, but unwilling to work at any of the thousands of jobs available to her; she is fundamentally lazy and civically irresponsible; she spends her days doing nothing but sponging off the government's largesse. Despite the societal pressure to be gainfully employed, she enjoys her status as a "dependent" on the state and seeks at all costs to prolong her dependency. Promiscuous and shortsighted, she is a woman who defiantly has children out of wedlock. Without morals of her own, she is unlikely to transmit good family values to her children. She lacks the educational skills to get ahead and the motivation to acquire them. Thus, she is the root of her own family's intergenerational poverty and related social ills. She is her own worst enemy. And she is Black.[25]

Fundamentally, the "Welfare Queen" comes of the premise that mothers who need welfare are not only bad mothers, but also irresponsible citizens—bad citizens in need of punitive measures to get them out of the home and into the wage-earning economy. Thus, Aid to Families with Dependent Children (AFDC), the cash assistance program primarily for mothers of children under eighteen, was reformed from an entitlement program to keep poor families from abject poverty to a system of welfare-to-work, a program of limited assistance with the sole intent to move women into wage-earning jobs outside their homes; the program is known as Temporary Assistance to Needy Families (TANF).

The welfare-to-work approach was based fundamentally on a moral doctrine of marriage, two-parent families, and the sanctioning of single mothers. PRWORA explicitly begins with the statement "Marriage is the foundation of a successful society; and Marriage is an essential institution of a successful society which promotes the interests of children."[26] Following the construct of *family values,* the congressional report presents data citing the increase of children utilizing AFDC, and proposes that children born to unmarried women are responsible for the rise in AFDC benefits among children. The report does not consider the existing gender and racial disparities in the labor market for women, or the systemic reasons and conditions of poverty for women; instead, a list of social maladies supposedly resulting from children born "out-of-wedlock" is given as explanation for poverty, poor educational attainment, crime, and teen pregnancy. Arguing that two-parent families tend to have lesser rates of poverty, and that single-parent families tend to breed neglectful, abusive, and deteriorating situations, the report claimed that "in light of this demonstration of the crisis in our Nation, it is the sense of the Congress that prevention of out-of-wedlock pregnancy and reduction in out-of-wedlock birth are very important Government interests."[27] Thus, PRWORA's amendments to the Social Security Act, which first established federal responsibility to poor mothers, claimed that government responsibility is to:

(1) provide assistance to needy families so that children may be cared for in their own homes or in the homes of relatives;

(2) end the dependence of needy parents on government benefits by promoting job preparation, work, and marriage;

(3) prevent and reduce the incidence of out-of-wedlock pregnancies and establish annual numerical goals for preventing and reducing the incidence of these pregnancies; and

(4) encourage the formation and maintenance of two-parent families.[28]

Given the moral reasoning that established "out-of-wedlock" births as the main cause of the "crisis in our nation," the actual provisions set forth in PRWORA presented notable contradictions to legitimize cruel sanctions for poor families, particularly those headed by single mothers. If problems of crime, poor education levels, poverty, and teenage pregnancy stemmed from neglect in homes headed by single mothers, why did Congress force women to leave their homes and their children so as to engage in mandatory work or community service that did not enhance the economic well-being of most recipients, given the low wages (in some cases, no wages) received? Work requirements forced single mothers to leave their children for thirty hours per week in order to receive cash assistance.[29] Rather than addressing low wages, inadequate child care, domestic violence, or poor health care as existing factors in structural disparities, Congress established a punitive system for women in poverty with children and needing assistance. Ninety-five percent of adult AFDC recipients were women; the punitive consequences of this law made poor mothers more vulnerable to state surveillance, labor exploitation, sexual harassment, and domestic violence.

Welfare-to-work was not always the logic behind assisting poor mothers. In fact, the origins of welfare for poor mothers emerged out of a concern that single mothers *not* seek paid labor but focus on the healthy reproduction of future citizens, at a time of industrialization and nation building. Like T. H. Marshall in his concerns about unequal access to resources and participation as a result of class inequalities, early welfare advocates and supporters argued that welfare for poor mothers was essential for a solid American citizenry. The projection of single motherhood as a recognized "social problem" did not emerge until the early decades of the twentieth century. Commonly conceptualized single mothers of the early 1900s were widows, deserted women, "illegitimate" mothers, and, rarely, divorced women.[30] A brief look at the historical formation of welfare for mothers leads to fundamental questions regarding American citizenship. This background reveals the gendered and racialized underpinnings that led to the demise of welfare with PRWORA in 1996.

THE EMERGENCE OF WELFARE AS CITIZENSHIP-MAKING

Concern over the increasing visibility of urban-dwelling impoverished women and children led to the maternalist reform movement for mothers' aid programs, the earliest precedent of the contemporary welfare state. The discourse over the struggle for Mothers' Pension programs revealed a deeply embedded racial, gendered, and class politics of citizenship formation that would continue to impact the structure of public welfare as well as its implementation. Maternalist definitions of *moral motherhood* constituted standards of class, ethnic, and religious constructions that did not always coincide with those of the children or parents being "saved."[31] Consequently most laws administered social provisions through systems of casework where social workers would determine *who* was a single mother "deserving" of benefits, through biased middle-class, Protestant-valued moral testing; "suitable home" provisions could refuse aid to any mother who failed to provide an environment meeting the social worker's standards.[32]

Although the platform of moral motherhood stressed women's gender difference and special needs within the domestic sphere, it also appealed to the Anglo-Saxon concern about the quality of the citizenry and the future of democracy, with an implied "racial uplift" and American quality of motherhood.[33] The women policy innovators drew from a broad tradition of maternalist thinking rooted in republican ideology of gendered citizenship that invoked the morality of the domestic sphere and asserted white women's political significance to "the race" and the nation.[34] Within the context of essentialist racial beliefs that perceived an increasing threat of "racial inferiority" and cultural deterioration of American society, these white middle-class reformers played on racial anxieties by focusing ostensibly on the sake of the children as well as of the republic, where motherhood became a cultural project.

Through the notion of conformity, caseworkers would determine which poor single mothers were deserving or worthy of provisions, based upon the mother's ability to prove her assimilability and her ability to reform into the dominant Anglo-Saxon culture. As a result, mother-directed policies "claimed only certain kinds of women as their subjects and the management of cultural diversity as a major objective, targeting poor, single mothers and offering means-tested benefits to compensate for an absent paternal wage, thereby to reduce the single mother's need to work outside of the home."[35] Pervasive racial ideologies held by officials that perceived women of color as inassimilable reflected the nature of early welfare construction as not only a gendered project of women's subordination but also a racial project that perpetuated the "othered" noncitizen status of women of color as workers rather than mothers.

The racial politics that materialized through the movement and construction of Mothers' Pension programs persisted and informed the federally funded ADC (Aid to Dependent Children) program under the larger Social Security Act of 1935. A two-tiered system, Social Security policy installed programs that would systematically perpetuate and reinforce existing racial and gendered exclusions and inequalities, by working primarily to insure the economic security of working white men. On one level, the Social Security Act established two social insurance programs, Unemployment Compensation (Title III) and Old-Age Insurance (Title II), that based entitlements on "(white) masculine employment categories and patterns—primarily full-time, preferably unionized, continuous, industrial, breadwinning work."[36] ADC (Aid to Dependent Children, Title IV), Old-Age Assistance (Title I), and other "public assistance" programs, on the other hand, were left with more local control, were means-tested, and were more parsimonious in providing sustenance.

The entitlements provided through the social insurance programs were limited by imposed occupational exclusions that denied benefits to most working women as well as women and men of color. White women's citizenship based on motherhood became increasingly tied to men's wages, and the labors and lives of people of color and poor single mothers were not granted the same entitlement to higher-level forms of economic security. Instead they were relegated to the social-assistance programs, where local welfare authorities could determine benefit levels and set eligibility rules.[37] Although the construction of ADC existed to provide public assistance and protection to needy children under the age of sixteen in single-parent families, the program continued to systematically discriminate against women of color and their children through means-testing and through locally determined eligibility requirements. ADC became the last resort for divorced, single, and deserted women, many of them women of color, but states often created additional restrictions that systematically discriminated against racial minorities and single mothers of color.

EQUALIZING WELFARE: WOMEN OF COLOR AND DIFFERENTIAL CITIZENSHIP

It was not until the 1960s that welfare rights advocacy groups mobilized on a mass scale and were able to pressure Congress to loosen requirements for ADC eligibility.[38] In the context of the Civil Rights Movement, Black radical politics, and civil unrest, the National Welfare Rights Organization (NWRO) staged sit-ins, confrontations in welfare offices, and collective challenges to individual grievances, resulting in an increase of welfare recipients from 7.8 to 8.4 million.[39] Significant legal battles over the constitutionality of state regulations successfully challenged discriminatory requirements that systematically excluded single mothers of color. In 1968, the case of *King v. Smith* ruled unconstitutional a state regulation that made certain children ineligible for welfare assistance whenever their mother was cohabiting with a man other than her husband.[40] Likewise, in the cases of *Shapiro v. Thompson* and *Reynolds v. Smith*, the court ruled that regulations that denied welfare assistance to individuals who had not resided in state for one year immediately preceding application were an unjustifiable pretext for denial of benefits.[41]

With the lifting of these barriers, and with the expansion of Aid to Families with Dependent Children to include unemployed fathers and employed mothers, AFDC assistance became more accessible to women of color. By 1970, 12.4 million people were on welfare. The moment Black discontent and radical social change resulted in the liberalizing of eligibility requirements for public assistance, a racialized backlash ensued. The drastic increase in welfare rolls inflamed the antiwelfare backlash, leading to calls for reform almost as soon as welfare became available to women of color.[42] The controversial Moynihan Report, "The Negro Family: The Case for National Action," written in 1965 by Daniel Patrick Moynihan, later a senator, and originally initiated by President Johnson's War on Poverty campaign, was critical as an official government publication that "scientifically" put forth the "culture of poverty" thesis as explanation for the continued poverty faced by African Americans. Whereas the origins of public assistance advocated by early maternalists developed programs that would institute dependency on the state in the absence of a male wage-earner, the Moynihan Report stressed a racially politicized alarm of "overdependency" by Black single mothers on welfare.

The power of the Moynihan Report was in its appeal to popular assumptions of Black pathology based on racial stereotypes, and to the image of dependency as deleterious for the American economy. In the rubric of social science research, the "Moynihan Report and the general discourse on the *culture of poverty* and the *welfare queen* became synonymous with *economic dependency*—the lack of a job and/or income, the presence of a child or children with no father and/or husband (moral deviance), and, finally a charge on the collective U.S. treasury—a human debit."[43] Thus, the move toward work-not-welfare worked in tandem with racialized condemnation of the so-called cycle of dependency related to worklessness and a "pathological" Black family structure. The welfare queen was politically situated, by mainstream discourse, in conflict with a newly recognized group, the *deserving working poor.*

In his 1986 State of the Union Address, President Reagan blamed welfare for "the breakdown of the family" and said the "welfare culture" was responsible for "female and child poverty, child abandonment, horrible crimes, and deteriorating schools."[44] Further, a White House report published in 1986, *The Family: Preserving America's Future,* reported that AFDC worked as an "enabler—a program that enables women to live without a husband or a job."[45] The Family Support Act of 1988, written by Senator Daniel Patrick Moynihan, reflected the belief that welfare dependency was a societal problem requiring a dramatic reorientation of welfare policy. The Act's primary objective was to link poverty with the lack of a work ethic, thereby channeling welfare recipients into a new workfare scheme. This was accomplished in two arenas: by mandating that single mothers whose youngest children had reached the age of three must work (or train for work); and/or by replacing state support with support from fathers, transferring a child's primary source of support from public to private hands.[46]

The thrust of the Family Support Act marked a direct reversal from the original construction of Mothers' Pension as provisions meant to allow the mother to stay at home to raise her children without severe economic hardship. The *undeserving* status of single-mother families in this new context was established both by their lack of relationship to the work force (either through their own jobs or through attachment to a male breadwinner) and by their asserted role as mothers in the perpetuation of poverty.[47] The meaning of *needs* versus *rights* was essential in the mandated coercion of single welfare mothers to "work off" their benefits via workfare.[48] Instead of providing women with a guaranteed income equivalent to a family wage as a matter of right, the system stigmatized, humiliated, and harassed them. In effect, it has decreed simultaneously that these women must be, and yet cannot be, normative mothers.[49] Eight years before PRWORA, the Family Support Act had already transformed welfare from what used to theoretically be *entitlement* to the underlying concept of "mutual obligation."[50]

PRWORA[51] made the 1988 Family Support Act seem a mild attack on public assistance. The reform in the 1990s was the triumph of a thirty-year reaction against the gains of the 1960s, once African American women finally shared in AFDC and welfare finally became a right or entitlement."[52] The historical trajectory of welfare reform culminated not only in mandatory welfare-to-work programs, with stricter sanctioning rules, but also in the five-year lifetime limit of TANF. Although it was widely understood and agreed that AFDC was plagued with myriad flaws in need of reform, that system at least provided an essential economic safety net for low-income families, especially those headed by single mothers. Ironically, in the face of much harsher welfare-to-work requirements, of the loss of formal education to fulfill work requirements, and of the five-year lifetime limits, Senator Moynihan was on the other side of the fence in PRWORA's congressional debate. The five-year lifetime limit mandated that TANF was only a temporary means for mothers to utilize public resources, with the sole intent being that they find and obtain paid work and move off welfare. The language of the new law assumed that mothers were poor because they failed to take personal responsibility, by finding work and staying employed, for their economic conditions. However, the law did not prescribe outside work as a serious alternative to welfare, for it did not make work pay through wage protections and requisite social supports.[53] Mothers were forced to work off their cash assistance by engaging in some form of work *outside* their home, while having to leave their children in the care of some other person (who could be another welfare-to-work participant). Wage earning came to define one's standing as a responsible citizen—which means that one is a citizen only if one "earns."[54] With *good citizenship* defined as wage earning, mothers who used welfare were deemed irresponsible and in need of strict punitive measures to insure that they engaged in labor within the "public" realm to indicate a move away from "dependency" to self-sufficiency.

In addition to the revocation of a guaranteed assistance program, the gains established through the welfare-rights challenges in the 1960s were overturned with the devolution of TANF administration to the state level. Thus, PRWORA not only withdrew the safety net, but included no federal oversight to protect the poor against arbitrary bureaucratic decisions or other implementation problems.[55] The replacement of AFDC with TANF block grants for states allowed individual states to create their own programs and devise more stringent restrictions. Some states have required recipients to work longer hours than required by the federal law, or have reduced benefits should people not meet work requirements within two months.[56] The requirement for welfare participants to work for their benefits is not new, and some scholars have identified workfare as a form of indentured labor or slavery.[57] PRWORA, however, more stringent than previously established workfare programs, narrowly defined what could count as work, and eliminated support for college education.[58] Since PRWORA's inception, thousands of women have had to leave higher education, probably the only true means of acquiring the credentials to find sustainable employment down the road. Rather, women desperate for any form of work have created a steady stream of hundreds of thousands of poor women into the low-wage end of the labor market, competing with those already there.[59]

The requirement to establish the paternity of the father forces poor single mothers to exchange fundamental rights for subsistence.[60] Poor single mothers' decisions about child-rearing and family life, and the right to family privacy, including the determination of one's own family structure, have been abrogated by the welfare law, which compels them to establish legal relations between children and fathers. The welfare law thus activates constitutionally significant distinctions between mothers who need welfare and citizen mothers who don't, distinctions that enforce inequality.[61] Although independence is the hallmark of American citizenship, mothers must cede independence as persons and as parents, for they are forced into relations of economic dependence with biological fathers who then may claim rights to custody and visitation.[62]

With the ill-perceived premise that welfare induces childbirth and dependency, and that marriage can end child poverty, welfare has become a tool of social control, a means of "improving" the behavior of poor families, where even the neediest children are cast deeper into poverty if their mothers do not conform.[63] PRWORA took measures to prevent welfare recipients from having more children through Family Caps, the refusal to increase grants with the birth of another child. Family Caps operate under the premise that children born to mothers in poverty must pay the price for their mother's "irresponsible" behavior, as their family will have less per person on which to survive. Women must relinquish personal and intimate sexual details in order to request an exemption in cases of failed birth control or of rape. State-funded and state-administered forms of invasive birth control (like Norplant or DepoProvera) literally strip welfare mothers' physical autonomy over their bodies in exchange for financial support. Mandatory paternity requires women to identify sexual partners and binds women to men who may be harmful to their emotional or physical well-being. In general, grants were systematically reduced, and fathers' child support payments were funneled through the mothers' monthly grants.

Even though the majority of women using AFDC were white, the racial constructions of irresponsibility and over-reproduction pervaded arguments for a more punitive welfare system, which failed to address lack of jobs through a family wage and benefits. Whereas a strong welfare state was required to make Blacks full participants in the political economy, whites' refusal to extend full citizenship rights to Blacks has persistently blocked efforts to establish an inclusive welfare system. Racial justice demands aggressive government programs to relieve poverty and redress longstanding barriers to housing, jobs, and political participation, yet white Americans have resisted the expansion of welfare precisely because of its benefits to Blacks. "Black citizenship is at once America's chief reason for and impediment to a strong welfare state."[64] An article in the *New York Times* brings this point home, through a photograph of a poor white woman in Louisiana taken shortly after the former KKK Grand Wizard David Duke lost the election for governor. Duke had campaigned on a pledge to reduce the number of Blacks on welfare by cutting benefits and by offering female recipients a monetary bonus to use Norplant. In the caption beneath the photograph, the woman explains that, although she has relied on welfare herself, she voted for Duke because Blacks "just have those babies and go on welfare." This woman was willing to reduce programs that benefited her in order to ensure that Black people could not benefit from them.[65]

Welfare reform demonstrates one way that full membership within the community has moved backward where social citizenship has little weight in the face of the moral obligation of *good citizenship* completely defined by one's independence as a wage-earning American. The issues presented in this section demonstrate the ways in which welfare reform focused on citizenship in terms of *responsibilities* to the nation rather than in terms of rights, membership, and participation. Fundamentally, these critiques are premised on the social configuration of those involved as citizens within the community who, due to discriminating factors, are not granted their full citizenship status. The fact that states were granted the choice to include noncitizen immigrants for TANF shows how citizenship is multilayered. Membership and participation in the nation is determined, in this instance, state by state by political interests, who decide whether to include their noncitizen legal residents in a public support system that their tax dollars help fund. Looking more closely at the multiple layers of citizenship in welfare and immigration reform, it becomes clear that immigrants were moved further outside the community collective as inassimilable outsiders responsible for their own poverty. In addition to the further devaluation of social citizenship of *citizen* welfare recipients, PRWORA established new eligibility criteria and more stringent exclusionary provisions directed at *noncitizens*. How do we continue to engage in questions of rights and justice when the "members" of the community vary in citizenship status?

Although all families in poverty were affected by the implementation of TANF, immigrant women were central to other forms of welfare reform that excluded particular groups from benefits on the basis of citizenship status. Critical feminist welfare scholarship provides a working model in which to engage state-sanctioned unequal citizenship, but an examination of noncitizen immigrants within a citizenship framework requires bringing together two distinctive areas of citizenship scholarship. Although we still lack an encompassing framework that considers the histories, politics, and global relations of immigrants in relation to the welfare state, significant work has been done to critique the growing question of belonging and entitlement for the millions of migrants who live outside their country of citizenship. With a more complex and multilayered framework of community, belonging, and entitlement, we can better incorporate "differently papered" people (i.e., those having differing forms of residency and citizenship documentation)[66] into discussions of social policy and political formations.

IMMIGRANTS OUT! PRWORA'S EXCLUSION OF NONCITIZENS FROM WELFARE

The anti-immigrant movement in many ways paralleled the antiwelfare movement, ignited in a racial backlash with the opening of accessibility to barred migrants in the 1960s. The convergence of these two policies was synergistic, with public sentiment demonizing welfare recipients and immigrants alike and thus holding that immigrant welfare recipients constituted a group that should be excised without question from public support. As stated in chapter 1, quasi-social-science research charged that welfare had become a magnet for poor third world immigrants, attracting them to the United States to receive benefits. Consequently, Title IV, Restricting Welfare and Public Benefits for Aliens, codified the immigrant threat by stating that it was "a compelling government interest to enact new rules for eligibility and sponsorship agreements in order to assure that aliens be self-reliant in accordance with national immigration policy."[67] The notion of *self-reliance* coincided with broader assumptions about people in poverty and the assumed lack of individual responsibility.

The once-touted "Give me your tired, your poor, your huddled masses yearning to breathe free," which characterized this *nation of immigrants,* was clearly intended for racially/ethnically desired immigrants. The Immigration Act of 1965, which eliminated the national-origins quota, led to an unexpected drastic increase of immigrants from Asia on the bases of family reunification and of occupational needs, established by the law's seven levels of preferences for immigration. Between 1953 and 1965, about 19,000 Asians annually were immigrants (about 7 percent of the immigration flow). In 1966, the number of Asian immigrants rose to about 40,000, or 12.3 percent. In 1967, the total jumped again, to 59,000 immigrants (16.4 percent). In the last year of the transition, 1968, the Asian total was 57,000, or 12.6 percent.[68] The point here is to emphasize the relatively short period of open immigration, followed by a backlash with an increasing third world immigrant presence.

The loosening restrictions on racial categories and the more gender-neutral provisions of the Immigration Act of 1965 also opened immigration from Asia to women. Immigration through family preference categories led to the entry of large numbers of "immediate relatives" (parents, spouses, and unmarried minor children of United States citizens) who could enter in unlimited numbers.[69] In addition, the employment-based preference categories directly impacted the large-scale migration of women from Asia to the United States, particularly to fill employment areas where skilled and unskilled laborers were in high demand. The dominance of women in immigration flows reflected the growth of female-intensive industries in the United States, particularly in service, health care, microelectronics, and apparel manufacturing. To escape the tightening labor market, employers in the United States (and other "developed" countries) have opted either to shift labor-intensive processes to less-developed countries or to import migrant labor, especially female labor, to fill low-wage, insecure assembly and service sector jobs. Consequently, between 1975 and 1980, women (twenty years and older) constituted more than 50 percent of the immigrants entering from China, Burma, Indonesia, Taiwan, Hong Kong, Malaysia, the Philippines, Korea, Japan, and Thailand.[70] Thus, the dual goals of the 1965 Immigration Act, to facilitate family reunification and to admit skilled workers needed by the U.S. economy, dramatically increased the number of Asian women immigrants.

Although the Asian immigrant population continued to increase dramatically through the decades of the 1970s and 1980s, public attention toward the increasing use of public assistance programs by Asian Americans was not seriously aroused until the 1980s. This low profile has to do with the impact of the United States in Southeast Asia, the war in Vietnam, and the refugee/asylum policies after 1975. In the immediate aftermath of the Vietnam War and the pull-out of U.S. forces from Vietnam, as part of their anticommunist stance policymakers stressed that public assistance was a necessary entitlement in the resettlement process. The Refugee Assistance Acts of 1975, 1980, and 1982 brought forward another wave of Asian immigrants from war-torn Southeast Asia. Here I want to note the trajectory in which immigrants from Asia were increasingly perceived as foreigners overusing the American welfare system. By the 1990s, the higher rates of welfare use by these visible inassimilable foreigners fed the nativist resentment demanding that noncitizens not have access to public resources at all. Thus, the compelling government interest set forward in PRWORA was based on arguments that positioned immigrants as outsiders leeching off public resources and costing hardworking American citizens' tax dollars.

The connections among immigrants, race, and citizenship drove public concern over immigrant access to public benefits. Like the welfare reform movement based on racist constructions of African American single mothers as welfare queens, the anti-immigrant antiwelfare movement centered on Mexican immigrant women as illegal border crossers giving birth to citizen children, and on Asian immigrants and refugees cheating the system rather than economically adapting to the nation and working their way out of poverty. Thus, although the decision to bar immigrants from specific public benefits was established through lines that distinguished between "citizen" and "alien" recipients, the logic of this demarcation was racially driven. As with most immigration policy, lines that appear based on citizenship can cover up lines based on race. In the case of welfare reform, where the two largest immigrant groups were Asian and Latino/a, citizenship was defined by "race"; *citizenship* thus became the innocuous demarcating line in lieu of the odious race.[71]

Drawing thoroughly confusing lines of eligibility among immigrants, Congress further distorted the demarcations by creating differently qualified and nonqualified categories of noncitizens. Legal permanent residents and refugees constituted the largest group within the qualified category. Nonqualified immigrants included undocumented immigrants, asylum applicants, immigrants formerly considered Permanently Residing under Color of Law (PRUCOL), and those with temporary status, such as students and tourists. Through the PRWORA, nonqualified immigrants were barred from most federal, state, and local public benefits except emergency medical care. Likewise, immigrants who fell into the qualified category were also barred from several federal programs. Even qualified immigrants were no longer eligible for Supplemental Security Income (SSI, assistance for the blind, elderly, and disabled), Medicaid, or food stamps, and states could choose whether to allow qualified immigrants eligibility to TANF. Qualified immigrants who entered after the passing of the law (August 22, 1996) were barred from federal means-tested public benefits for their first five years following immigration, and then were subjected to much more stringent sponsorship deeming rules, making eligibility nearly impossible.

Exceptions within the qualified category included active-duty service members, veterans, and their direct family members; refugees, asylum seekers, and individuals granted withholding of deportation, but only for the first five years after being granted that status; and permanent residents who could prove ten years, or forty quarters, of employment through Social Security verification. These exception categories for qualified immigrants reflected ideas of belonging and membership in the nation. Active military service or veteran status reflected the ultimate expression of patriotic loyalty (although, as we shall see in chapter 3, veteran status is not always objectively defined). Wage-earning for ten years (or forty qualified quarters) also provided license to use public services. In the venue of American citizenship, wage-earning superseded legal citizenship as a form of duty, given employment contributions to taxes, Social Security, and health care; however, many immigrants were unable to demonstrate forty quarters of employment, given their tendency to work in the invisible employment sector or to pull together odd jobs that did not provide accountable recordkeeping. And refugees, although by definition victims of displacement, were only granted five years of assistance, though, realistically, five years would be too little adjustment time for people having few marketable job skills in the post-industrial U.S. economy, low education levels, and trauma from war and displacement. As will be seen, this implementation of time limits led to a retraumatizing of entire communities of refugees who were once promised refuge in acknowledgement of their loyalty to U.S. imperial military efforts.

By distinguishing between legal immigrants and citizens, welfare reform tightened the circle of full membership within the nation. By linking access to the safety net with citizenship, welfare reform elevated the importance of citizenship in a nation where its value had been limited primarily to exercising political rights, holding (some) government jobs, and obtaining certain immigration privileges.[72] Through constitutional protections, legal permanent residents had previously expected to be treated equally with citizens. In addition, although immigration policy was typically a federal affair, welfare reform gave more power to states to determine the lines of eligibility for immigrants living within their jurisdiction. PRWORA authorized state and local governments to deny locally funded benefits to legal immigrants, transgressing the long-held constitutional requirement that states treat citizens and legal immigrants alike in terms of public benefits eligibility.[73] The power given to the states to determine eligibility for qualified noncitizens coincided with states having to take on increased financial responsibility if they chose to extend benefits to noncitizens.[74] The racial implication of what is referred to as "immigrant exceptionalism," or the process of singling out immigrants for differential treatment,[75] was embedded in the exclusionary anti-immigrant narratives claiming that Latinas/os and Asians were abusing the welfare system.

The legislation was pointedly complex in: creating new categories of qualifications; differentiating among particular programs, governmental levels, and *alien* categories; creating varying forms of exceptions; inserting "grandfather" clauses; including special transition rules.[76] These provisions resulted in the immediate cut of five hundred thousand elderly, disabled, and blind immigrants from SSI and nearly one million immigrants from food stamps. Given these drastic cuts alone, it is clear that the $23.7 billion savings from PRWORA in the first six years came off the backs of immigrants. Until PRWORA, legally resident immigrants were treated on par with citizens in terms of eligibility. Never before was naturalization held as a requirement to become part of the nation as a resident or community member. Although newcomers had been recognized at one time for their contributions to the economy and culture of the nation, the anti-immigrant disdain for immigrants assumed that immigrants until naturalized remained outside the imagined community, and therefore were not welcome to use public resources, even though their day-to-day economic contributions contributed to the very resources they were now denied.

The simultaneous subject of welfare mothers and poor immigrants reveals the more complex workings of differential citizenship that encompassed "offenders" of differing citizenship status. Both groups found themselves disbarred from the ideal model of American citizenship, for the imagined political community was reshaped with tighter boundaries of belonging, instilling a common identity to wage-earners and the economically independent.[77] For immigrants, citizenship status operated as a firmly entrenched demarcation excluding thousands of U.S. residents from public resources they desperately needed to support their families.

MULTILAYERED CITIZENSHIP AS AN ANALYTICAL FRAMEWORK

Harking back to T. H. Marshall's idea of full membership within the community, we may ask: how are the social, civil, and political rights of immigrants negotiated in an age of renationalization and fortification of borders? Two primary issues arise: how are noncitizens protected by the laws within nation-states, and what social rights to services should immigrants claim? Challenges to the injustice of domestic social policies for citizens are usually couched in terms of civil rights. For immigrants, who are increasingly positioned outside of legal guarantees for equal protection, the venue of human rights becomes the place to address these issues. Except in extreme circumstances, a human rights argument challenging federal legislation usually appeals to moral sensibilities rather than to legal prescriptions.

Current trends in transnational migration for a significant portion of persons who retain ties in, and navigate among, multiple communities and nations further complicate the notion of citizenship as membership in the community in which one lives. Given the prevalence of conflict between nativist interests and immigrant rights, a broader tension has emerged between the role and responsibilities of nation-states and those of supranational entities in regulating membership and protecting the rights of all people residing within the nation-state. The new global economy is contributing to new forms of race, class, and gender inequality by widening economic disparities based on citizenship status. Concerns for economic justice and human rights, thus, need to be addressed at the transnational level.[78] With well over 100 million people now living outside their country of birth or citizenship, millions of women are resident in countries where they have no citizenship rights and either no or uncertain residence and labor rights. Every state assumes the right to treat citizens and noncitizens differently.[79] Although marginalized groups and women are already subjected to the exclusionary tendencies of the welfare state, welfare policies nonetheless work as entitlements that serve ipso facto to accentuate territorial boundaries by demarcating an exclusive space of privilege for full citizens through the distinct exclusion of noncitizens.[80] With the intensification of globalization and the consequent impoverishment of certain populations, women who form a transnationally exploited class of workers are disproportionately affected by the breakdown of welfare and public services.[81] Recent trends show a reduction or loss of social welfare and services (such as education and health care) in developing countries through the direct mandate of structural adjustment policies. Not only have migrant-receiving countries greatly reduced social welfare services to their citizens; they have simultaneously restricted access by noncitizens whose migration is due to economic necessity as a result of neoliberal policies.[82]

Considering more specifically the issue of rights for citizens and noncitizens within the nation-state, we see how human rights begin to impinge on the principle of nation-based citizenship and the boundaries of the nation.[83] In the context of increasing globalization, national immigration policies are increasingly shaped by an understanding of immigration as the consequence of the individual actions of emigrants; the receiving country is taken as a passive agent, one not implicated in the process of emigration.[84] Such emphasis on the individual allows countries, such as the United States, to legislate levels of rights and entitlements to immigrants that are shaped by economic and political interests. The neoliberal logic embedded in immigration policy places exclusive responsibility for the immigration process on the individual, and hence makes the individual the site for the exercise of the state's authority. Individualization places responsibility for survival on each individual immigrant, rather than recognize the larger national or global processes that have led to particular collective circumstances.

In addition to the neoliberal project of individualization, the ideological and technological shift to *responsibilization* cohered to situate poor, working-class immigrants as anticitizens.[85] As personal responsibility became the hallmark to good citizenship, and *dependency* the marker of anticitizenship, this anticitizenship signaled not only the need for containment of immigrants who already existed within an outsider position, but additionally the need to be protected from them, for their very existence became seen as a threat to the responsible citizen. PRWORA can be seen as an anticitizen technology that on one level worked to ethically reconstitute wayward citizens into work and responsibility,[86] and on another level worked to police the boundaries of entitlement by seeing immigrants in need of assistance as immigrants threatening the privileges of citizenship.

Although immigrants have never enjoyed the full privileges of political participation as citizens (hence the significance of American citizenship), within civil society generally, immigrants have had the same rights as citizens to equal protection under the Fourteenth Amendment.[87] Given the promise of naturalization, the condition of *alienage* with limited rights was only temporary, and the line demarcating *citizen* and *alien* was seen as soft. The processes that shape and determine the level of permeability of rights granted to citizens and noncitizens are inherently shaped by racial politics. Restrictive immigration laws produce new categories of racial difference,[88] and whether intentional or not establish new hierarchies of racial belonging or intrusion. Although national origin quotas were abolished with the Immigration Act of 1965, subsequent immigration policy has intentionally responded to perceived threats of alien invasion by particular racially constructed groups. Thus, whether the targeted group is migrant agricultural workers, welfare recipients, or refugees from various political circumstances, policies invariably establish hierarchies of noncitizenship, usually based on racially charged concerns. It is my task here to examine these multiple layers of difference that have so drastically reshaped the rights of immigrants to equal access to public benefits.

When the *nation of immigrants* was the prevailing American construction, it was understood that immigrants were future citizens. The question, in such a situation, over whether noncitizens should be equal to citizens (just short of political enfranchisement, as the vote has been reserved for full membership) is barely disputable. However, when the predominant image is *immigrants as threat* (whether economic or terrorist), noncitizens quickly lose grounds on which to demand equal rights.[89] The devolutionary aspects of welfare reform, by putting more power over immigration policy in state hands, allowed for social experimentation over the granting of eligibility for immigrant residents. Consequently, the local fabric of state demographics and racial politics has determined the rights and eligibility of immigrants in economic need. With citizenship as a proxy for racial exclusion, the devolutionary aspects of welfare reform further jeopardized vulnerable noncitizens in particular. Although one might hold out hope that the devolution of power over immigration policy into state hands could lead to progressive practices in states with strong commitments to their immigrant constituents, still—if racism within immigration law and policy is systemic—devolution will not cure the problem, but rather both federal and state governments are likely to employ racist policies.[90]

Since 9/11, the further erosion of immigrant rights has crystallized. However, these erosions were readily available given the slippery foundation on which noncitizenship rights rest, determinant on the racial politics of any given historical moment. If we think about *citizenship* as a proxy for *race,* racial profiling of immigrants is easily disguised by the seemingly benign category *citizenship.* With the national identity of the United States constructed in opposition to *foreigners, aliens,* and *others,* the use of racist tropes works to establish legitimacy in racial profiling. Citizenship identity within the transnational context further strengthens the salience of the nation, both in terms of shaping identity (belonging) and in the form of governmental control.[91] The ability to claim American identity as *citizen* is only made possible through the power to subordinate and constitute the subject *noncitizen* (irrespective of actual citizenship status). Citizenship identity is established through a process of interpellation where subjects are positioned, if of selected racial backgrounds, as antithetical to the assumed citizen.[92] Just as citizenship is not equal among all citizens, within a transnational context, noncitizens face differential interpellations that shape beliefs about their perceived threat to the nation, and thus must negotiate differing degrees of policing and exclusion. Although this has become much more apparent with the massive sweeps of Arab, Muslim, and South Asian noncitizens into detention centers after the attacks on the World Trade Center,[93] we can apply this same logic to the massive cuts of primarily immigrant women of color (Asian and Latina) from welfare benefits.

Throughout this book, I utilize such analytical tools as *multilayered citizenship* to examine the loss of immigrant rights and entitlements through PRWORA. Contextualized within a transnational context, an examination of immigrants and welfare entitlement needs to be conceptualized within a multilayered construct, in which one's citizenship, or noncitizenship, always occupies different layers—local, ethnic, national, state, cross- (or trans-) state, and supra-state—and is affected, and often at least partly constructed, by the relationships and positionings of each layer in a specific historical context.[94] To deal with the multilayers of inclusion and exclusion, we can think of immigration policies as a logic of encompassment[95] dialectical in nature to the politics of citizenship. Moving beyond the notion of the *politics of closure,* the logic of encompassment is an approach that pushes immigration scholars to examine citizenship as a dialogical and relational process embedded in cultural and associational life.[96] As a conceptual framework, the logic of encompassment incorporates the hierarchical and dialectical nature of citizenship formation.

With the recognized feminization of migration[97] in current conditions of globalization, a dialectical and relational approach to examine the varying levels of citizenship within the national context allows for a more complex analysis of the rights and entitlements of immigrant women. Even while simultaneous projects are at work to diminish the social and public resources for citizens, immigrants and/or racialized/ethnic minorities become targets, in postindustrial economies, as competition or threat. "Besieged" majority members mobilize against "outsiders" and claim the state as theirs only.[98] Contemporary mobilization efforts have concentrated in political arenas where impoverished migrants remain the most vulnerable: labor, public assistance, education, and naturalization. To discuss the multiple levels of welfare dismantling that simultaneously marginalized citizen and immigrant welfare recipients, we need to incorporate the racial and gendered politics of legal citizenship within conceptualizations of social citizenship both as multilayered, and as dialectically situated within their respective historical political trajectories.

ASIAN IMMIGRANTS, CITIZENSHIP, AND WELFARE REFORM

The meaning of citizenship remains dialectical to the noncitizen. Thus, the rights bestowed upon citizens are placed in contradistinction to the rights not granted to noncitizens. Policies that demarcate by *citizenship* define *belonging* through its contrast with the oppositional concept of the *noncitizen* as one who lacks the essential qualities needed to exercise citizenship.[99] The question of democratic citizenship—who is allowed active participation and full membership in the social polity—is further complicated by contemporary demographic shifts and the growth of Latina/o and Asian immigrant communities. With the dismantling of AFDC, increased economic insecurity affected all poor single mothers and their children; however, the immigrant provisions, which clearly demarcated *otherness* and the utilization of public services by "non-deserving/non-Americans," also formed a cornerstone for the passing of the welfare act. The underestimation of the anti-immigrant movement contributed to the relatively easy and unpredictable passing of a devastating welfare law that left hundreds of thousands of immigrants in peril regarding their livelihood. Along with the attack on single motherhood, a simultaneous focus on conditional immigrant eligibility for Supplemental Security Income, food stamp assistance, TANF, and Medicaid clearly revealed the racist tactics mobilized in a nativist welfare reform that directly impacted all recipients, immigrants as well as so-called citizens. Of course, the trajectory of the welfare state reveals a long-standing system of denying women of color full citizenship status.

Along the historical continuum, PRWORA employs the decisive tool of citizenship in terms of motherhood and nationhood. Through racialized and gendered constructions that placed the blame for poverty on women of color, these women's "dependency" was constructed as a threat to the nation's well-being by virtue of their reproduction. For Latina and Asian immigrant women, the constructed threat consisted of a foreign invasion by racial outsiders coming to this country specifically to abuse its overgenerous welfare system. Asian immigrant and refugee women were seen as welfare cheats guilty of pathological family patterns, lacking a work ethic that would make them take personal responsibility for their families' well-being. However, the loss of benefits ignited a terror that would reverberate to devastating levels.

The specific historical context of Asian immigration to the United States reveals patterns of recruitment, exclusion, inclusion, and resentment. The politics of Asian immigration and citizenship reveal formative moments in this nation's history in shaping American citizenship. As noted in the previous chapter, Lisa Lowe argues that "In the last century and a half, the American *citizen* has been defined over against the Asian *immigrant*, legally, economically, and culturally."[100] Contemporary transnational politics has led to a racial and gendered politics of citizenship where belonging and entitlement are in constant tension with globalization, and where nativist movements want to "Keep America for Americans." PRWORA demonstrated the ability of the racial state to legislate the positioning of the alien Asian subject: to confer differential citizenship based upon the Asian's foreign *otherness*, and to deny protection on the basis of a missing citizenship. Both notions of citizenship remain embedded and inseparable as political assumptions underlying the harsh changes in welfare, its implementation, and the reaction from Asian immigrant communities.

To date, very few studies exist that examine Asian immigrants and the politics of citizenship, race, gender, and welfare. For Asian immigrants in poverty, the global economic conditions of exploitive labor are coupled with state technologies in social services that shape the circumstances and day-to-day experiences for noncitizens negotiating the public welfare system.[101] Aihwa Ong's 2003 publication, *Buddha Is Hiding: Refugees, Citizenship, the New America,* focuses on refugees from Cambodia and their experiences in war, refugee camps, and settlement in San Francisco and Oakland, California. Ong presents a complex examination of citizen-making through the day-to-day negotiations of everyday citizenship in America. In terms of the welfare system, Ong presents the everyday interactions with welfare agents, bureaucratic rules, and individual acts of agency that shape the refugees' negotiations to get the economic resources they need for their families. Ong puts forth the notion of "practical citizenship," as produced in the everyday domains, which can be highly unstable and open to modification.[102] With this logic, citizenship is negotiated through everyday practices—a logic that allows a clearer analysis of how state power is enforced, as well as how it is resisted or manipulated by noncitizens.

Useful in Ong's approach is the complexity in which she engages in the varying levels of economic positioning of newcomers that shape their negotiations with state technologies and their relative formations of citizenship, as felt through experience and as inscribed by common assumptions of deservingness.[103] In addition, her conceptualization of welfare state practices through social service offices and agents reveals the embedded levels of power noncitizens must conform to as they negotiate the cultural and economic landscape to receive their public assistance. However, much has changed since Ong's research (during the era before welfare reform). The Cambodian refugees accessing public assistance and negotiating with welfare technocrats in the 1980s would face a completely new system after 1996. The orientalist constructions that plagued the politics of early immigration foreground the complex yet resurgent notions of *inassimilable, foreign,* and *undeserving* that play out with welfare office technocrats. How these negotiations shape immigrant and refugee citizenship is a conceptualization that proves helpful in more direct examination of Asian immigrant and refugee women and welfare reform.

Practical citizenship is one level of belonging and entitlement to be engaged here. However, within a broader multilayered framework, I examine the politics of citizenship for Asian immigrants by focusing on the interacting elements of social policy, enforcement, and resistance.

Global patterns of migration and the movement of peoples across borders raise fundamental issues of how we incorporate legal or formal citizenship into discussions of deservingness, belonging, and entitlement. Thus far, I have established a framework that incorporates the racialized gender politics of public assistance generally, and the implications of citizenship for poor immigrant women of color specifically. In the following chapter, I look more deeply into the immigrant welfare provisions that proved devastating for Southeast Asian refugees. Citizenship politics played out in varied and unexpected ways. Incorporating the rights of the disabled as non-wage-earners, the establishment of veteran status, and the process of using voice and testimonial as membership credentials (regardless of formal citizenship status) all proved instrumental in regard to the immediate legislative challenges that imposed serious damage on the lives of poor noncitizens.

3

Refugees Betrayed

Chia Yang lay in the dark and waited for her husband to fall asleep. Then she got up and changed her clothes. She slipped past the bedrooms of her son Yia, 21, and daughter Jamie, 14, sleeping in their American beds, steeped in American culture.

Mrs. Yang had endured war in Southeast Asia, walked miles through rotting corpses and lived four years in suffocating refugee camps. A Hmong tribeswoman from the mountains of Laos, she was 36 before she first saw a water faucet.

But at 54, after bearing seven children and more heartache than most, she looped a cord around her throat, tied it to an overhead beam, and jumped off the trunk of her husband's Toyota.

She ended her life because she believed the United States betrayed her by cutting her family's welfare benefits.

—Deborah Hastings, *Asian Week,* February 10, 1998

Chia Yang, a Hmong woman who found refuge in the United States, committed suicide in her Sacramento, California, home in October 1997. About forty thousand Hmong, including Mrs. Yang's husband and her two brothers, were enlisted by the CIA from 1961 to 1974 as guerillas in the Vietnam War. In return, they were given rice and an average salary of three dollars per month.[1] After the CIA lost its covert war in Laos and abandoned the Hmong hill tribal villages in 1974, Chia Yang, her husband, and six children fled across the Mekong River and into the jungles of Thailand. She, along with thousands of other refugees, walked for days, passing the bodies of perished men, women, and children, and dodging land mines, as they fled for survival. After living and waiting for four years in refugee camps, Chia Yang and her family found permanent refuge in the United States.

After arriving in the United States, Yang's husband, Sua Chai Vue, was rarely able to find work, and the family relied on public assistance. Like most Hmong displaced from their homelands, they came from villages with no electricity, toilets, or locks, and no written language. While Yang grew vegetables, her husband Vue studied English and eventually got a job as a dishwasher. They were first resettled in a two-bedroom flat in San Diego, California; then in 1987 they moved to Sacramento, where their oldest son, Toby Vue, became a registered nurse. The son bought two modest tract homes in Sacramento, renting one to his parents for $460 a month.[2] According to Yang's son, his mother was very hopeful, before welfare reform, that her children would have better opportunities, and felt proud that she was able "to bring her children to a modern country where they could attend school and maybe one day do some good."[3] She lived to see two of her sons earn college degrees. In February 1996, Chia Yang passed the U.S. citizenship test, but because the Naturalization Assistance Service tested her in Hmong, the INS threw out her results. Twice, Yang took the test in English at INS headquarters in Sacramento, but each time she panicked and could barely utter a word. According to Yang's doctor, she suffered from high blood pressure, panic attacks, diabetes, kidney stones, bladder infections, arthritis, night sweats, and a stroke.[4] After PRWORA passed, Yang constantly worried about how she and her family were going to survive. Her son repeatedly told her not to worry, that they would manage, but she continued to feel helpless and hopeless.

At age fifty-four, and still living with her two youngest children, Mrs. Yang received a notice stating that her Supplemental Security Income (SSI) of $640 a month, granted due to her disability status, would be discontinued because she was not yet a naturalized U.S. citizen. The loss of her SSI benefits would leave only her husband's $400 welfare check and $180 in food stamps for the couple and their two youngest children to live on each month. Upon receiving these official notices, Mrs. Yang panicked, then slid into a depression. Already suffering from major health ailments, she fell deeper into despair when she repeatedly failed her citizenship test because of her limited English skills. She told her son, "I'm worthless. Maybe they are right, I'm just like a dummy," and for the first and only time she spoke of killing herself.[5] Shortly before she was to be cut off from her SSI, Chia Yang received another notice, stating that she would not lose her SSI since Congress was restoring the benefit to those noncitizens who were receiving assistance before August 22, 1996.[6]

However, only a few months later, Mrs. Yang received another letter stating that the family's food stamps were to be cut in half, because noncitizens between the ages of eighteen and sixty-four were no longer eligible. With the receipt of this third letter, Mrs. Yang became inconsolable. Yang's son, Toby Vue, told reporters that, after watching the late news, his mother and father went to bed. "My dad woke up at 3:30 and saw my mom wasn't in bed. He found her in the garage, hanging from a nylon rope."[7] Chia Yang's suicide captured public attention, particularly due to an audio tape she left behind blaming the U.S. government for her unbearable despair. Several newspapers presented her story, including some of the contents of her audio tape:

> In a farewell tape she tucked inside her traditional Hmong funeral clothes, Yang blamed welfare reform for pushing her over the edge. "It feels like I'm sitting in a pot of boiling water every day. What if I lose my SSI? What if my husband and children lose their AFDC grant? If they stop my grant I'm going to die anyway." . . . She also said she never would have come here if she'd known the U.S. government was going to change the rules and make it so hard for her to survive. "I hope I will be reborn as a smarter, healthier, more educated person, better able to help myself and others so my next family won't have to go through this. I'm sorry I had to bring you to this country and then leave you behind. Don't be angry at me, don't miss me too much, because even if I die my spirit will come back and help you to be strong and survive so you don't have to suffer like I did."[8]

Yang's son further emphasized that "the number one reason she took her life was because welfare reform had caused her so much stress she couldn't focus on anything else."[9] In the immediate aftermath of welfare reform, several other elderly and disabled refugees committed suicide in fear that the loss of their SSI would overburden their families. Ye Vang, in Fresno, and two elderly Hmong residents of Dane County, Wisconsin, killed themselves out of despair and fear that they and their families would starve.

I have begun this chapter with Chia Yang, a Hmong survivor of war and atrocity who left her voice behind to underscore the inhumane and unjust elements of American social policy. I think of Yang's verbal testimony as both a *shedding* as she moved her way into her next life, and an appeal to those who remained behind to make a difference. If we consider Chia Yang's life, testimony, and suicide as a moment to interrogate the complex relationships among race, citizenship, and social policy, what emerges are issues of obligation, responsibility, and betrayal within the context of national identity and refugee politics. However, moving from the end-of-life story of Chia Yang to a discussion of social policy proves a challenging undertaking. As scholars and researchers, we too often tend to disconnect the specificities of policy matters from the lived, emotional experiences of those impacted. In this instance, I am engaging in an analysis that involves a group of people who carry collective trauma and collective despair. This group consists primarily of elderly and disabled refugees from Southeast Asia who came to the United States after direct experience of war, flight from their homeland, and the wait in refugee camps for resettlement. In examining the racial and citizenship politics that surrounds their relationship to welfare policy, I rely on their testimony from forums and venues in which they felt safe or supported enough to make their feelings public. I analyze existing public testimony to consider how welfare reform as a legislative act became an act of betrayal for refugees who believed they were entitled to the benefits necessary for their survival in the postwar United States. This is a welfare story that rarely gets told and that remains poorly understood. By focusing on the particularities that Southeast Asian refugees faced in welfare reform, I hope to illuminate the multiple levels of complexity that led to such a catastrophic level of despair.

The use of testimony, a form and practice that has traditionally been excluded from empirical modes of evaluation, proves critical in this instance, for it extends the scope of what constitutes legitimate knowledge and gives voice to those who have been systematically rendered invisible.[10] We can use, read, understand, and locate institutional testimonies to decenter existing structures of power and inequality. The aim is "not just 'to record' one's history of struggle, or consciousness, but to examine how it is recorded; the way we read, receive, and disseminate such imaginative records is immensely significant."[11] Testimonies are "accounts in which the narrator is a central participant in the story or is close to the characters in the story."[12] Sociologist Eduardo Bonilla-Silva argues that testimonies "provide the aura of authenticity and emotionality that only 'firsthand' narratives can furnish."[13] Given my concern with the multifaceted issues for Asian immigrant communities, I have found testimony an essential forum to give voice and visibility to this group that had been popularly constructed as welfare abusers devoid of humanity and history. Through countless testimonies in welfare reform hearings, court cases, and social service administrative forums, Southeast Asian refugees told their stories of trauma, U.S. irresponsibility, and despair over welfare reform. These testimonies center the experiences of refugees, the geopolitical events that shaped their current circumstances, and their political vulnerability and agency.

In this chapter, I examine the ways refugee politics further complicates our understandings of immigrant rights and the significance of citizenship. Although my focus here is on Southeast Asian refugees, I am not necessarily making legal claims of grievance that would result in a specific exception or safeguard for only those refugees. Rather, my research demonstrates how social policies (welfare and immigration) merged and inflicted trauma and despair on a marginalized group of people, a group nearly invisible to the public. My point is to highlight the levels of complexity and degrees of trauma within the heterogeneous Asian immigrant community by showing how racialization interacted with the state to produce disparate and traumatizing realities for largely poor, disenfranchised members within the nation. As refugees from Southeast Asia experienced welfare reform, their welfare narrative emerged and held public notice for a brief moment in which some legislative changes were achieved.

First, I provide a brief background of the refugee politics that surrounded the granting of refugee status, of the process of resettlement in relation to welfare and public assistance, and of the subsequent backlash that led to punitive exclusions to all legal permanent residents. After giving this political backdrop, I then offer an analytical examination of the testimonies, statements, and narratives of refugees facing welfare cuts, an analysis that points to an increasing use of citizenship status to deny basic human rights to targeted racial groups. Through this focused discussion, I demonstrate how a particular group of refugees and immigrants experienced these policies as a form of betrayal, given their historical experiences of war, refuge, and resettlement, when they suddenly found themselves at particularly vulnerable moments losing the assistance that literally sustained them.

REFUGEE POLITICS AND SOUTHEAST ASIAN RESETTLEMENT

According to the United Nations, there were sixteen million formally recognized refugees worldwide by the end of the year 2000.[14] This statistic does not include the more than twenty million displaced persons lacking formal refugee status. Eighty percent of the world's refugees are women and children.[15] The U.N. Office of High Commissioner of Human Rights defines a refugee as a person who, "owing to well-founded fear of being persecuted for reasons of race, religion, nationality, membership of a particular social group or political opinion, is outside the country of his nationality and is unable, or owing to such fear, is unwilling to avail himself of the protection of that country; or who, not having a nationality and being outside the country of his former habitual residence as a result of such events, is unable or, owing to such fear, is unwilling to return to it."[16] Although political refugees flee their homelands due to a "well-founded fear of persecution," the politics regarding permanent resettlement in a receiving country is often fraught by that country's conflicted geopolitical relations with the refugees' country of origin.

The recent history of refugees from Southeast Asia presents a critical moment in refugee politics that was shaped by global political interests and notions of U.S. accountability and responsibility. Although numerous, detailed historical-political works have documented and analyzed the war in Southeast Asia, its political and military events, and its impact on Southeast Asians, I aim here to examine more deeply the construction of American obligation, the role of social services in the resettlement process, and the legislative acts of betrayal that left thousands of refugees in despair. Betrayal is a breach of trust. For many legal permanent residents from Southeast Asia, resettlement in the United States came with a governmental promise and acknowledged obligation to assist them as they adjusted to life in an economically competitive and culturally insensitive system. This was a promise that did not come with time limits or citizenship requirements.

The U.S. wars in Southeast Asia, memorialized in American history as the Vietnam War, encompassed direct military warfare in Vietnam, Cambodia, and Laos. Through anticommunist interests, the United States supported the installed South Vietnamese government from 1955 to 1961 with more than one billion dollars in aid, primarily in the form of military assistance.[17] When the North Vietnamese shelled an American destroyer, Congress passed a resolution that gave President Lyndon B. Johnson the authority to act as he saw fit in Vietnam. In February 1965, the United States began its bombing raids on North Vietnam. In 1969, the United States started bombing neighboring Cambodia to deny respite to North Vietnamese troops and to stave off the growing communist Khmer regime. By the time Congress ended the Cambodian bombing campaign, in 1973, more than half a million tons of bombs had fallen.[18] This parallel campaign killed more than a hundred thousand civilians and displaced traumatized Cambodians from the countryside to urban centers (such as the U.S.-funded Phnom Phenh). In Laos, the

Central Intelligence Agency, in violation of the agreements of the second Geneva Conference of 1962, which guaranteed Laotian neutrality, formed and utilized a mercenary army consisting of Hmong tribesmen and boys. In attempts to destroy the Ho Chi Minh Trail in Laos, between 1965 and 1973, the United States dropped more than two million tons of bombs.[19]

U.S. military efforts in Southeast Asia only strengthened the communist forces they set out to destroy, and those forces eventually took control of Vietnam, Cambodia, and Laos. With the departure of American troops from Vietnam and the fall of the South Vietnamese government in 1975, the newly empowered military communist regimes engaged in organized campaigns to root out pro-American army personnel and civilians. In the immediate aftermath of the fall of Saigon, President Gerald Ford authorized the attorney general to use his "parole" power to admit 130,000 refugees into the United States.[20] Thus began what is now called the first wave of refugees from Southeast Asia. With thousands of Vietnamese (primarily Sino-Vietnamese, seen as the more bourgeois merchant class) fleeing by boat, and thousands of Cambodians and Laotians (both high- and lowland) fleeing by foot to Thailand, a major refugee crisis ensued that would result in numerous policy changes to allow more Southeast Asian refugees into the United States. By the end of 1979 nearly 600,000 Cambodians were living in refugee camps along the Thai border. An estimated 300,000 Laotians (10 percent of the total population) became displaced persons.

The pullout of U.S. forces from Southeast Asia resulted in the abandonment of American ally forces in Cambodia, Laos, and Vietnam. The narrative of abandonment pervades the stories of airlifts that ceased to arrive to transport desperate people—people who knew that their alliance with the U.S. would lead to certain persecution. Anne Fadiman's journalistic account of the travails of a Hmong family, in the popular *The Spirit Catches You and You Fall Down,* retells the collective despair experienced by the Hmong left behind by CIA case officers who had promised protection in return for loyalty and manpower. When the Pathet Lao took over the preexisting Lao monarchy, the Hmong were declared enemies as a result of their collusion with the United States. In this most dire of circumstances, the Hmong discovered that the protection promised them would not include everyone. Between one thousand and three thousand, mostly high-ranking, officers and families were airlifted by American planes to Thailand. Fadiman presents the following haunting scene that illustrates the intense trauma and despair caused by America's breached promise:

> Hmong fought to board the aircraft. Several times the planes were so over-loaded they could not take off, and dozens of people standing near the door had to be pushed out onto the airstrip.... After the last American transport plane disappeared, more than 10,000 Hmong were on the airfield, fully expecting more aircraft to return. When it became apparent that there would be no more planes, a collective wail rose from the crowd and echoed against the mountains. The shelling of Long Tieng began that afternoon. A long line of Hmong, carrying their children and old people, started to move across the plateau, heading toward Thailand.[21]

In a clear anticommunist "pro-democracy" pretext, an empathic American government originally set out to rescue their unfortunate allies now facing political persecution. Between April and December 1975, the United States admitted 130,400 Southeast Asian refugees, 125,000 of whom were Vietnamese.[22] With the continued flows of refugees out of Cambodia and Laos, a series of Indochinese Parole Programs were established to allow entry of more of the wartorn, and annual arrivals jumped from 20,400 in 1978 to 80,700 in 1979, then to 166,700 in 1980.[23] By the summer of 1979, the number of arriving Southeast Asian refugees swelled to 14,000 a month.[24]

The opening of American borders to refugees of a special status was not without global political strategy. A nation touting itself as the leader of the "free world," America in its global anticommunist agenda fed a calculated kindness[25] that would result in a disproportionate admittance of refugees fleeing communist countries. Aiwha Ong argues that this purported kindness was characterized as a special consideration because of the ideological perception that refugees from communist regimes had undergone great suffering as symbolic or literal "freedom fighters."[26] According to Christain Joppke, refugee policy in the 1965 Immigration Act (unlike the liberalization that abolished national origins quotas) maintained discriminatory bias.[27] The Seventh Preference category of the 1965 act reserved 6 percent of Eastern hemisphere immigrant visas to refugees from "communist-dominated countries" or the Middle East.[28] It was not until the Refugee Act of 1980 that refugee policy was separated from immigration policy, in order for Congress to establish more control over the executive's discriminatory parole authority. Consequently, political exiles from countries such as Haiti, El Salvador, and Chile did not benefit from this calculated kindness.

From the 1950s until the present, the United States has admitted well over 90 percent of its refugees from communist countries.[29] According to Bill Ong Hing, "these figures betray any claim that refugee policy was based solely on humanitarian considerations."[30] In keeping with the calculated kindness extended toward refugees from Southeast Asia, during the first five years (1975–1980) of admittance they were granted several years of refugee assistance. With the understanding that public assistance would be essential to the resettlement process, Congress passed the Indochina Migration and Refugee Assistance Act of 1975 (P.L. 94–23). The 1975 act authorized $455 million for the performance of functions set forth in the Migration and Refugee Assistance Act of 1962, amended to include aliens who had fled Vietnam or Cambodia.[31] The act covers those who, because of persecution or fear of persecution on account of race, religion, or political opinion, fled Cambodia or Vietnam and could not return, and who were in urgent need of assistance for the essentials of life. The U.S. Department of Health, Education, and Welfare (now the U.S. Department of Health and Human Services) also gave grants to public or nonprofit private agencies to provide the refugees with English instruction, employment counseling, and mental health services.[32] The first wave of refugees to gain from less restricted federally funded services (public assistance, social and medical services) consisted of the more educated and professional classes from Vietnam and Cambodia.

As the more war-traumatized second exodus—a much more ethnically heterogeneous people consisting of ethnic Chinese from Vietnam, Kampucheans (usually still referred to as Cambodians), lowland Lao, and highland Hmong—began settling in the United States, their presence and visibility stirred public concerns of cultural conflict and racist resentment over public assistance to foreigners or so-called nondeserving outsiders. Policymakers' understanding of the need for public assistance for refugees (i.e., war victims with ties to the United States), was short-lived at best, and never quite accepted by the mainstream American public. Southeast Asians were soon accused, as Blacks had been in the construction of Black cultural pathology, of developing a "welfare mentality," since their relatively low rate of labor-force participation (primarily due to barriers of English, skills, education, racism, and discrimination) had inevitably led many refugees to depend on government assistance. Aiwha Ong argues that "as refugees settled down to become long-term residents, they lost their glow as freedom fighters, and congressional fears of communist subversion began to erode the unconditional welcome offered to escapees from communist regimes."[33] Although refugees from Southeast Asia were first embodied as highly principled victims of war, resentment and hostility by "American citizens" would soon manifest in an anti-welfare response resulting in changes in social policy.

With the enactment of the Refugee Act of 1980, the law mandated that refugee admissions be handled separately from immigration.[34] According to Park and Park, in response to the increased visibility of impoverished and inassimilable refugees, the 1980 Act greatly limited the number of refugees admitted from war-torn Southeast Asia.[35] The new act aimed to only admit displaced persons who were, in its terms, "persecuted," and could demonstrate they would be persecuted should they return to their country of origin. Of course this ruled out the larger universe of persons who were displaced but not individually persecuted. Even for those displaced directly as a result of war, destruction, and U.S. military campaigns, the burden of proof was on the asylum applicant to show continued danger from government authorities of communist regimes. With the grounds for asylum limited, the Act of 1980 sifted displaced persons such that a sizable fraction of asylum and refugee claims were subsequently denied, dismissed, or reviewed in greater detail. Since 1980, about 75 percent of asylum claims have been approved, the other quarter denied, dismissed, or withdrawn.[36]

In addition to legislating this overall reshaping of refugee admittance, Congress enacted sweeping changes in the domestic policies that aided refugees once they had been admitted.[37] To coordinate the federal resettlement programs, Congress established the Office of Refugee Resettlement (ORR) within the Department of Health and Human Services. The ORR had its own budget to administer assistance programs designed to help refugees achieve economic self-sufficiency as quickly as possible.[38] Through the 1980 act, refugees were given 36-month special refugee cash stipend, medical assistance programs, and other support services.[39] However, with the entry, in 1982, of the poorer, less educated, and more devastated "second wave" of refugees, popularly referred to as the boat people, amendments to the 1980 Refugee Act reduced the stipends to eighteen months to pressure refugees to become economically independent more quickly.[40] With limited English courses, job training, or educational opportunities, refugees were left to fend for themselves, with few marketable skills in an advanced capitalist

economy. Not surprisingly, poverty levels and welfare use among them remained significantly high.

PERSISTENCE OF POVERTY AND WELFARE

From the time of resettlement in the decades preceding welfare reform,
poverty among Southeast Asian families remained expectedly high. According to the 1980 U.S. Census, the percentage of Laotian and Hmong families
with income below the poverty level remained over 65 percent; this figure
was over 46 percent for Cambodian families and over 33 percent for Vietnamese families.[41] Ten years later, the 1990 U.S. Census showed that poverty
rates for Southeast Asian groups remained among the highest in the nation:
66 percent of Hmong, 47 percent of Cambodians, 67 percent of Laotians,
and 34 percent of Vietnamese lived in poverty. "A general assessment of
the economic patterns of Southeast Asians, conducted in 1987, revealed
that, nationwide, 64 percent of all Southeast Asian households headed by
refugees arriving after 1980 were on public assistance, a figure three times
the rate for African Americans and four times that for Latinos."[42] In fact,
Southeast Asians represented the largest per capita ethnic group receiving
public assistance.[43] As of 1991, the proportion of Southeast Asians utilizing
public assistance remained significantly high. Rather than acknowledging the
structural and racial factors leading to massive unemployment among the
recent refugees, many attributed this so-called dependency to a welfare
system that purportedly created disincentives to work.[44] Thus, after the
1982 amendments, when aid was reduced to eighteen months, most programs stressed employment-enhancing services such as vocational, English-
language, and job-development training. Most refugees were unable to acquire
the skills that would qualify them for anything other than minimum-
wage jobs, in eighteen months. They were nonetheless constrained to take
these positions, in the absence of continued public assistance.[45] As a result
of these more stringent and inefficient assistance programs, refugees were
relegated to entry-level jobs with minimal earnings (and lower for refugee
women than for refugee men), thus fostering the poverty rate of over 50
percent among Southeast Asian refugees by 1985. This proletarianization
of Southeast Asian refugees has led to a predominance of jobs in manufacturing, electronics assembly, home piece-work, and service sector jobs
among them.

Further studies indicated that, given the gravity of the situation faced by poor Southeast Asians—particularly language conflict, lack of marketable skills, illiteracy in language of origin, mental illness, and post-traumatic stress syndrome—their rates of public assistance use remained significantly high. A 1987 study conducted by Gong-Guy, which included a survey of 2,773 Southeast Asians between eighteen and sixty-four years of age in California, found that their economic problems and need for public assistance remained severely high. Examining family income and employment, Gong-Guy found that the percentage of families completely dependent on public assistance was 79.3 percent for Cambodians, 76.3 percent for Chinese-Vietnamese, 81.1 percent for Hmong, 81.1 percent for Lao, and 49.7 percent for Vietnamese.[46] Clearly, the most obvious correlate for such high rates of public assistance were the respectively high rates of unemployment. According to Laura Uba's examination of refugees and stress from a mental health perspective, "Unemployment among Southeast Asians for the first few months after settling in the United States has been almost 90 percent, and after more than three years in the United States, about one third are still unemployed."[47] Thus, pre–welfare reform research on Southeast Asian refugees clearly indicated a persistent level of poverty, of unemployment, and of numerous issues associated with mental health, physical health, language, and limited job skills continuing to contribute to the economic struggles within these communities.

The backlash following the early visibility of Asian refugees on public assistance would escalate, as many Americans felt that public assistance should not be spent on foreigners. An analysis of racial conflict and resentment, as expressed through anti-Indochinese incidents, by Jeremy Hein reveals the level of hostility over the increased numbers of Asian immigrants and refugees themselves (not to mention over their utilization of public benefits). The fall of the pro-American governments in Vietnam, Laos, and Cambodia led to the arrival of 147,000 refugees between 1975 and 1978; subsequent political turmoil and persecution resulted in another 453,000 refugee arrivals between 1979 and 1982. Finally, migration, primarily based on family reunification, brought 350,000 refugees between 1983 and 1990. According to Hein:

> Each wave is associated with a different pattern of aggression toward the refugees. The earliest period was marked by protest over the refugees' arrival. The next period produced conflict over jobs and social services—as large numbers of refugees arrived during a severe recession—and a rise in violence.

The final period, when Vietnamese, Laotian, and Cambodian communities took root in the United States, is characterized by destruction of property, harassment, assaults, and murders.[48]

By 1984, 700,000 refugees from Southeast Asia had resettled in the United States. As Southeast Asian refugees began settling in as U.S. residents, the memory of their characterization as freedom fighters quickly waned. The sudden visibility of Southeast Asian refugees became a reminder of the U.S. defeat in Vietnam, and resentment over U.S. involvement "to free those people over there" permeated middle-American sentiment.[49] In light of economic recession and the increase in unemployment, this resentment shifted to what was perceived as unfair access to a welfare system unavailable to hardworking Americans (read: white Americans). Southeast Asian refugees were soon subjected to a welfare racialization in which their foreignness and perceived inassimilability became tropes for a familiar narrative of "learned dependency," "freeloading laziness," and "irresponsibility." Aihwa Ong describes the growing public resentment and the emergence of a more definitive climate of antagonism toward Southeast Asian refugees as "compassion fatigue."[50] The image of *welfare-dependent* superseded any common awareness of language and skill barriers, poor education levels, or a racist marketplace. Negotiating confusing, foreign, and bureaucratic institutions, as well as American resentment toward their assistance, Southeast Asian refugees discovered they had fled from their original harrowing experience simply to one of a different form.

In spite of welfare reform, the drastically changing demographics within Southeast Asian populations caused their poverty levels to decline by the year 2000. According to the 2000 U.S. Census, the percentage of Southeast Asians living below the federally established poverty level had decreased (although it remained significantly higher than that of the overall U.S. population, which was 12.4 percent). From 1990 to 2000, the level of poverty went from 66 percent to 37.6 percent among Hmong Americans, from 47 percent to 29.3 percent among Cambodians, from 67 to 19.1 percent for Laotians, and from 34 percent to 16.0 for Vietnamese.[51] Although these poverty rates remained notably high (and still are distressingly high, in some cases), clear reasons for the somewhat astounding drops in poverty levels are due to the changes in age demographics with the maturation of 1.5 generation arrivals; cohorts who came as infants or young children had at this point gone through the American school systems, acquired high school degrees, and had entered the labor force. Yet poverty persisted, and even with this persistence of poverty, welfare use declined drastically; in the years 1990 to 2000, public assistance rates declined from 16 percent to 10.2 percent for Vietnamese, 39.5 percent to 22.2 percent for Cambodians, 53.4 percent to 30.2 percent for Hmong, and 28 percent to 14.2 percent for Laotians.[52] These figures indicate a serious discrepancy from the U.S. average for those Southeast Asian groups that still maintained high levels of poverty and who did not receive public assistance. Thus, the overall decline in poverty rates among Southeast Asian refugees does not correspond to welfare reform; in fact, the lack of access to resources may perpetuate the lingering persistence of poverty among groups not benefited by the natural shifts in demographic shifts.

Even less examined are the gender implications for Southeast Asian refugees struggling to adapt and survive in the United States. Although an estimated 80 percent of the world's refugees are women and their dependent children, very little attention has focused on the specific forms of trauma, adjustment, and needs of refugee women. Because of their gender, refugee women were more likely to experience sexual assault and trauma during the process of escape, yet policies and programs failed to recognize the complexity that these issues would raise in the resettlement process. Four of the five grounds for persecution that are specified in the 1967 United Nations Protocol as defining refugee status—these four being race, religion, nationality, and membership in a particular social group—are *givens,* identities into which a person is born. Although sex is a given and refugee women are at special and often high risk of sexual abuse, the Protocol does not include sex as grounds for persecution.[53] Although Southeast Asian refugee women were admitted on the basis of political persecution, their widespread experiences of sexual trauma have gone ignored in both social policy and social services. There has been some attention given to post-traumatic stress syndrome through the study of mental health and social adaptation, but the particular circumstances and experiences of Southeast Asian women refugees continue to need greater understanding and exploration.

GENDERED TRAUMA AND SOUTHEAST ASIAN REFUGEE WOMEN

Testimonies by Southeast Asian refugee women around sexual trauma and torture, rape, stigma, and community sanctions reveal an ongoing dilemma for these women. Although they must deal with the sexual violence they survived, many are unable to talk of their experiences, for varied reasons. Most obviously, they dread reliving their nightmares; further, they risk severe repercussions within their communities based on cultural traditions of sexual purity. It is known that the flight from Vietnam by boat was fraught with peril. Numerous publications document the long voyages on overcrowded boats in poor condition, and the insufficient provisions of food and water on perilous journeys to Thailand, Malaysia, and other adjacent countries.[54] Refugee boats were often repeatedly attacked by Thai fishermen and pirates who roamed the South China Sea preying on these boats during the early 1980s. Between 1980 and 1983 alone, more than 2,200 women were raped and another 500 abducted, presumably to work in Thai brothels.[55] Altogether, more than 600,000 refugees arrived by boats in other Asian countries. Refugees escaping from Laos and Cambodia, including the Hmong, fled toward Thailand and were often harassed by government troops; many died crossing the Mekong River, the principal waterway in mainland Southeast Asia.[56] Frequent sexual abuse of women and girls by peacekeepers working in the refugee camps contributed to a growing distrust and sense of betrayal by government figures.[57]

Important theoretical work has emerged to explain the social and emotional complexities of sex/gender expectations, manifestations of silence, dismemberment, and distrust emerging in narratives by women refugee survivors of trauma, sexual assault, and torture. Although in medical parlance the silence surrounding the sexual atrocities is psychosomatic, this silence may be a continual manifestation of the process of dismemberment. For example, fifty-four Cambodian women over age forty who presented with psychosomatic blindness at a Los Angeles eye clinic had experienced physical trauma, starvation, and the loss of family members, often in their presence. Refugee women survivors, understandably, can experience therapeutic probing or social scientists' investigative interviews as a continuation of overwhelming intrusions into the most intimate aspects of the self. However, their attempt to repress memories of sexual violation and wartime trauma (in order to proceed as culturally virtuous women within the community) has led to psychosomatic forms of physical disability or illness.[58] The mix of trauma, violence, and sexual violence among the resettlement communities created physical, mental, and emotional maladies that compounded the problems of language, employment skills, and arrival in a racially hostile, xenophobic climate. Many of the women who survived physical, sexual, and mental abuse were left to cope and adjust in their country of resettlement while also negotiating multiple forms of discrimination and oppression based on their racial, gender, class, and citizenship status.

Research on Southeast Asian refugee women in the United States tends to focus on patterns of adaptation and the role of family, kinship, and community.[59] Examinations of resettlement life for refugee women commonly point out a shift in gender roles attributed to different forms of subordination by men in the U.S. context. While adapting to a social system that positions women differently from their homeland, researchers and social service providers agree, Southeast Asian women have experienced a dramatic shift in gender roles as a result of their men's inability to provide for their families in customary ways. Hein reports that a "liberalization of gender roles" has occurred among Southeast Asian refugees, primarily because refugee families have had to collect welfare to survive while the men remain unemployed for lack of necessary skills in a tough labor market. Simultaneously, some women are given more access to outside education and training than was permitted in their home countries.[60] However, some researchers argue that the shift in gender roles, the increase in autonomy, and the sometimes-reversed position of women earning more income than their male counterparts often contribute to family conflict and, in some cases, domestic violence.[61] As women have gained more economic autonomy and cultural familiarity with U.S. practices, the reporting of domestic violence to service providers (although still underrepresented) has increased. In 1992 the severity of domestic violence among Southeast Asian immigrants gained public attention when a man set fire to the family home to commit suicide and to kill his four children following a dispute between him and his wife. He was distraught because his wife was contemplating divorce after he objected to her plans to work outside the home and to continue her education.[62] Although this scenario was described in the *Los Angeles Times,* August 3, 1992, as an extreme case, the prevalence of domestic violence within the Southeast Asian community and the cultural implications of silence and stigma among battered refugee women became a serious topic of concern. Community organizers have had to negotiate the delicate and taboo subject of domestic violence slowly and sensitively; nevertheless, advocates have seen the need for concealed shelters specifically for battered Asian women, and many such shelters have been established in major metropolitan areas.

Although many women found refuge in this country with their husbands and families, others had to leave their spouses behind or fled after losing them to war. By 1980, in the initial years of resettlement, 23 percent of the Southeast Asian population in the United States were single female heads of household, constituting 51 percent of all Southeast Asian families below the poverty level.[63] Economic survival for Southeast Asian refugee women in general has been an enormous struggle. Although some have been able to integrate more easily into the workforce, often at the expense of underutilizing the educational or professional credentials obtained in their homelands, many more have had to survive with limited education and literacy, working in minimum wage jobs to supplement other forms of insufficient income. Early examinations of Vietnamese women in the U.S. labor force, funded by the federal government, found that the earliest women entrants from Vietnam experienced the highest level of economic integration. In 1983, 52 percent of Vietnamese women participated in the labor force, while 18 percent were unemployed. Relative success in the labor market for women still trailed behind that of Vietnamese men, who had a rate of 65 percent of labor force participation and 16 percent unemployed. Further, average wages for men were nearly a third higher than those of their female counterparts.[64] Studies also found that Vietnamese women were not only participating in the labor force at lower rates than men, but were having a much more difficult time finding employment.[65]

By the 1990s, staggering rates of unemployment and poverty prevailed for Southeast Asian refugee women. The Southeast Asian population in general possessed the highest sector of the U.S. population with less than a high school degree (64 percent) and with limited English-speaking ability (55 percent). They also had the highest rate of joblessness (33 percent for males and 58 percent for females).[66] Those who were employed typically remained in service sector occupations (hotel, restaurant, janitorial, or garment or electronics assembly), a figure including 52 percent of Laotians, 47 percent of Cambodians, and 42 percent of Vietnamese.[67] By the year 2000, per capita income for Southeast Asian groups showed an extreme lag in economic stability. Cambodians, Hmong, and Laotians had average per-person incomes below $12,000, and Hmong Americans had the lowest average per-person income of any ethnic group described in the 2000 U.S. Census: $6,613. Vietnamese Americans had an average per-person income of just over $15,000, compared with a per-person income of more than $21,000 for the U.S. population overall.[68]

As indicated earlier, shifts in educational attainment have reshaped the working demography among all Southeast Asian groups. According to the 2000 U.S. Census, the ratio of high school graduates to those with no formal schooling had shifted significantly. For persons aged twenty-five years and above, among Cambodians, Hmong, Laotians, and Vietnamese, the percentage of high school graduates increased. However, percentages of people with no formal education still remained fairly high (see table 1), and women continued to lag behind their male counterparts significantly among Cambodians and Hmong. These educational figures also corresponded to the decreased poverty levels and to the significant decrease within the Laotian population. Thus, although Southeast Asian women (and men) made strides in educational attainment and have become more integrated into the labor market, with economically viable employment or businesses, the correspondingly high rates of poverty still indicated a strong need for public assistance.

The Personal Responsibility Work Opportunity Reconciliation Act (PRWORA) of 1996 moved far beyond the original limits established in the Refugee Act of 1980 and its subsequent amendments. For the first time, legislation clearly demarcated Southeast Asian refugees (among other noncitizens) as no longer worthy of public support. Two decades after the first arrivals of Southeast Asian refugees, the U.S. government felt entitled to base eligibility on citizenship status, abrogating its protection of the vulnerable populations residing on U.S. lands as a result of trauma perpetrated by the United States in their countries of origin. My examination of welfare reform, containing a consciousness of refugees' historical experiences of war, trauma, and displacement, diverges from existing critical feminist scholarship that cogently critiques the further loss of rights and liberty for mothers in poverty. Focusing on Southeast Asian refugees further complicates concerns about immigrants and noncitizens in general. In discussing the immediate aftermath on Southeast Asian refugees of welfare reform, I show how the role of citizenship as a demarcating principle clearly established a proxy to push thousands of refugees off assistance regardless of the inherent cruelty and denial of U.S. responsibility.

TESTIMONIES OF BETRAYAL

The audiotape left behind by Chia Yang to tell her family good-bye, to express her sorrow to leave them, and to explain her despair over her impending economic insecurity is perhaps the most direct condemnation of welfare

TABLE 1. Gender Differences in Southeast Asian Educational Attainment (in percentages)

Group	High school graduate	No formal schooling	Women High school graduate	Women No formal schooling	Men High school graduate	Men No formal schooling
Cambodian	47.1	26.2	39.5	31.6	55.9	19.8
Hmong	40.7	45.0	28.5	56.4	53.1	33.4
Laotian	50.5	22.7	45.5	27.6	55.5	18.1
Vietnamese	61.9	8.0	56.7	9.7	67.3	6.2

Source: The Southeast Asian American Statistical Profile, Southeast Asian Resource Action Center (SEARAC), Washington, D.C., 2004. This profile covers ages 25 years and older. All figures based on 2000 U.S. Census.

reform on record. Anne Anlin Cheng asks, "How does an individual go from being a subject of grief to being a subject of grievance?"[69] I argue that Chia Yang's decision to end her life, leaving testimony behind, was an act of will in the face of insurmountable government circumstances—an act she saw as truly the only form of grievance left to her agency. As scholars we are often faced with the dilemma of stripping our subjects of their agency and constructing an overt characterization of victimization. I find Cheng's analysis of what she refers to as the *morphology of ghostliness* helpful in an understanding of suicide as an act of grievance. Arguing that a broader racial melancholia elicits a particularized melancholic response by the racial minority, Cheng argues for new ways of thinking about what agency means for one stripped of it. Paul Gilroy, in *The Black Atlantic,* makes similar arguments in his examination of slavery and slaves' *choice* of death. According to Gilroy, for the powerless, the association of death with freedom is not one of mere morbidity. Gilroy does not see the turn toward death as a giving up or empty victory; he sees it as an active act of will in a situation devoid of will.[70]

Chia Yang articulated in her testimony that she could not bear the pain of starvation or that of having to watch her family suffer once again. At the hands of a legislative act, Chia Yang recognized the "changing of mind" by the U.S. government as an act of betrayal. In ending her life, Chia Yang chose to end her suffering as a powerless political subject of governmental forces that could easily determine the fate of her family. I do not claim to make a psychological assessment regarding the state of Chia Yang's mental health or level of depression, nor is it my intention to engage in a causal argument. Rather, the narrative of Chia Yang's life and death inspires exploration of the implications of the racialized betrayal that persists in American social policy decisions through acts that intentionally exclude or target specific groups of people deemed suspect by dominant racial assumptions.

For the thousands of refugees made ineligible for the benefits that had sustained them since their arrival, the 1996 act of Congress was a broken promise. Narratives from distraught refugees began to flood community organizations and immigrant rights groups. A recurring theme told a common story of U.S. military involvement in Southeast Asia, the establishment of trust and loyalty, the first act of betrayal when American troops pulled out, and then the second act of betrayal—removing the only form of economic security for survival in the United States. A deep onslaught of despair reverberated through entire communities, and detrimentally impacted family members from all generations. Few examinations of welfare reform have included the narratives of refugees whose welfare loss was experienced as a specific form of trauma; given the distinctive circumstances experienced by Southeast Asian refugees in the face of welfare cuts, quite unforseen responses emerged that challenged the loss of benefits to which these refugees believed they were entitled. In this examination, I argue that multilayered citizenship shaped not only the policy targeting specific immigrant groups, but also the particular responses of refugees positioned categorically as noncitizens. The experiences of Southeast Asian refugees reveal the complexities of the multifaceted impact that welfare reform had on noncitizens.

As the cutoffs for SSI approached, the level of anxiety, fear, and mistrust among refugees culminated in an immigrant rights campaign that gained national attention. Stories of elderly and distraught refugees acquired media attention, largely in light of the rash of consequent suicides. Asian immigrant community mobilization efforts centered the experiences of refugees from Southeast Asia through a narrative of betrayal that emerged from frantic refugees and their advocates. Community forums, hearings, and protests became venues where refugees could express their anger and indignation toward the U.S. government for changing the rules and making them ineligible on the basis of citizenship status.

Given the high concentration of Southeast Asians in the Bay Area, organizations like the Asian Law Caucus were instrumental in interpreting, nationwide, policy implications for Asian immigrants, and in providing forums and services for those facing welfare cuts. Similarly, the Asian Law Alliance in San Jose, California, and Catholic Charities, the Northern California Coalition for Immigrant Rights, and the Southeast Asian Community Center in the Tenderloin District of San Francisco were all important in coalition efforts to raise public awareness of welfare reform and to pressure legislatures to rescind the harshest cuts to noncitizens. Organizations used testimonies to show Congress and the public what the cuts were doing to noncitizens, and to portray how welfare reform equaled a violation of human rights.

Newspapers began printing these stories across the nation, as the human drama intensified with the approaching implementation of citizenship requirements. What resulted was the restoration of Supplemental Security

Income to those who were residing in the United States on or before the passing of PRWORA on August 22, 1996. Food stamps were not restored, and the struggle for those restorations continued. The narratives of betrayal also continued, even after SSI was restored. The fundamental fact that Congress decided to cut aid to noncitizens was seen as an unforgivable and unforgettable act of discrimination. What emerged was a rearticulation of the "immigrant welfare problem," but this time not as a narrative of immigrants overusing an overgenerous welfare system, but rather as the tale of a murderous government that was essentially leaving people to starvation, homelessness, and death—a clear violation of human rights. Thus, the "Immigrant Rights Are Human Rights" campaign encompassed most specifically the betrayal of Southeast Asian refugees who had fought for the United States and ultimately arrived in it out of a necessity caused by American actions.[71] Much of the material throughout the following sections draws directly from my ethnographic field work with this campaign's community mobilization efforts.

Operating through both racial and gendered experiences, the two most critical narratives representing the Asian immigrant community voiced the despair of elderly and disabled immigrant and refugee women without other means of support, as well as of betrayed veterans who fought for an American government that easily reneged on its promises and obligations. I will first discuss the testimonies and stories of elderly and disabled immigrant and refugee women, many displaced from Southeast Asia, who found themselves with only the option of obtaining U.S. citizenship. This requirement would prove an insurmountable barrier to many, leaving them in terror of the impending loss of SSI and food stamps. About 72 percent of the immigrants expected to lose SSI were women.[72] Women stood to gain less from the few exceptions allowing some immigrants to remain eligible for assistance; they had more difficulty demonstrating forty qualified quarters of documented work outside of the home or, alternatively, lacked a living spouse who was on active military duty or a veteran. As a result, the greater proportion of elderly and disabled immigrant women losing their assistance evidenced a collective panic as they rushed to attempt naturalization, seeing it as their only hope for survival. Stories of women too old or disabled to fulfill the naturalization requirements were disseminated by community organizations and soon appeared in local and national newspapers. Stories similar to Chia Yang's claimed national attention.

NARRATIVES OF WELFARE DESPAIR

Chia Yang was not the only Hmong refugee to fall so deep into despair that she chose suicide to end her suffering. Ye Vang, a 59-year-old Hmong immigrant, despaired over the loss of the welfare benefits that had enabled her to live in relative peace since arriving in the United States in 1993. Despite assurances by relatives that she would be taken care of should the benefits be cut, Vang felt her future was bleak. She worried that in her old age she would be a burden to her extended family. In September 1997, Vang hung herself outside of the Fresno, California, home that she shared with a brother, a sister-in-law, and eight nieces and nephews.[73] After fleeing Laos in 1975, and living in a refugee camp in Thailand for eighteen years, in 1993 Vang had moved to Fresno to live with her brother, who had moved there three years earlier. She acted as a second mother, providing care to her nieces and nephews. For the first few years of her life in the United States, her family said, Ye Vang was happy, at peace, and content with her new life. However, when the welfare law passed she became distraught, worried, and anxious.

Ye Vang received Supplemental Security Income due to disabilities. Unable to read or speak English, she needed translation and explanation of letters from the Social Security Administration. She tried to pass a citizenship course, but, unable to understand the lessons, stopped attending classes after three weeks. She became demoralized and fearful that she would not be able to survive in the United States. Even though SSI was restored before the cutoffs would take effect, she feared that the nation would stop this support or send her back to Laos. The change in rules implemented by the welfare law fundamentally signaled to Vang, and to others like her, that the promise by the United States to provide refuge could change at any moment. Spreading into hopelessness, the vulnerability established through the passing of PRWORA proved irreparable. Community organizations within the Fresno area indicated that Hmong leaders said they received daily calls from frightened older immigrants afraid they would not be able to survive the new welfare provisions, with some contemplating suicide.[74] The Asian Law Caucus also reported the need to set up hotlines for distraught and confused immigrants contemplating suicide.

Even though death by suicide in Hmong culture is considered potentially detrimental for surviving relatives, community service providers argue, many Hmong in America were so paralyzed by fear, depression and helplessness that they saw suicide as the only way out.[75] In each suicide resulting from welfare reform, the distraught person perceived the burden she or he might become on the family to be more taxing and detrimental than the curse caused by suicide. Suicide by hanging is seen by the Hmong, it should be noted, as the worst possible way of taking one's life, because, it is believed, the person's soul may not be reincarnated; however, a person might choose to end her or his life by hanging out of concern for the family. Hanging, as opposed to other means, signifies that the suicide is due to an *issue* rather than to a personal or familial problem.[76] Both Yang and Vang chose to end their lives by hanging, and left behind messages to their families not to blame themselves, but it was clearly the U.S. government's bad faith that drove them to end their lives. The suicides reflect a heightened level of despair felt by the most vulnerable and hopeless communities affected by welfare reform. In particular, elderly and disabled women with physical and mental health problems feared becoming burdens on their families and feared for the well-being of their own children. True, thousands of refugee women did not choose to end their lives, but they nevertheless expressed a great level of stress, anxiety, and emotional trauma as they faced the loss of benefits.

In attempts to prevent more suicides among distraught elderly and disabled immigrants, advocates stepped up efforts to pressure Congress to restore benefits. Legal advocates from such organizations as the Asian Law Caucus, Asian Pacific American Legal Consortium, and Immigrant Legal Resource Network filed class action lawsuits on behalf of particular immigrant and refugee groups, claiming that the cuts to benefits for noncitizens imposed a violation of equal protection. In addition, coalition groups engaged in massive demonstrations in cities and state capitol buildings across the country. Advocates and immigrants filed through state legislative offices in massive lobbying efforts, pushing for the rescinding of immigrant benefits cuts. Hearings, forums, and workshops provided arenas for legal advocates to better inform frightened noncitizens, and community spokespersons provided testimonies and backgrounds on the impact of the law on their constituencies. Soon to emerge would be a broadbased resistance movement that worked to rearticulate dominant assumption of "welfare fraudulent immigrants" with the counter construction of destitute immigrants as victims of social policy.[77]

In a food stamp appeal hearing in Marysville, California, a tearful Hmong mother threatened to kill herself and her five children if her food stamps were not restored. She told the judge, "You might as well send a soldier to just kill us because that's what you're doing."[78] The situation was especially dire for those elderly and disabled that used their assistance to provide their care in skilled nursing facilities, nursing homes, or convalescent hospitals. The following excerpt from the *San Francisco Chronicle* emphasized the increased awareness of the terrible circumstances some immigrants faced since unable to acquire citizenship: "Because of her disabilities, she has never been able to take the U.S. citizenship test. Without her SSI check, Fong said, the woman would have to leave the rest home and would probably end up in a state mental hospital—assuming she would be admitted. 'She is not abusing the system,' said Fong. 'She truly needs society's care.'"[79] In a *New York Times* article of February 14, 1997, "Administration Welfare Plea Is Scorned in Congress," Robert Pear reported on the battle in Congress to restore SSI benefits:

> It is possible that sentiment on Capitol Hill may change if there is a public outcry when elderly and disabled immigrants actually lose benefits in a few months under the new restrictions on the Supplemental Security Income program. "One of our greatest fears is that the United States will have a rash of suicides among the very old and disabled immigrants who are left without any source of income or medical care," said Sharon M. Daly of Catholic Charities.[80]

The potential reality stirred the question whether such social policy should be reconsidered, at least for the most vulnerable. Placing life-or-death responsibility in the hands of legislators became a prominent theme in major newspaper stories. For fear of being perceived as cruel and inhumane, legislators began to shift their positions to express sympathy for "those most vulnerable, and who were about to lose their only means of survival."

IMMIGRANT DAY II

To increase the visibility of the thousands of elderly and disabled immigrants about to be cut from lifesaving benefits, organizations orchestrated major demonstrations at state capitals and the national capital. With the implementation of SSI cuts only a hundred days away, a major protest, Immigrant Day II, in Sacramento, California, May 28, 1997, pronounced the immigrants' heightened level of anxiety, intensity, and insistence on restoration of benefits. The day, in which I participated, began with a press conference in which community activists clarified the fundamental need for a safety net for immigrants

FIGURE 1. This three-by-four-inch sticker was worn by demonstrators in Sacramento. The slogan was reproduced on t-shirts, posters, and handouts.

and for all poor Californians. Coalition organizers had developed a movement platform, "Immigrant Rights Are Human Rights," framed in bold letters in five languages, displayed on posters, t-shirts, and large signs. Immigrants from all over the world stood together, but the two most visible groups were Asian and Latinas/os. And elderly Asian immigrant women held signs that read "YOUR SSI CUT IS KILLING US!!!"

Throughout the demonstration, groups of five to ten advocates and immigrants conducted legislative visits to California Assembly representatives to demand a real safety net and to urge reinstatement of benefits through existing proposals facing the California budget. In the halls of the capitol, Assembly members, confronted with crowds too large to fit in their offices, stood outside their doors surrounded by immigrants of all ages and from many countries, some in traditional dress, who asked such questions as "Where is our safety net?" "What are you going to do about the hungry and starving when food stamps are cut off?" Conservative representatives tended to blame the situation on President Clinton. Numerous times throughout the day, I heard: "Our hands are tied, and we are under direct stipulations that have been federally mandated. We are doing the best we can, given the federal law."[81]

In one hallway, a group of about twelve, including Hmong women wearing traditional headdress (Mien), Laotian women and advocates, and elderly Latinos wearing jeans and plaid shirts, had surrounded a befuddled young white legislator wearing suit and tie. As I stopped to observe, an older Hmong woman in her seventies shook her head as the young man continued to explain the federal rules, trying to impress upon people that his own hands were tied, and interrupted him to yell "Where's our safety net?" Exasperated, the young man continued to explain some legislative rules, then said abruptly, "I have to go now. My time is up." He swiftly moved into his office and shut the door behind him, but the women and men in the corridor smiled at each other, aware they had given him a new perspective.

Outside the Capitol, elderly East Asian, Southeast Asian, and Latino immigrants stood side by side. They covered a range of ages but the vast majority were elderly. Young advocates accompanied groups of elderly immigrants, some disabled and walking with canes and walkers into the Capitol to await a legislative visit with their assigned Assembly member. As people filed into the building, speakers at the podium at the top of the Capitol stairs addressed the thousands of cheering demonstrators. Buses from throughout California had brought these immigrants, about to be cut from SSI, to show legislators the real people about to lose these life-sustaining benefits.

To end the demonstration, the executive director of the Coalition for Immigrant Rights, a young Latina lawyer, took bullhorn in hand to urge the massive crowd to line up at the steps of the Capitol; then, with Coalition organizers in special t-shirts assisting elderly and frail protesters, the line began moving around the building, with thousands of immigrant women and men and their advocates waving signs high and chanting "Immigrant Rights Are Human Rights!!" The crowd was dense, the hot air stifling. The urgent call for benefits restorations focused on the frailty and vulnerability of elderly and disabled immigrants, pinpointing the gravity of the impending loss of benefits through the slogan "Your SSI cuts are killing us." For all

FIGURE 2. The Sacramento Immigrant Day II march marked the 100-day countdown to the Supplemental Security Income cut for noncitizens. The sign slightly cut off on the right reads "I HELPED YOU IN THE VIETNAM WAR BUT NOW YOU WANT TO KILL ME." Photograph by the author.

present, the historical and political experiences of the thousands of refugees from Southeast Asia who had fled from genocide resonated with conflicted perceptions of American involvement in the war in Vietnam.

FURTHER TESTIMONY OF DESPAIR

The testimonies by and about elderly and disabled women already suffering from the atrocities and displacement of war demonstrated the level of terror and trauma imposed by new citizenship enforcements. As the individual testimonies accumulated into a collective testimony of despair, the grief arising from welfare reform channeled into a grievance against the U.S. government. The testimonies left behind by suicide victims, along with the voices of the thousands of surviving women about to face the very cut-offs that drove their counterparts to end their lives, surfaced as a welfare story on a public scale heretofore never heard. The concept of a welfare-abusing foreign woman was reconstructed into a figure who had already suffered more atrocities, loss, and violations of war and displacement than any person should have to bear. To endure the loss of benefits that for thousands had been the primary means of survival became a criminal act for which Congress would have to hold responsibility.

This narrative was enough to rescind the harshest cuts. As implementation neared, and pressure from the immigrant rights movement became more visible, legislators began making public statements of support for the restoration of SSI for elderly and disabled immigrants.

Through the Balanced Budget Act of 1997, weeks before the cut-offs of SSI were to begin, Congress restored benefits so that those receiving benefits at the time, August 22, 1996, that the law passed would not lose their monthly checks even if they did not meet the Act's exemptions. The terms of the Balanced Budget Act afforded immense relief that at least those already receiving SSI would not lose their life-sustaining benefits. Community organizations recognized the significance of the testimonies and stories presented by the immigrants and refugees. In an issue of the Asian Law Caucus newsletter, The Reporter, one month after the Balanced Budget Act, the Caucus's executive director stated:

> It took the courage of those immigrants and refugees who spoke publicly about their plight, along with the suicides of others, to preserve SSI assistance for immigrants. Now there still remains the balance of cuts imposed by welfare reform, some which have yet to be phased in. As our article on the loss of assistance to refugees describes, thousands are now losing their eligibility for Food Stamps. The battle to prevent or ease some of those cuts is our next major challenge in what promises to be a long and painful process known as "welfare reform."[82]

A prominent theme to emerge in the aftermath of PRWORA was the significance of women's agency throughout the community advocacy efforts. The move from *silence to voice* and from *invisibility to visibility*[83] required change in the public image of the Southeast Asian refugee soon to lose her benefits. The hearings and forums where women spoke of their dire circumstances became the fodder for community organizations to push advocacy efforts. Even the suicides by distraught women afraid to see their families again suffer became instrumental for organizations in pressuring legislatures to turn back the harshest cuts. Until this moment, most elderly and disabled Southeast Asian women preferred little public attention. However, at this point their own agency and voice became the only means for these women to survive. A new form of politicization emerged, one that led them to demonstrate at capitols, yell at country officials, and talk to the press. The *agency* utilized by elderly and disabled Southeast Asian women in the "Immigrant Rights Are Human Rights" campaign demonstrates Lisa Lowe's point that Asian immigrants and Asian Americans have not only been "subject to" exclusion and restriction but have also been "subjects of" the immigration process, and have been agents of political change, cultural expression, and social transformation.[84]

In addition to the stories of despair and trauma that all elderly and disabled noncitizens faced from loss of benefits, the narratives and testimonies by Southeast Asians as betrayed veterans complicated assumptions that noncitizens were not entitled to public benefits. The testimonies of betrayal by Southeast Asians specifically provided a public rearticulation and reeducation for collective memories of the U.S. war in Vietnam. The American collective memory of that war usually centers on the plight of U.S. veterans. With the cutting of welfare to noncitizens, however, an unrecognized Vietnam veteran emerged. Hmong and Laotian soldiers who fought for the United States sought refuge here with the understanding that the U.S. government owed them assistance and support. The loss of welfare for Southeast Asian veterans demonstrated a problematic practice of defining the citizen *patriot* by pushing out those who did not fit the national masculinist and racialized idea of the American soldier.

VETERANS BETRAYED

In a newspaper interview, Chia Yang's son Toby Vang clearly saw the loss of welfare as the cause of his mother's suicide. In his indictment, he articulated the profound sense of betrayal from which his mother could not recover. Vang stated, "She lost her country because we fought on the American side. Then she loses her benefits because she wasn't a U.S. citizen."[85] As noncitizens faced the impending loss of SSI and food stamps, the testimonies of Southeast Asian veterans exposed the hollowness of the U.S. promise. As the mission statement of the U.S. Department of Veterans Affairs states,

> "To care for him who shall have borne the battle and for his widow and his orphan."
>
> These words, spoken by Abraham Lincoln during his Second Inaugural Address, reflect the philosophy and principles that guide VA in everything we do, and are the focus of our endeavors to serve our Nation's veterans and their families.[86]

The Department's statement of commitment claims, "Veterans have earned our respect and commitment, and their health care, benefits, and memorial services needs drive our actions. We will value our commitment to veterans through all contingencies and remain fully prepared to achieve our mission."[87]

The notion of respect, gratitude, and obligation for veterans of war has remained a steadfast principle in U.S. politics. The government's commitment to fully care for and compensate the nation's veterans has, however, not been consistent or universal. The demarcation of noncitizen veterans as no longer deserving of government assistance struck a familiar chord in U.S. veteran politics, as charges of racism have been waged against the U.S. military throughout history. The racialization of Hmong and Laotian veterans as not fully American veterans jabbed a particularly hurtful nerve among the thousands of refugees struggling to survive in an unwelcoming and fiercely competitive advanced capitalist country.

At the crux of the Southeast Asia veteran's struggle is a deeper problematic of a racialized gendered construction that worked to emasculate Southeast Asian men as *nonprotectors* and *nonheroes* of the nation. Since they are welfare recipients, as opposed to beneficiaries of veteran benefits, they have a status as *nonproviders* that goes against the predominant assumption of manliness as independence and being a provider. Thus, in a book that focuses on the implication of welfare reform on immigrant women, the issue of Southeast Asian veterans inserts an important gendered dialogue regarding citizenship, nation, and entitlement. A historical precedent exists where the "feminization" of Asian immigrant men was seen through their relegation to such feminized industries as laundries, restaurants, or live-in "house-boys." Important scholarly work by David Eng demonstrates the ways that intersecting forces of race, gender, and sexuality come together to shape, represent, and organize Asian American male subjectivity.[88] Southeast Asian men fighting to retain their welfare benefits could be seen as racially emasculated, such that social agencies easily dismissed their claims to veteran status and, thus, their entitlement to public benefits—in a stereotype reminiscent of the "feminized" occupational ghettoization that was experienced a century earlier. Like elderly and disabled refugee women, Southeast Asian men had to go public as war veterans enlisted by the United States—but had also to confront a racialized emasculation as poor men in need of continued benefits for their families' survival.

Testimonies before a California food stamp appeals hearing included one Hmong veteran producing death certificates of fifty-two relatives he said were killed as a result of his family's service to the CIA.[89] Another Hmong veteran, whose military service includes a congressional Defenders of Freedom citation and seventy-two months in a communist reeducation camp, said that before he came to the United States, he never asked anyone for help. "Now I have to depend on my children for everything, such as translating, shopping or going anywhere. My children are my parent and I am their child. I take ESL classes, but it does no good."[90] Having to acknowledge the fact of his children taking the parental role demonstrates the profound gendered implications for refugee men of the struggle for survival in the United States.

Like the narratives of Chia Yang and Ye Vang, the story of Sai Chou Lor evokes the overwhelming sense of despair and betrayal resulting from welfare cuts. Lor fought for the CIA against the Laotian communists and resettled with his wife and four children as legal immigrants in the United States. Because of a serious war injury, Lor was unable to work, and received SSI. Two years after his arrival, Lor received a notice saying that he would lose his benefits if he could not prove his U.S. citizenship. Having only been in the country for two years, Lor was not even eligible to apply for naturalization. A few days after receiving his ineligibility notice, he attempted suicide but was unsuccessful and remained in a Stockton hospital. In this case, the fear for survival and dread over the loss of benefits played out in ways that remain unrecognized among impoverished men.

From 1961 to 1975, Hmong and Laotian men and boys were recruited by the CIA and trained to fight the North Vietnamese Army and to rescue downed pilots in Laos and Vietnam, suffering nearly thirty thousand casualties. The men were on the Pentagon payroll—yet their veteran status has been disputed. The Department of Veteran Affairs has fought against granting veteran status for Hmong and Laotian soldiers, stating that veterans need to show a document of honorable discharge from military service to be eligible for benefits available through the G.I. Bill.[91]

Jim Parker, one of the few surviving CIA advisors who served in Laos, argues that the Hmong should not be granted veteran status. Parker claims he made no promises to the Hmong, that the Hmong and Americans were fighting a common enemy: "I don't feel like we abandoned them." He later stated, "The United States is not the best home for them. They're a stone age people. Bless their hearts, I love the Hmong, but they complain a lot. It's their nature. They're very fatalistic."[92]

Working with the broader movement to restore benefits, Hmong and Laotian veteran groups began mobilizing and sought legal redress to confront the loss of support they deserved for their veteran status. Asian Law Caucus managing attorney Victor Hwang led a mass legal effort to challenge the loss of food stamps for Hmong and Laotian veterans. The specific nature of the Hmong and Laotian veterans' cases dealt with the purposely ambiguous nature of their veteran status. Although the restoration of SSI meant that most Hmong and Laotian veterans residing in the United States on or before August 22, 1996, did continue receiving this assistance, thousands lost theirs. To establish exceptions for veterans, PRWORA had defined a veteran as "a person who served in the active military, naval, or air service, and who was discharged or released . . . under conditions other than dishonorable." By this definition, Hmong who aided American forces during the Vietnam War were not "veterans." The Balanced Budget Act of 1997, in restoring SSI for some noncitizens, established that Hmong veterans did qualify to remain eligible for benefits cut to most noncitizens. Congress made the following findings in the Balanced Budget Act to set forth its intent that those refugees who served with U.S. forces in Laos should be considered veterans:

- Hmong and other Highland Lao tribal peoples were recruited, armed, trained, and funded for military operations by the United States Department of Defense, Central Intelligence Agency, Department of State, and Agency for International Development to further United States National security interests during the Vietnam conflict.

- Hmong and other Highland Lao tribal forces sacrificed their own lives and saved the lives of American military personnel by rescuing downed American pilots and aircrews and by engaging and successfully fighting North Vietnamese troops.

- It is the sense of the Congress that Hmong and other Highland Lao veterans who fought on behalf of the Armed Forces of the United States during the Vietnam conflict and have lawfully been admitted to the United States for permanent residence should be considered veterans for purposes of continuing certain welfare benefits consistent with the exceptions provided other noncitizen veterans under the Personal Responsibility and Work Opportunity Reconciliation Act.[93]

However, the U.S. Department of Agriculture (USDA) insisted that since Congress did not provide a budget to implement its intent, benefits could not be extended to the Hmong and other refugees from Laos. The Clinton Administration also agreed that the statement did not amend PRWORA, thus lacked the force of law, and left approximately sixteen thousand Laotian veterans and their family members without food stamps and other benefits.[94] Thus, even though Congress established the recognition of Hmong and other Highland Lao veterans as in fact U.S. veterans, this mandate was not enough to secure exceptions for these veterans and their families. In fact, the USDA continued to disavow Hmong and Laotian veterans as U.S. veterans. In California an immediate appeal was made to the California Department of Social Services (DSS) following the Balanced Budget act, but the administrative law judge involved ruled that the plaintiff's federal food stamp benfits were correctly being terminated because he was a legal noncitizen between the ages of eighteen and sixty-five who did not fall within any exception to the PRWORA.[95] On September 1, 1997, approximately twenty thousand Hmong in California lost their food stamp benefits.[96] The loss of food stamps was not only nutritionally detrimental to entire families, it imposed a devastating level of emotional and physical stress. At this time, the poverty rate among Hmong in the nation as a whole was 60 percent.

California civil rights lawyers filed at least thirty-five hundred appeals in Fresno, Los Angeles, Sacramento, Yuba, Alameda, Butte, San Joaquin, and Orange Counties alone. In addition to the appeals, Victor Hwang filed a class action lawsuit against collective defendants DSS, DSS director Eloise Anderson, the USDA, and USDA secretary Dan Glickman on behalf of Chong Yia Yang, a Hmong veteran whose food stamps were cut for himself and his two children on September 9, 1997. Yang was recruited by the CIA in 1971 when he was only fourteen years old. When the United States pulled out of Laos, he was forced to flee. In an editorial published by the *Fresno Bee* on November 11, 1998, Yang said "the Americans told them that if the Americans win the Vietnam War, then the Hmong people can live in peace in Laos. On the other hand, if the Americans lost the war, then they agreed to take all the Hmong people out of Laos to live in their country, and would make sure that every Hmong would live like American citizens."[97] Yang's attorney Victor Hwang believed that this case was an excellent test for welfare reform: "If we win on his behalf, then we can win for everybody."[98] The lawsuit challenged the ambiguous "sense of Congress" doctrine established in the Balanced Budget Act of 1997. The lawsuit, if successful, would have consolidated Hmong and Laotian veterans as U.S. veterans for the purpose of remaining eligible for the benefits denied to noncitizens by PRWORA.

In addition to the class action lawsuits, the public demonstrations (previously described) integrated the testimonies of betrayed veterans. Southeast Asian refugee veterans who had fought for the United States articulated in their signs HMONG VETERAN DENIED FOOD STAMPS, while wearing U.S. army fatigues and their military ribbons. The notion of obligation and betrayal was also invoked as elderly Southeast Asian refugee women and veterans held signs that said REMEMBER US? WE ARE THE CIA, AND WE WANT OUR FOOD STAMPS. The trials experienced by the thousands of refugees from Southeast Asia who had fled from genocide severely tested American ideals of loyalty and obligation to those who had protected American interests and citizens. The assertion of these veterans' American military membership directly challenged attempts to write them out of U.S. military entitlement.

With heightened exposure of the unique situation faced by these Hmong veteran refugees, the media elevated public awareness over the contradictory nature of welfare reform and the reform's harsh impact on legal immigrants. Within months of the immigrants' being cut from food stamp benefits, articles in major newspapers focused on the sense of betrayal, abandonment, and injustice experienced by affected Hmong refugees. Revisiting the bloodiest years of the Vietnam War, the "secret war" in Laos, and the devastation, trauma, and genocide faced by entire families and communities left behind when America pulled out in 1975, news articles exposed the hypocrisy of the U.S. government's denial of food stamps to deeply impoverished veterans' families. Yee Xiong, the president of the California Statewide Lao/Hmong Coalition, told *Asian Week* on November 13, 1997, "The Hmong people were targeted for persecution and execution in Laos because of their service on behalf of the CIA. Many have [staked] the lives of their parents, brothers, sisters, sons, and daughters on the promise the United States would care for their families. All we ask is to honor that promise."[99]

A front-page article (December 27, 1997) in the *New York Times*, "Many Laotians in U.S. Find Their Hopes Betrayed," reported on the suicides of elderly Asian immigrants. Throughout, the article explains the historical circumstances of the war in Southeast Asia, the harrowing journey to refugee camps, and the difficulties in resettlement in great detail. In this article, three months after immigrants began losing food stamps, journalist Tim Weiner explained how the Hmong were a casualty of U.S. involvement in the Vietnam War.

> Some 36,000 Laotians battled North Vietnamese troops, rescued downed
> American pilots and guarded the radars that guided Air Force bombers.
> Thousands of tribesmen died. In return, the United States gave the tribes-
> people rice and promised them refuge if things went badly. . . . The Laotians,
> most of whom are members of the Hmong tribe, were migratory slash-and-
> burn farmers with only the rudiments of a written language when the CIA ar-
> rived to teach them the art of modern war in 1961. . . . They [the Hmong]
> were left behind when the United States left their country in 1974. Thou-
> sands of them, many physically or mentally wounded by war and exile, trekked
> through jungles to refugee camps in Thailand in the late 1970s. They settled
> in California, Minnesota, Wisconsin and a handful of other states, and have
> tried to overcome high barriers of skill, education, language and culture in a
> land far from their roots.[100]

Weiner reported that the thousands of Laotian veterans and their families
that resettled in the United States faced benefit cutoffs that "led to despair
and suicides among the refugees." Quoting several Lao and Hmong community representatives, Weiner reported:

> "You can't believe the level of desperation and the level of betrayal they feel,"
> said Jayne Park, attorney for the Laotian veterans. . . . "Survival of the tribe
> was becoming a major concern by the time the United States began with-
> drawing from the war," according to an Air Force study. A quarter-century
> later, the Laotians say their prospects for survival have been damaged by wel-
> fare reform. "We feel that we have been betrayed," said Blong Lo, a leader of
> the Coalition for Hmong and Lao Veterans in Chico, CA.[101]

According to Khao Insixiengmay, a veteran of the CIA war in Laos, interviewed for the *New York Times* article:

> When they came here they have had little education, little skill. Many became
> mentally and physically unstable due to the trauma of war and dislocation.
> Now with the cutbacks, people are under the poverty line and they have a
> problem to survive in this new society. They do not know who to turn to.[102]

Similarly, Yia Noei Her, who worked for the CIA from 1967 to 1975, stated
that many former soldiers suffer from physical and psychological wounds
from the war.

> Many soldiers think there is nothing left for them in this country. Either you
> give them the benefits or not. They don't want to suffer anymore, so they say
> they might as well die.[103]

In public hearings before administrative law officials across California
counties, Hmong veterans and their families testified about the aggressive
enlistment of Hmong men and boys by the CIA, the arduous journeys away

from their homeland, and the difficulties they encountered in their attempts to secure self-sustaining employment in their new country. According to Ernest Velasquez, the former welfare director in Fresno County,

> The Hmong should have a special dispensation. . . . The reality is, this wasn't their war. We brought the war to them. We recruited them. We made them our secret army and now all of a sudden we aren't even going to give them food stamps.[104]

Less heard are the stories of Hmong and Laotian women veterans who were also recruited by the CIA. In a hearing before California administrative law judge Robert Fugina, a woman testified that she was recruited by the CIA and served as a nurse, ministering to wounded combat troops and downed U.S. fliers. Her husband fought nearby in a CIA-led combat unit. She pleaded with Judge Fugina not to cut her food stamps because of the great hardship it would cause her and her four children. Although Judge Fugina approved her appeal, the state denied the ruling, stating that the language of the federal law ("the sense of Congress") left them with no choice.[105]

The movement to restore benefits for Southeast Asian veterans emerged as an independent entity. The Lao Veterans of America, based in Washington, D.C., organized hearings before the USDA to demand that USDA Secretary Dan Glickman follow through with the intent of Congress to restore food stamps to Lao and Hmong veterans, as put forth in the Balanced Budget Act. South Vietnamese, Hmong, and Laotian veterans joined the preexisting struggle by Filipino soldiers of World War II who had been denied their U.S. veteran status. In light of the massive demonstrations and publicity regarding the denial of formal veteran status to Hmong and Laotians, nationwide veterans' campaigns influenced sympathetic legislators, often veterans themselves, to recognize the hypocrisy and injustice being enacted toward a group that sacrificed so much to save the lives of downed American soldiers. In September 1997 at the capitol building in Madison, Wisconsin, a state tribute was held on behalf of Lao and Hmong veterans. Veterans Affairs Secretary Raymond Boland and other elected officials spoke before approximately a thousand Lao veterans and relatives. About five hundred veterans stood in formation in military fatigues and medals, as state officials and veteran officers paid them tribute. Boland told the audience, "You have a distinguished tradition as true freedom fighters," and acknowledged that this tribute should have come much sooner.[106]

As the veterans issue continued to gain publicity, the Agriculture Research, Extension, and Education Reform Act, proposed in the Senate, offered a remedy specific to Hmong and Laotian veterans. First introduced in September 1997 by Senator Richard G. Lugar, R-Indiana, the provisions clarified the more ambiguous "sense of Congress" by specifically defining members of a Hmong or Highland Laotian tribe at the time the tribe assisted the U.S. military during the Vietnam War, as veterans entitled to welfare benefits. If this bill passed, the class action lawsuits on behalf of Hmong and Laotian veterans would become moot, as food stamps would be systematically restored to Hmong and Lao veterans, including spouses and dependent children. On June 23, 1998, President Clinton signed the Agriculture Research, Extension, and Education Reform Act of 1998, Public Law 105–185. In fact, the Act also restored eligibility for those noncitizens who were under eighteen and over sixty-five. In light of the new Act, the class action lawsuit *Yang v. California Department of Social Services* narrowed the plaintiff's claims to retroactive payment of benefits for the period when his benefits were cut off (September 1, 1997, to November 1, 1998). A primary argument for retroactive payments was that the new bill clearly demonstrated that Congress fully intended to restore benefits to Hmong and Laotian veterans unfairly denied food stamps and veteran status by the USDA. Ultimately the district court did not grant in favor of Yang, and ruled that through the Balanced Budget Act's sense of Congress provision "amounted to no more than nonbinding legislative dicta."[107] Although the restoration of food stamps to Hmong residents was clearly a success made possible by much collective effort, the residents' veterans status was not yet formally recognized, nor has it been at the time of this writing. The language in both the Balanced Budget Act and the Agriculture Research, Extension, and Education Reform Act extends their recognition of the sacrifices made by Hmong soldiers on behalf of U.S. military efforts, yet both bills stop short of granting formal veteran status. An act of this magnitude would open up a wide host of benefits that the U.S. government appears evidently unwilling to extend.

The extraordinary efforts by Southeast Asian veterans to publicly state their grievances, as rightfully deserving the public assistance from which they were cut, challenged the racial and gendered emasculation that denied them their veteran status. Yet the persistent refusal to grant these men their veteran status points to ongoing racialized and gendered assumptions about who gets declared *protector* and *hero* of the nation.

Although some benefits were partially restored, the levels of hunger and food insecurity among immigrants continued to rise. This was primarily because the piecemeal restorations to select groups of noncitizens were not enough. They still did not provide enough purchasing power for immigrants to adequately feed their families. The struggle to retain food stamps for Hmong and Laotian veterans reflects the harsh levels of indignity that the U.S. government was willing to impose on people on the basis of citizenship status. That these veterans had to prove their U.S. veteran status was a historical denial negating an entire set of obligations and promises; in this instance, legislators had attempted to place citizenship status over veteran status in demarcating entitlement. The political vulnerability refugees faced as they lost their benefits revealed the troubling implications for immigrants when *legal* citizenship becomes, through social policy, the differentiating principle for entitlement.

REFUGEES AND CITIZENSHIP, SOCIAL POLICY AND IMMIGRANT RIGHTS

The testimonies and reports from Southeast Asian refugees confronted with losing life-sustaining benefits revealed a less known story of welfare reform. This story reflects the complicated nature of refugee matters subsumed within broader anti-immigrant legislation and citizenship politics. The lumping of refugees and immigrants together in matters of social policy proves problematic on numerous counts. However, to argue that refugees should, due to their refugee status, not be cut from assistance is not intended to argue that benefits may be cut from immigrants who are not refugees. Although my research shows that neither immigrants nor refugees should have been eliminated from welfare programs, the arguments for each group differ, given the groups' divergent political experiences and migration backgrounds. Researchers have documented that a substantial reason for the rise in immigrant welfare utilization between the 1970s and the 1990s was the rise in refugee and asylee admittances.[108] For Southeast Asians in the United States, this demographic is undercounted, as a significant proportion of legal permanent residents from Southeast Asia did not enter the United States through refugee status but rather through family reunification status. Even after spending decades in refugee camps, these residents' official status is not "refugee or asylee." However, given these persons' historical and political experiences, researchers consider those who entered from 1975 through the 1990s as refugees displaced by political upheaval and war. Although PRWORA made some distinctions for recently arrived refugees, the policy generally treated refugees like all other immigrants. To consistently ignore the particular circumstances that refugees face in terms of economic and social integration is to impose a malevolent blindness that leads to significant and avoidable damage. As a primary receiving country of the world's refugees, the United States only commits to temporary assistance, few resources, and a self-sufficiency model that leads a great many refugees to survive in low-skill, low-wage employment. The cuts to welfare retraumatized displaced refugees, doing permanent damage to hope, trust, and security.

The two dominant narratives of despair and betrayal, that of the refugee veterans and that of elderly Southeast Asian women, that emerged with the implementation of PRWORA further demonstrated the effects of heterogeneity within the Asian immigrant community. Elderly and disabled Southeast Asian women lost their SSI benefits because they were demonized as unfairly utilizing an overgenerous welfare system; along with other racialized and gendered constructions of women (e.g., as dependent on the state when they should rely on their husbands—or, in this case, on their offspring), these claims fitted with a broader politics of dismantling welfare as a system of entitlement. Welfare reformists in favor of drastically reducing and eliminating benefits to immigrants argued that welfare had become a magnet attracting migrants from Asia and Mexico. As discussed earlier, the works of Norm Matloff and George Borjas helped fortify the idea that the increase in immigrant welfare participation within the past few decades somehow proved that immigrants' access to public benefits allowed them to exploit the welfare system rather than rely on their families or sponsors for economic support. The problem with this argument was that, by and large, immigrants and refugees did not choose to enter the United States to receive welfare. Noncitizens resorted to welfare for much the same reasons that most poor citizens needed to utilize assistance. Economic conditions, a changing work force, loss of jobs, and devaluation of blue collar skills resulted in people fluctuating in and out of employment. For elderly Southeast Asian women, SSI was essential for basic survival. Nevertheless, immigrants were charged with using welfare benefits with no incentive to work—yet the very basis of SSI was that recipients are unable to sustain employment due to their age or their physical or mental health conditions. The use of citizenship as a demarcating factor served a two-fold purpose: one, to reap a significant savings in welfare reduction at the expense of immigrants; two, to reformulate immigration policy so that noncitizens' welfare use would impede their future naturalization, which in turn would discourage entrance into the nation.

The narratives of betrayal articulated by Southeast Asian veterans presented a dilemma common for veterans of color, consistently marginalized by the U.S. military complex. In this instance, citizenship was utilized as a definitive axis on which to deny veteran status; this compounded problems not only for the veterans, but also for their wives and dependent children, likewise denied the privileges stripped from their husbands and fathers. When it came time for formal recognition and the right to benefits, the racial foreignness of the thousands of Southeast Asians who fought for the United States trumped what was due their loyalty. Although systematic forms of racial and gendered discrimination have plagued U.S. military programs, it was the use of citizenship status, in the case of Southeast Asian refugees, that marked them as "other," not truly veterans, and thus undeserving of government support. For a moment, economic support was recognized as an essential element of restitution and successful resettlement for those refugees who sacrificed their lives and country to assist American military efforts to fight communism in Southeast Asia. Yet along the way, not only did refugees from Southeast Asia become racialized as inassimilable and undeserving foreigners, Southeast Asian veterans of U.S. military service were forgotten and subsumed into a broader rhetoric of foreign dependency on American resources. This anti-immigrant/antiforeigner mentality stripped these men and their families of veteran status despite their sacrifices to support the U.S. government.

The compassion fatigue that Aiwha Ong discusses in her work on Cambodian refugees applies in this instance; however, welfare reform moved beyond exhaustion and resentment to a more definitive notion, *foreigner undeservingness*. The broader racial politics of welfare reform that demonized, primarily, women of color in a linguistic framework of *overdependency, irresponsibility*, and pathological *laziness* drove the mandates that ultimately dismantled welfare as a system of entitlement. However, the anti-immigrant veins of reform used coded racial meanings that included *foreigner dependency, transnational fraudulence*, and *welfare as a magnet for immigrants hoping to scam an overgenerous assistance system*. Citizenship became the logical marker with which to eliminate the perceived drastic increase of welfare utilization by Asian and Latina/o immigrants.

For the refugees whose situations and perspectives were presented in this chapter, the logic of welfare reform made no sense. Although some might argue that these particular refugee groups could be seen as innocent bystanders or unintended victims of a broader political anti-immigrant mandate, the demographic information was always available, and legislators were responsible for the cuts they mandated. Within the politics of any given historical moment in the United States, choosing to act in support of popular tides of anti-immigrant sentiment, and of a retrenchment of Americanism through citizenship entitlement, reflects the broader tendency to demonize particular immigrant groups. In the immediate state of expanding global political and economic interconnections, and of massive numbers of refugees and displaced persons, noncitizens remain truly vulnerable to political tides within the U.S. domestic sphere. Southeast Asian refugees were retraumatized when they found themselves suddenly cut from the benefits critical for their survival. Even with the restorations of the harshest cuts, the emotional and economic damage, political insecurity, and mistrust remain irreparable.

4

The Rush for Citizenship

Naturalization as a Technocratic Apparatus of Exclusion

> What Congress and President Clinton didn't realize when they
> passed this law [PRWORA] was the thousands of elderly, disabled,
> and indigent immigrants who are physically and mentally unable to
> obtain citizenship through the naturalization process. Even if they
> qualify for the disability waiver making them exempt from the English
> requirement or the civics exam, some immigrants are so cognitively
> impaired that they aren't able to take the required oath of allegiance.
> We are basically hearing from people who are terrified because they
> are going to lose the income that provides their in-home health care,
> or payment for their convalescent care. But they are so mentally
> impaired [that] it is going to be absolutely impossible for them to
> be naturalized. But the only recourse they have right now is to
> gain citizenship. . . . It's a state of forced citizenship.
>
> —Legal Assistant, Asian Law Caucus

When the Personal Responsibility Work Opportunity Reconciliation Act (PRWORA) first passed, the only assured advice that community service providers and legal advocates could offer to their confused and panicked constituents was to naturalize. Once the law was enacted, immigrant rights organizations began large-scale citizenship drives to expedite the naturalization process for numerous immigrants, by helping them complete their paperwork and by answering their questions in a less intimidating and more supportive environment. Record numbers of immigrants began filing for naturalization, producing a two-year waiting list within months of the law's passage. This timeframe proved detrimental for those immigrants losing benefits long before they would be able to naturalize. In this context, citizenship took on a precise new meaning: survival, prevention of hunger and malnutrition, continued nursing care, and housing.

The immediate panic that led to the massive rush to naturalize illustrates the increasing significance of citizenship status as a formal prerequisite of entitlement. Although formal citizenship does not guarantee all the rights of citizenship status (many groups continue to experience unequal access to resources, and endure discriminatory exclusions), citizenship as a formal demarcation for rights and liberties has further eroded immigrants' political rights. As already noted, elderly and disabled Southeast Asian refugee women struggled to pass the citizenship exams, but failed repeatedly, leading to greater despair and in some cases suicide.

The difficulties, challenges, and obstacles immigrants faced in the naturalization process demonstrate the state's power in granting or denying citizenship. The citizenship politics to emerge with the welfare and immigration reforms of 1996 represent struggles that continue to shape the experiences of Asian immigrants in relation to broader state and cultural politics. And the politics of citizenship has been a prevailing theme of significant concern in Asian American studies. This chapter focuses specifically on *citizenship*, in this global contemporary moment of continued heightened immigration from Asia and Mexico, as a state technology to differentiate rights, liberties, entitlement, and exclusion. As Mai Ngai so cogently articulates, "Immigration policy is constitutive of Americans' understanding of national membership and citizenship, drawing lines of inclusion and exclusion that articulate a desired composition—imagined if not necessarily realized—of the nation."[1] The politics of citizenship and naturalization run deep and persistent through the history of Asian America, and the implications of welfare and immigration have stirred a reemergence of this politics for Asian immigrants. Thus, this chapter aims to examine the way the convergence of welfare and immigration reform resulted in very specific technologies that produced contemporary forms of exclusion for the most vulnerable immigrants seeking citizenship.

In the face of lost benefits, the process that Asian immigrants undertook to naturalize, in hopes of maintaining crucial assistance, revealed a technocratic system of rules, requirements, and contingencies that further complicated the obtaining of citizenship, and that systematically excluded large groups of vulnerable immigrants. The racial and gendered politics embedded in this process were hidden by government regulations, rules that ostensibly pivoted on "general applicant criteria" but which primarily worked to keep out poor women of color as potential "dependents" of the state. What constitutes a good or desired citizen did not include most of those facing the cut-offs in the first place. Thus the convergence of welfare and immigration reform was a clear step to further divide those able to claim full legal status and public resources from those who were not.

According to Aihwa Ong, "What matters is to identify the various domains in which these preexisting racial, ethnic, gender, and cultural forms are problematized, and become absorbed and recast by social technologies of government that define the modern subject."[2] Although citizen welfare recipients were subjected to racialized and gendered demonizations of *laziness, irresponsibility,* and *pathology,* noncitizens were also embedded in a narrative of *national threat to economic security* and thus of nonbelonging in the nation in general. Thus, increasingly, citizenship came to be defined as the civic duty of the individual to reduce his or her burden on society, and instead to build up his own human capital—in other words, to "be an entrepreneur of her/himself."[3] Although this notion of responsible citizenship was applied to all welfare recipients at the time of welfare reform, for noncitizens, human capital became more significant not only in terms of ineligibility for benefits but also for naturalization.

To reiterate the point made by Stuart Hall and David Held, "The issue around membership—who does and who does not belong—is where the *politics* of citizenship begins."[4] As I have argued earlier, it was the convergence and intersection of welfare and immigration reform that established new criteria for legal belonging in the United States. Just as citizenship status became more firmly integrated into welfare eligibility, so welfare use and poverty became more clearly integrated into naturalization and citizenship eligibility. The notion of racial fairness in immigration policy (exemplified by the elimination of national quotas in the Immigration and Nationality Act of 1965, formally ending exclusion from Asia) had reached its demise, as the anti-immigrant advocates prominent in the 1990s rearticulated the "unfairness to Americans" of allowing immigrants room in this country even if they are not economically self-sufficient. Nira Yuval-Davis argues that one of the most important factors shaping national-level issues over citizenship involves the relationships between the two countries involved and their relative positions of power in the international social order. In this situation, Asia (although a heterogeneous group of independent nations) and Mexico were seen as dependent third world nations sending their countries' poorest to claim American jobs and American resources. But, in fact, throughout the welfare and immigration debates, the history of refugee politics has usually been ignored, along with the global economic policies shaping economic and political relations that have made the United States the imperial center driving migration to fill needed areas of labor. To understand the significance of citizenship politics for Asian immigrants facing welfare and immigration reform in 1996, it is important to contextualize PRWORA's broader political implications within the long trajectory of citizenship exclusion that has shaped Asian American politics.

ASIAN IMMIGRANTS AND THE POLITICS OF CITIZENSHIP

Legacy of Aliens Ineligible for Citizenship

The politics of exclusion based on immigration and citizenship rights has clearly shaped Asian immigration politics in the United States. This history is well documented and has been laid out in much more elaborate and in-depth analysis than I present here. Rather, I revisit the course of naturalization and citizenship for Asian immigrants to draw out the continuities through the 1996 welfare and immigration policy reforms. More specifically, I examine here the politics of belonging, and how the state uses its power to define the specific criteria allowing some immigrants in and excluding others. I note how, with increasing global economic expansion and the displacement and migration of women, the convergence of U.S. welfare and immigration policy sought to tackle the perceived threat of poor foreign women dependent on the nation's welfare system.

Asian immigrants have historically faced numerous struggles surrounding naturalization rights and equal protection under the law, and their U.S.-born offspring have encountered only questionable rights and protections from the state in spite of their citizenship status. As the United States was securing and protecting its white Anglo-European identity (nearly one hundred years prior to the anti-immigrant movement that characterized the 1990s), Asian immigrants were central figures in the government's establishment of control over the nation's racial configuration.[5] As is widely known and well documented, the Naturalization Act of 1790 stipulated that naturalization of alien residents required that they maintain a certain period of residency and that such a resident be "a free white person." Although this law was first intended to exclude African slaves, American-born African Americans, and Native Americans, it would prove the most readily available shaper of anti-Asian immigration laws, and of whatever protections or entitlements, Asian immigrants might be accorded or denied.

The definition of *white* citizenship became more complicated with the Civil Rights Act of 1870; whereas men of African descent were made eligible for citizenship, the racial bar persisted for Asians. Through numerous lawsuits and challenges to the existing naturalization laws, the courts consistently isolated Asians as the one racial group ineligible for naturalized citizenship.[6] Although full citizenship, with all its rights and protections, was continually denied to residents of African descent despite eligibility for formal citizenship status, Asian immigrants bore a separate distinction as "inassimilable foreigners," seen as "heathens" by nativists. This distinction, however, contradicted capitalist desires for an ongoing exploitable labor pool; in what represents a common narrative, Representative William Higby of California stated, in response to a proposed amendment concerning Chinese immigrants in California: "The Chinese are nothing but a pagan race. They are an enigma to me, although I have lived among them for fifteen years. You cannot make good citizens of them; they do not learn the language of the country; and you can communicate with them only with the greatest difficulty, as their language is the most difficult of all those spoken."[7] Making the case for why Chinese should be denied naturalization even though Africans were granted naturalization rights, Higby stated that he opposed naturalization for the Chinese because "they are foreigners and the Negro is a native."[8] This *foreigner* racialization pervaded nearly all immigration and naturalization laws pertaining to Asian immigrants, who were positioned in the perpetual category "aliens ineligible for citizenship." This status impeded Asian immigrants,' and their citizen children's, abilities to own property, testify in court, or attend public schools; it eventually led to the complete exclusion of immigrants from Asia, through the Immigration Act of 1924, which decreed the permanent exclusion of all aliens ineligible for citizenship.

At the core of anti-Asian sentiment was the issue of racial assimilability. The racial requirement for naturalization presumed a status of innate inferiority that contradicted the more democratic premises of citizenship for immigrants in general. Assimilative practices emphasized Americanizing immigrants through teaching the English language, the work ethic, the Constitution, and other American democratic values.[9] Europeans could become Americans through such educational practices—but Asians could never achieve Americanness because their racial identity kept them outside the boundaries of the nation.[10] Asians in industrial America were seen as strangely foreign, exotic, and the antithesis of what it meant to be American.

The foregrounding of a foreigner racialization of Asians as inassimilable and un-American took on particular gendered constructions in relation to Asian women. The earliest U.S. presence of Asian women stirred racial and gendered nativist hysteria in a way that sexualized Asian immigrant women as immoral, "lewd," and a threat to the moral fabric of the expanding West Coast. Aimed to deter an inflow of Chinese women immigrants, the Page Act, enacted in 1875, was the first federal regulation of immigration. Although white prostitution was equally if not more prevalent than Asian, at least eight laws, including the Page Law, were passed between 1866 and 1905 to restrict the importation of Chinese women for prostitution or to suppress the Chinese brothel business. Apparently, Chinese women in this industry were perceived as constituting a more damning influence on white men than were white female prostitutes.[11]

Rigorous enforcement of the Page Act resulted in a drastic restriction in Chinese women's admission into the United States. By making the assumption that most Chinese women were entering as prostitutes, this law denied entry to nearly all these women, greatly intensifying the gender ratio imbalance and hindering the establishment of communities of Chinese families. Closely following the Page Act, in 1882 the Chinese Exclusion Act prohibited the entry of all Chinese laborers, as well as laborers' spouses. Congress's rationale for the Chinese Exclusion Act specifically stated that "in the opinion of the Government of the United States the coming of Chinese laborers to this country endangers the good order of certain localities within the territory thereof."[12] The Chinese Exclusion Act would begin the large-scale dismantling of a short-lived open immigration policy with Asia, at a time when European immigration was encouraged.

Of course, women's citizenship in general was unevenly developed, in comparison to white men's full citizenship status. However, not only were Asian immigrant women shorn of the right to naturalize, but even their presence heightened nativist concerns—by virtue of their capacity to bear citizen children. The Fourteenth Amendment, enacted in 1868, guaranteed that anyone born in the United States would be an American citizen, though this guarantee was not fully established for American-born Asians until 1898, thirty years later. Wong Kim Ark, born in San Francisco, was detained and prevented from entry into the United States after a trip to China, when the Immigration Department claimed that he was not an American citizen. Ark's case went to the U.S. Supreme Court in *United States v. Wong Kim Ark,* and the court determined that a person born to parents ineligible for citizenship in the United States was still a citizen. With the recognition that Asians born in the *United States* would be American citizens, the movement to exclude women from Asia heightened. Visas for women were curtailed through specific acts and agreements with source countries to send, instead, sojourning men who would return after laboring in the United States.

Concerns over the settlement of Asian communities and families in the United States escalated in 1906, over the issue of Japanese children in the public schools in San Francisco. Charging this group with crowding out and holding back "American" children, the San Francisco school board proposed a resolution to relieve congestion, "but also for the higher end that our children should not be placed in any position where their youthful impressions may be affected by associations with pupils of the Mongolian race."[13] Following a ruling that established the legal right to segregate white from Mongolian school children, "based on a school law which authorized school boards to establish separate schools for Indian, Chinese, and Mongolian children, at their own discretion," the board ordered all Japanese children to attend the Chinese School in Chinatown.[14]

The drive for total exclusion of Japanese immigrants, a drive based in issues of labor competition and agricultural gains by Japanese families, found popular consent among those concerned over white American children's educational resources and "protection." Japanese school children, immigrant or American-born, were seen in California as a threat to white privileges and as spearheading an Oriental invasion.

Japan's angry response set the San Francisco school board's actions in direct conflict with the federal government. As a compromise avoiding politically risky immigration legislation, the Gentlemen's Agreement of 1907, between the United States and Japan, resolved that the Japanese government would refrain from issuing travel documents to laborers destined for the United States. In exchange for this severe but voluntary limitation, Japanese wives and children could be reunited with their husbands and fathers in the

United States, and the San Francisco school board would be pressured into rescinding its segregation order.[15] Yet, although the focus of the San Francisco actions centered on Japanese school children and the increasing presence of Japanese families, this legislative agreement addressed only other anti-Japanese arguments, those against "unfair" labor competition from Japanese migrants. Thus, the Gentlemen's Agreement did not accomplish the intended goal of limiting the entrance of Japanese women and preventing more Japanese family formations in the United States.

With the successful exclusion of all South Asians by the 1917 Immigration Act, which established the Asiatic Barred Zone, the only group from Asia still allowed to immigrate[16] was Japanese women reuniting with spouses. Domestic cries for more stringent policy against Japanese immigrants remained, primarily because of this continued immigration of Japanese wives and children. With the continued and growing community of Japanese families, the fear of a permanent presence elevated white nativist concerns over the nation's "racial purity." The practice of *picture brides* became a centerpiece for nativist morality about women and for cultural constructions of property and family. Ethnocentric unfamiliarity with the so-called foreign practice of arranged marriages through photographs led to public outrage over the "indecency" of such practices and a call to ban them within the United States. Thus, the Immigration Act of 1924 successfully banned all Asian wives of Asian immigrants in America from joining their spouses. To bypass problems with imperial Japan, the U.S. government adopted language in this Act barring all "aliens ineligible for citizenship," halting immigration from Asia altogether.

The formal categorization *aliens ineligible for citizenship* persisted until a series of repeal acts emerged after World War II, in the face of greater international scrutiny over the apparent hypocrisy of the nation's racially discriminatory immigration policies. The first removal of the category was granted to Chinese immigrants through the Magnuson Act, which also repealed the Chinese Exclusion Act, in light of increasing ties with China as an allied force against Japan during World War II. Noting Japan's plans for Pan-Asian unity, Neil Gotanda cites the importance of Japanese propaganda emphasizing anti-Asian laws and policies of the United States, especially the exclusionary acts. According to Gotanda, "in the battle for moral superiority among allies, the American position was further undermined by its racially discriminatory domestic policies."[17]

In the international context of World War II, the United States posited freedom, equality, and democratic values in response both to Nazi Gemany's appeals for Aryan supremacy and to Japanese imperialism. Thus, as an exhibit of a national shift toward more open and fair immigration policy for Asian nations, the Magnuson Act was passed in 1943. Presented as necessary for war efforts, the Magnuson Act repealed existing Chinese exclusion acts, established a token quota that made very little difference in the Chinese immigrant community, and allowed Chinese to become naturalized citizens. Soon to follow in this moment of public scrutiny of democratic principles in U.S. immigration policy was the Act of July 2, 1946, allowing Asian Indians and Filipinos to become naturalized citizens, and establishing a small quota for Asian Indian immigration. On July 4, 1946, immigration quotas for the newly independent Filipinos were enacted. Still, it was not until 1952 that the McCarran-Walter Act nullified the portion of the 1790 Naturalization Act stating that only whites could be naturalized as citizens, and thus allowed all Asian immigrants the right to naturalize.

Immigration and Nationality Act of 1965

Driven by the international politics surrounding the United States' continued regressive race-based exclusionary immigration policies, the Immigration and Nationality Act of 1965 was intended to end the long history of discrimination aimed particularly at Asian countries. The elimination of the national origins quota meant to remove all remaining, offensive racial provisions. Using a preference system based on seven selective categories including family reunification, employment needs and opportunities, and other criteria,[18] this new immigration act nullified birthplace and ancestry as the primary selection mechanism. As a result, persons from Asian countries could emigrate to reunite with family members or seek new opportunities, especially in occupations where labor was in short supply.

Policymakers, nativist organizations, and other supporters of the new law did not foresee the drastic effect of this final removal of directly discriminatory provisions[19] upon immigration flows from Asia. Because of prior Asian exclusion, Asians in America numbered approximately 1.4 million, constituting less than 1 percent of the nation's population.[20] A percentage ceiling was given each preference, and the four family reunification preferences in the new bill added up to 74 percent of quota immigrants. It was perceived that the minuscule population of Asian American citizens and legal resident aliens at the time could make wide use of the family reunification provisions of the new law, but also that there were few Asian Americans available to sponsor relatives, as compared to citizens and legal residents with European backgrounds.[21]

However, as stated in chapter 2, regardless of what the Act's proponents predicted, the demographic shifts in the Asian Pacific American population were dramatic. There were multiple reasons for the unexpectedness of this surge. Policymakers did not understand how the political, economic, and social dynamics in Asian countries would influence immigration. They knew little about Asian American communities, Asian countries, and the relationships between the two; and their analyses by and large were cursory and highly inaccurate.[22] The family reunification provisions would be highly utilized as families reunited, and, as these new immigrants naturalized, sponsorship and thus naturalization would continue to elevate at an increasing rate. From 1960 to 1990, the 1965 Immigration Act helped set off a chain migration that led to an increase from one million persons to over seven million persons in the Asian Pacific American population.[23] While the number of U.S.-born Asian American citizens doubled from 1970 to 1990, the Asian immigrant population grew more than eight-fold.[24] In addition, the employment-based preference categories led to the entry of many immigrant professionals and technicians, particularly in the sciences and health-care fields, categories with a large proportion of women. From 1961 to 1970, 12.88 percent of immigrants came from Asia, but from 1971 to 1980 the percentage from Asia increased to 35.35 percent of all immigrants. These figures varied moderately in ensuing decades, rising in 1981–1990 to 38.39 percent; by 1991–1994, 30.50 percent of all immigrants to the United States came from Asia.[25] By 1980, 70 percent of the total Asian American adult population consisted of immigrants, and by 1990 this proportion had increased to 79 percent.[26]

With the massive shift in immigration flows from Asia, a shift in naturalization would be likely to follow. However, given the legacy of ineligibility for naturalization that existed until 1952, the naturalization process among Asian immigrants lagged. According to Ong and Nakanishi, in 1970 the Asian rates were consistently lower for all cohorts, with the largest difference among long-term residents.[27] The long-term legal permanent residents, probably the most ready to meet the citizenship requirements, were alienated from political belonging and participation, a stance that delayed their decisions to naturalize once the option became available. By 1980, naturalization rates for Asian immigrants had significantly improved, and a steady level of about 40 percent of the 18-and-older Asian immigrant population were naturalized through the 1990s. Given that immigrants were a significant proportion of the Asian American population, naturalization directly and powerfully determined the size of the population eligible to vote, and directly shaped broader political concerns and interests.

Naturalization since 1965

Although naturalization was seen as a right granting the ability to vote—in other words, access to political participation—it was never established as a requirement for immigration or residency purposes. In 1994, 55 percent of adult Asians were not citizens.[28] It was the welfare and immigration reform in 1996 that for the first time established citizenship as a criterion of eligibility for public benefits; until the passage of PRWORA, legal permanent residents were recognized as people who participated and contributed to the economic, social, and cultural fabric of the country; and they were granted the same (if few) rights as U.S. citizens to welfare assistance. In general, welfare and immigration reform catalyzed a major increase in naturalization among all immigrants; from the mid-1990s to the year 2002, the number of naturalized citizens rose for the first time in decades—from 6.5 to 11 million.[29] From 1995 to 1996 alone, the number of naturalizations went from 488,088 to 1,044,689.[30] Of all immigrants naturalizing in 2002, 2003, and 2004, 40 percent annually were from Asia. By 2004, the percentage of naturalized Asian immigrants increased to 48 percent of all Asian immigrants; the overall immigrant average remained at 37 percent.[31] Thus, even with continuing levels of immigration levels from Asia, naturalization rates among Asian immigrants steadily increased after the mid-1990s.

Whether or not recently naturalized immigrants have used their acquired citizenship status to retain public benefits is still to be determined. Earliest reports from the Urban Institute convey that there is not yet clear data to conclude that immigrants have sought more public assistance since becoming naturalized. However, should they become disabled or elderly, or should their incomes fall below the poverty level, they will not confront the same barriers to SSI or food stamps that they would have without citizenship status. Of significance here is the demarcation of citizenship status that sent so many immigrants to the naturalization process who might have opted away from it in the past. For some, this decision was based on witnessing the erosion of their rights as noncitizens. Education level, income level, and age played critical factors in the ease of obtaining citizenship, and so, for those who were previous welfare recipients, the quest for citizenship was particularly stressful and intense. The process of acquiring citizenship proved challenging on multiple levels. Community organizers struggled to assist elderly, disabled, and less-educated immigrants to interface with state technologies. Hard cases emerged unexpectedly from the Asian immigrant community, as Asian immigrant women struggled to become citizens and have some assurance of survival.

CITIZENSHIP DRIVES AND INFORMATION FORUMS

Acquiring Citizenship

Aside from the historical trajectory of race-based exclusions from naturalization, certain set requirements have long defined the naturalization process for eligible immigrants. To be eligible to apply for naturalization, an immigrant must be at least eighteen years of age, have been lawfully admitted to the United States for permanent residency, and have resided in the country continuously for at least five years (three years for sponsored spouses of citizens). Additional requirements include the ability to speak, read, and write the English language; knowledge of the U.S. government and U.S. history; demonstration of a good moral character; a declaration of attachment to the principles of the U.S. Constitution; and a favorable disposition toward the United States.[32]

The application process involves first submitting the application form N400, Application for Naturalization. At the time of my field research from 1996 to 1998, the standard N-400 was a four-page form in 8-point font, with twelve parts each consisting of many questions.[33] The application filing fee has risen since, from $95 to $320. Completing the N-400 successfully required an understanding of the documentation process to gain legal permanent residency, and a precise memory of all absences from the United States (including how long away), regardless of how many times one had left and for what reasons. Questions covered full details of residences and employment during the past five years, a marital history and information about any spouse or spouses, and detailed information about each child. Additionally, good moral character had to be established through fifteen questions, some containing as many as five subquestions, ranging from "Have you ever been affiliated with or a member of the Communist Party?" to "Have you ever been a prostitute or procured anyone for prostitution?"

Filling out the forms, for a person familiar with U.S. institutions, language, and writing literacy, requires approximately an hour. However, for an immigrant unfamiliar with the spoken or written language, or with the question format, the N400 proved a major initial hurdle in applying for naturalization. In addition to the completed N400, necessary accompanying documents included photocopies of the front and back of the applicant's Alien Registration Card ("Green Card"), two photographs meeting INS standards, and fingerprints taken by a certified INS fingerprint official. To expedite the process of filling out the N400 and obtaining all other necessary information, intake specialists (often trained volunteers) were alerted to possible "red flag" situations where the applicant might need to consult with an immigration lawyer. In situations where the applicant might have a criminal record or a history including tax evasion, draft evasion, failure to pay child support, absence from the United States for more than six months, or fraud committed either to obtain legal residency (for self or others) or to collect public benefits, for instance, naturalization could be in jeopardy, necessitating consultation with an expert before filing with the INS.

Once an applicant's set of forms was filed and reviewed by the INS, an interview would be scheduled (if the N-400 was thus far approved). In addition to explaining any questionable items on the N-400, the interviewee had to undergo an English literacy test and U.S. civics/history exam. The applicant had to be able to read, write, and speak in English during the interview. In addition to speaking in English, the applicant was required to read some basic text in English and to write a dictated sentence. The applicant was given three chances to write the sentence correctly; the applicant's speaking abilities were being judged by the interviewer through the course of the interview. The history/civics exam consisted of ten questions, taken from a list of one hundred questions (thus, the applicant needed to learn all one hundred questions). To pass the test, the immigrant had to answer seven out of ten questions correctly.

Given the daunting nature of the application process, numerous organizations across the nation held large-scale citizenship drives. As noted in previous chapters, within months of the passing of PRWORA, immigrants began receiving notices stating that, to continue receiving their SSI assistance checks, they would have to prove citizenship status or qualify for one of the exemptions as legal permanent residents. In panic, the immigrants overloaded social service providers and community organization with phone calls and appointments; existing citizenship programs needed somehow to address this sudden surge of applicants within an intensified period. In the San Francisco Bay Area of California, immigrant rights organizations worked in coalition with service centers and legal advocacy groups to create information forums and drives assisting immigrants with the N-400 and related requirements. To gain more insight into how these organizations were providing naturalization services and support, I participated in citizenship drives as an intake volunteer. I also taught a citizenship course to immigrants who had filed the N-400 and were waiting for the INS interview that would include their English, U.S. history, and U.S. government tests. I attended regularly scheduled community information forums, participated in citizenship trainings, and observed legal workshops by organizations dealing with difficult cases. This work allowed me to see and experience the process of obtaining citizenship. Applying for and obtaining naturalization proved much more difficult for Asian immigrant and refugee women than legislators had predicted.

Community Organizations Fostering Naturalization

The citizenship drives were established to expedite the large numbers of immigrants needing to naturalize, and also to provide a more comfortable, less intimidating, and more language-accessible environment for the daunting experience. The citizenship drives held by the San Jose Center for Employment Training Immigration and Citizenship Project were held in a large room with multiple stations for immigrants to file through. They came first to the intake table, a long table with volunteers sitting on one side facing the open room. Approximately ten to fifteen volunteers awaited the immigrants, who had taken a number and were waiting in the rows of seats facing the table (these seats were usually full, as people entered throughout the day). The volunteers' tasks at the intake table were to fill out, as much as possible, the N-400 with the applicant, check for any red-flag problems, and answer any immediate questions. The next station was for anyone flagged with an issue or problem that might raise difficulties in his/her naturalization or lead to its denial. The third station was a quality-control check consisting of more experienced and credentialed immigrant legal advocates. In the case of the citizenship drives in San Jose, this station was usually filled with legal advisors from the Asian Law Alliance, a community-based legal organization modeled after the Asian Law Caucus of San Francisco. Once the N-400 forms were completed, the applicants moved on to have their pictures taken and green card photocopied, and to be fingerprinted right there by an INS-certified fingerprinter. (This latter service, however, was disallowed, and could only be conducted at an INS office.) With all necessary documents compiled, the N-400 packet was ready to be sent on to the INS for processing. Given the crowds and waiting time between stations, the entire process usually took several hours.

Smaller-scale citizenship drives and workshops provided the same level of service. These were usually housed within the organizations' own buildings, and immigrants often came to packed rooms with few staff and volunteers, but were nevertheless able to get their N-400 forms completed, along with other necessary documentation. In a visit to the Immigration Program of Catholic Charities in San Jose, I observed a typical workshop and assistance drive for naturalization applicants. Immigration lawyers, translators, and volunteer assistants were ready to help some forty applicants at a time, in a large, overcrowded classroom filled with approximately one hundred immigrants, who might come from anywhere in the world. On this day, the majority of applicants were of Asian and Latina/o descent.

> The room was so crowded that some people were sitting and standing out in the hall area trying to hear the instructions inside. The gentleman speaking to the class in the front of the room spoke slowly, and frequently wrote important terms on the board. The Asian applicants carefully and attentively watched him speak, but their expressions revealed confusion, stress, and anxiety as the instructions for the N400s became more complicated and confusing. Walking through the process step by step, the Latino immigration lawyer wrote out and, in the most simplistic form possible, tried to explain all the necessary documents people needed to fill out the naturalization form. "How many times you've left the country, for how long, and why you left," he repeated slowly, emphasizing the need to be honest and to remember all possible occasions because the INS would try to verify this information. At one point when he was explaining possible "red-flag" problems (problems that could prevent one from naturalization), such as failure to file taxes, any felonies, drug convictions, DUI's (driving under the influence), or any form of fraud claiming to be a citizen to receive benefits, some people in the room began to shift, and a few people raised their hands to ask questions about their own circumstances (in their own languages, with interpreters).
>
> In the back of the room was a Southeast Asian middle-aged couple with the woman's mother, who sat slumped in her wheelchair with head tilted over the armrest, appearing unaware of her surroundings. When I asked the volunteer coordinator, who was showing me around the Immigration Project offices and facilities, about the elderly woman in the wheelchair, she very solemnly stated that this was an example of their most difficult situations. "At this point

we are just advising everyone to apply for citizenship. This woman will no doubt qualify for a disability waiver, but she will most definitely be unable to take the oath. We aren't sure what's going to happen yet, that's why we just have to keep pressuring Congress to make more exceptions."[34] The volunteer explained that they frequently see elderly clients who are in need of one-on-one tutoring in the civics and English requirements. Part of her job was re-cruiting and coordinating volunteers from the community to provide more one-on-one tutoring for very small groups and individuals who could get totally lost in the larger English/civics classes.[35]

While providing citizenship assistance at the Asian Women's Resource Center, I had the opportunity to observe the weekly English/civics classes offered in the room next to my office. The regulars consisted of five elderly women, three middle-aged women, and two elderly men. The instructor was a middle-aged woman, herself a Chinese immigrant who had recently natu-ralized. From my office, I could hear the instructor, in a very loud tone, read out questions in English in hopes of a response back from her students. "DO YOU HAVE A PASSPORT?" the teacher exclaimed over and over until some-one very quietly replied, "Do you have a passport." "YES, I HAVE MY PASS-PORT!" "Yes I have my passport."

When I looked inside the classroom, I saw one gentleman, appearing to be in his seventies, at one side, sleeping with his head leaning up against the wall. The four women, all in their late sixties or seventies, were scattered in the back with their books in front of them, trying to read the English print. The middle-aged women in their early fifties, closer to the front, were the only students responding to the instructor. In contrast to the instructor with her booming voice, the class remained intently and hesitantly quiet. Appar-ently hoping that eventually her students would gain a better feel for the language, she continually repeated questions, working on one citizenship question at a time.

As elderly and disabled immigrant women began to fill up citizenship and English classes, the absurdity and cruelty of welfare reform's making the naturalization process the only means to these women's survival became evi-dent. One of the first major stories in the Bay Area was *SF Weekly*'s cover story in February 1997, six months after the passing of PRWORA and about seven months before SSI cut-offs were to begin. The full-cover photograph, a facial close-up of an elderly Asian immigrant woman in her late seventies or early eighties, conveys her years of struggle and hard living. Her facial expression conveys a proud sternness, yet her sparse gray hair, worn wrinkled skin, and tired eyes reveal the vulnerability of her position and the impossibility of trying to acquire citizenship before losing her benefits. Next to the image are the bold title words, "The Welfare Crackdown Arrives," announcing the cover story by Tara Shioya, "Immigrants Desperately Seeking Citizenship." This cover image represented San Francisco's oldest and poorest who were running out of time.

The image of the grandmotherly woman in this feature article highlighted the cruelty of the law, the nation's unrealistic expectations for citizenship, and the stress these women were forced to endure as a result of inhumane social policy and its legislative enforcers. The article in this edition, "Immigrants Desperately Seeking Citizenship," exposed the impossibility for most elderly Asian immigrant women of successfully learning either the necessary questions for the civics exam or enough English to prove English literacy. The article focused on the seventeen thousand elderly, disabled, and blind legal immigrants, of whom 60 percent were Asian, who depended on federal aid. Visiting a civics and English class at the North of Market Senior Services in the Tenderloin District of San Francisco, Shioya revealed the grave situations women faced in trying to learn and comprehend the civics fundamentals the INS required for citizenship:

> At 9:30 on this gray Thursday morning in January, Tuan Van Dang is setting out to accomplish what some have called an impossible task. He is trying to teach women old enough to be his grandmothers—women who can't read, write, or speak English—the civics fundamentals the INS requires for citizenship. Van Dang's deadline is tight—and, like the law that spawned it, unforgiving.[36]

The invocation of "grandmother" provides a humanist's universal connection; nearly all people can identify with family concerns over aging grandparents or parents. These are not just immigrants being denied life-sustaining benefits, they are *grandmothers, grandfathers, mothers, fathers*. Grandmothers as ethical figures conjure a special person to be honored and cared for, as the bearers and caretakers of the larger family imaginary. The idea that Congress can impose such cruel suffering on grandmothers evokes a sharpened level of moral degradation and worsened violation of human rights.

According to Janet Griffiths, the director of the citizenship project at the North of Market Senior Center, "Only a fortunate few of the center's male clients—and almost none of the women—are literate in their native Vietnamese, Chinese, Khmer, or Lao."[37] Griffiths explained that many of her

FIGURE 3. This photograph appeared on the front cover of *San Francisco Weekly*, February 12–18, 1997.

Photograph by Pamela Gentile; reproduced with permission of the photographer.

students had taken years of English as a Second Language (ESL) classes with little success. In her interview with Shioya, Griffiths argued that the new citizenship requirement was unrealistic: "How can you expect them to pass an interview when they don't have the language skills to be able to remember or understand what someone is asking? They try, but they just can't remember."[38]

Shioya's *SF Weekly* article quotes one woman faced with an overwhelmingly stressful situation beyond her managing skills:

> Kiev Lim, a 79-year-old former refugee from Cambodia, can tell you the basic details of her life in simple English. She lives alone in an Ellis Street apartment with no kitchen, where the rent is $375 a month. She's been here seven years. She is sharp-eyed and lucid. Yet Lim has failed the citizenship test five times.
>
> "I was scared. I got nervous and I forgot everything," Lim says with the help of a translator. "Even before the examiner asked me anything, I was already shaking." . . . "I'm very worried," she says. "Learning English is so difficult." . . . Struggle is nothing new to Lim. To escape the Khmer Rouge, she walked from her village in Cambodia to Thailand one night, eight hours over dozens of miles without stopping. Like many of the city's elderly immigrants, Lim has known war and dire poverty. She wonders what will happen to her next.[39]

The *SF Weekly* article reflected the level of trauma imposed by U.S. military operations in Southeast Asia, and the second trauma imposed by the U.S. legislation denying the benefits once promised to those who sought refuge from the results of those actions. In detail, Shioya's article rearticulated the historical circumstances of Southeast Asian refugees, a vulnerable group that had endured the lasting traumas of war, of tyranny, of refugee camps. The stress of having to prepare for an interview with an American INS agent, and of needing to respond to any one of a hundred possible questions, created a crisis situation with few avenues for coping: reason for some to choose suicide. The story of Kiev Lim reveals the intense anxiety spawned by a harsh welfare policy that purposely chose to exclude her because of her citizenship status. The narrative of trauma that began with war was cojoined with another obstacle to survival—American social policy.

As discussed in the previous chapter, the level and form of stress exerted on an already frail and vulnerable community would have deep and lasting impact, impact not necessarily reversible with a mere change in policy. Considering the struggles that Chia Yang and Ye Vang faced as they attempted to acquire citizenship, how do we make sense of the broader naturalization process for immigrants with disabilities, those who are elderly, those who are cognitively impaired? These subjects, primarily women, were the welfare reform targets with the least ability to gain citizenship. The demarcation of citizenship for receiving benefits put these women in intractable binds with broader detrimental implications. Even though the cuts to SSI were rescinded, thousands of women like this realized that, as noncitizens, they could find their fates changed at any moment. Naturalization remained the only guarantee that their legal citizenship status would not be the basis for the loss of economic support.

From Aliens Ineligible for Citizenship to a State of Forced Citizenship

Although the naturalization process might not, given the many volunteers and staff available for assistance, appear that taxing, many cases revealed the difficulties, pressures, and anxieties that pursued immigrants trying to naturalize. The situation for elderly Asian immigrant and refugee women illustrates the cost that citizenship imposed on people worried about survival yet not fully capable of naturalizing. Immediate advocacy efforts pressed for more generous disability and age waivers. The INS allowed three possible exceptions (still in effect), based on age and length of permanent residency, to the English requirement. Two exceptions, known as the 55/15 and the 50/20, allow a legal permanent resident applying for naturalization to qualify for an English Language waiver if the applicant is at least fifty-five years old and has been a legal permanent resident (LPR) for fifteen years or more, or if the applicant is at least fifty years old and has been an LPR for twenty years or more. In these cases, applicants can have a translator present to answer all questions in their native language. Another exception, the 65/20 history and government rule, allowed LPR applicants at least sixty-five years of age and living in the United states for at least twenty years since obtaining legal permanent resident status, to be tested from a standard list of twenty-five questions, from which they had to answer six correctly to pass.

Applicants with a more serious disability might file for a disability waiver, N-648, along with their N-400 certifying possession of a serious medical disability that prevents their learning English and the U.S. civics/history requirements. Although disability waivers existed prior to 1994, it was not until 1996 that the INS more formally activated the official disability waiver guidelines. Until then, the disability waiver was primarily used in cases in which a person was legally blind or clinically deaf, and INS officers used their own discretion with disability waivers of other sorts. In 1994, Congress passed the Immigration and Nationality Technical Corrections Act, which specifically provided that persons with developmental disabilities or mental and/or physical impairments might also be eligible for a medical waiver.[40] Until advocates made more concerted efforts for the use of medical waivers, the Technical Amendment was little used. Until 1997, though, by law, persons with a disability preventing them from learning sufficient English and U.S. history for naturalization should have been able to receive a waiver of those requirements, but the process was fraught with delay and inconsistency. In 1996, the Asian Law Caucus served as co-counsel in a class action against the INS, *Chow v. Meissner,* which resulted in the issuance and dispersal of formal regulations by the INS for disability waivers. Since this issuance of formal regulations in 1997, the Asian Law Caucus has conducted trainings for doctors, nurses, lawyers, and other immigration advocates working with disabled naturalization applicants, and has directly represented more than two hundred immigrants with mental, physical, or developmental disabilities in successfully applying for disability waivers and becoming naturalized U.S. citizens.

Within the Asian immigrant and refugee constituency, the issue of disability and age remained a primary concern. Since, in San Francisco, 72 percent of the immigrants to be cut off SSI were elderly and disabled women, the naturalization efforts there had to deal with high levels of cognitive impairment and physical disability. The narrative by the Asian Law Caucus legal assistant that begins this chapter reflects the dilemma of those trying to naturalize with a disability; later in our interview, she explained that she was primarily assisting elderly and disabled Asian immigrant women. For her, the situation of the mentally disabled was the most problematic.

> It's a state of forced citizenship, and the mentally disabled will be totally unable to obtain citizenship. They are going to be completely left without support, except for smaller GA (General Assistance) payments provided by the county. Most of these women are taken care of by families who need the income or by facilities that are paid through their SSI benefits. In general, more women receive SSI than men, so more women are going to be impacted.[41]

Throughout the campaign to make visible the immigrants soon to be cut off from SSI benefits, the exposure of elderly and disabled immigrant and refugee women became central to clarifying the complexities involved in obtaining citizenship. In a phone interview in San Francisco with Deeana Jang, member of the board of directors of the Asian Women's Shelter (and project coordinator of the Asian-Pacific Islander American Health Forum),[42] she emphasized that "many women can not qualify for exceptions because they can not document forty quarters of work outside the home or do not have a living spouse who is on active military duty or a veteran."[43] With longer life expectancies, and fewer exception categories available to women, Asian immigrant women were going to need to naturalize at a greater rate than were immigrant men, who were more likely to document forty quarters of work.

In a discussion with the coordinator of the Health Education Projects of the Southeast Asian Community Center in San Francisco,[44] I learned that in February 1997, when people were just beginning to receive their SSI cut-off letters from the Department of Social Services, the level of panic was astounding. Throughout our discussion, the coordinator, a Ms. Loretta Kruger, had to fight back tears while describing the situation of people coming into the office with official government letters telling them that they would no longer receive benefits if they could not prove citizenship. The majority of those who called would most likely be unable to meet the qualifications.

> We've already started to see the impact of the SSI benefits [being cut] because the letters started going out and [there are] a lot of people who are calling up. We're listed as a community agency to contact when Social Services sends out the letters; they also send a cover sheet telling people that if they have questions they can contact different community agencies that speak languages other than English, and we're one of the ones listed for Southeast Asian languages, and Chinese too—Cantonese.
>
> So we've been getting a lot of phone calls from people that are most likely going to have a very difficult time becoming naturalized citizens, which is people's only recourse, and to become naturalized for the SSI population is going to be very difficult. I read the commission on aging estimates that two-thirds of the SSI population will be unable to become naturalized.
>
> Because the standards for disability that SSI uses are a different standard than immigration uses to waive . . . only the civics and literacy requirement, you can get that waived, you can get a disability waiver for that, but even though you're on SSI for disability it doesn't automatically qualify you for the disability waiver, and the disability waiver requirements of immigration are very strict.

Throughout our discussion, Kruger stressed the devastating impact that welfare reform was going to have on entire family units.

> It is scary, and when you have families who are living in extended families, like a lot of Asian families do, it may be a family of eight people and maybe only

> one of them is receiving SSI but that's crucial—I mean, that pays the rent, the
> SSI check buys the food and pays the rent. So the whole rippling effect is
> going to be very severe. And then if you put the loss of food stamp benefits on
> top of that . . .

Her emphasis on families and the overall impact on the Southeast Asian
community of the loss of SSI benefits often going toward a much-needed
household income, belies the assessment given by Norm Matloff that naturalized children were abusing the welfare system by inappropriately putting
their elderly parents on public assistance.

In contrast with Matloff's claim of relative ease in obtaining citizenship,
a claim used to justify denial of SSI to immigrants unless they naturalized,
Kruger provided a scenario faced by a family because their cognitively impaired mother, who lived in a nursing facility and required 24-hour care would
have to move home. This would occur since, Kruger noted, the mother's
state of cognitive impairment rendered her incapable of naturalizing, and
hence she would lose her SSI assistance.

> There's a lot of people that just can't be naturalized under the current natural-
> ization regulations. The older people are gonna have a very hard time, espe-
> cially the ones that are not literate in their own language, or have different
> alphabets than we do. . . . Somebody came in the other day with a letter I've
> never seen for their mother who is in a nursing home and is totally disabled
> from a series of strokes, and because she's not a citizen, she will not be natu-
> ralized because she can't take the oath. I mean she's really in a vegetative state,
> and you can't become naturalized if you can't take the oath. So there's like this
> catch-22, you have to be so disabled that you meet the [disability] criteria but
> you can't be so disabled that you can't meaningfully take the oath. She's losing
> her SSI benefits; they're cutting off her Medi-Cal. And this family, there's
> no way—it's a very poor family, they can't take her in, they live in a studio in
> the Tenderloin, they can't take her in . . . their . . . mother.[45]

An important discrepancy to emerge from the efforts to naturalize immigrants was the disparate education level between men and women immigrants
and refugees. Especially among rural immigrants who had migrated through
economic necessity, rejoined naturalized children within the past twenty years,
or had fled as refugees, women tended to have less education in their country
of origin than had men. Patriarchal systems tend to emphasize the education
of sons rather than of daughters when economic conditions require families
to make such a choice. Thus, many of the Asian immigrant and refugee
women in citizenship classes, forced to memorize one hundred questions

about the U.S. government and history in English, were not literate in their own language.

In an interview, Duron Le of the Asian Advocates of Marin County's Catholic Charities Organization[46] explained the difficulty for the majority of women aged sixty-five and older faced with studying for the civics and English literacy test for naturalization. According to Le, suddenly having to study for an exam is a shock for most of her clients. She explained that there was not only an age problem, but also a cultural assault: "You know, a lot of the Asian people believe that when they get older they cannot study—you know, not like here. Here they leave it open. So they lock that brain over there, and after fifty they think they are too old to learn new things, so it's different, so they just cannot remember, and they struggle with . . ."[47] I asked Le how many of the women she thought would pass the exam; thoughtfully she said "Maybe 50 percent."

Le also emphasized the cruelty of the time factor to immigrants trying to gain citizenship. The time to obtain citizenship would far exceed the time left to receive benefits, so, even though actively going through the process of citizenship, these immigrants would have no income or support while engaged in seeking and waiting for citizenship status.

Advocates soon found filing for disability status a dilemma in itself. An applicant needed to prove that her disability impeded her from being able to fulfill English and history/civics requirements, but she could not be too disabled to take the oath of allegiance. If the disability diagnosis was determined so extreme by the INS official that the applicant is unable to demonstrate an understanding of the oath of allegiance, her application could be denied. In response to a request to waive the oath of allegiance for applicants with disabilities, Acting U.S. Assistant Attorney General Dawn Johnson, in a memo dated February 5, 1997, ruled that the oath of allegiance was too integral to the naturalization process to be waived. Citing the Naturalization Act of 1790 and court precedents, Johnson stated:

> As "a promise of future conduct," the oath of allegiance has been, and remains, an "indispensable legal requirement" of naturalization. "The alien makes a contract with the government of the United States. In return for the benefits and high privileges bestowed upon the alien, he makes a solemn agreement expressed in the oath required of all who become citizens." "Citizenship is membership in a political society and implies a duty of allegiance on the part of the member and a duty of protection on the part of the society. These are reciprocal obligations, one being a compensation for the other."[48]

This ruling on the necessity of declaring allegiance remained unchanged by the Justice Department in spite of community outpouring on behalf of disabled immigrants. These immigrants and their advocates were in a bind that did not yield any viable solutions. The ruling stood until November 2, 2000, when Public Law 106–448 finally authorized the attorney general to waive the oath requirement for an individual with a developmental or physical disability or mental impairment making him or her unable to understand, or communicate an understanding of, the meaning of the oath.[49] This time frame did not benefit, however, the immigrants and refugees facing immediate cuts in the first years following welfare and immigration reform.

The situation confronting the majority of elderly and disabled Asian immigrant and refugee women as they attempted to acquire the necessary citizenship status that would allow them to retain their life-sustaining benefits points to a paradox: fewer than fifty years earlier, most would have been considered aliens ineligible for citizenship. Although SSI was eventually restored to those noncitizens residing in the United States on or before August 22, 1996, citizenship status nevertheless had taken on new meaning in regard to protection, equal rights, and equal access to resources.

Good Moral Character

Perhaps more than any other requirement for naturalization, the proof of good moral character reveals the state's idea of who makes a good citizen. According to the application's questions, good moral character means someone who has never been arrested or convicted of any crime, who has paid his or her taxes, who (if male and over eighteen) has registered with the Selective Service, who has no alcohol problem, who has never engaged in prostitution, and who has never been affiliated with the Communist Party or supported communism in any way. It was this section, known simply as "part 7," that caused the most anxiety for the applicants whom I assisted as an intake volunteer at citizenship drives.

The first question under part 7 on the N-400 was "Are you now, or have you ever been a member of, or in any way connected or associated with the Communist Party, or ever knowingly aided or supported the Communist Party directly, or indirectly through another organization, group or person, or ever advocated, taught, believed in, or knowingly supported or furthered the interests of communism?"[50] For applicants from Asia, the issue of Communist affiliation proved complex and difficult. For those who entered the country as refugees, the assumption was that they were fleeing Communist persecution for their anti-Communist political beliefs. Yet applicants I assisted often expressed concern, as their political affiliation did not always form an unambiguous, distinguishable set of beliefs. Although no applicants answered yes to this question, they would ask me what kind of background checks would occur regarding their political affiliations back home. I would explain that, unless some concrete action had been documented with the FBI (documentation that would turn up with the submission of their fingerprints), they would not have anything to worry about. And if an applicant was a member of the Communist Party (or engaged in activities supportive of communism) within the past ten years *involuntarily,* then an exception could be made. The applicant would have to show that the Communist Party was the acting governing force of the nation where he/she had lived, with affiliation necessary for basic needs such as work. This exception would prove instrumental primarily for applicants from Southeast Asia and China. In spite of such reassuring factors, the scrutiny over their past political affiliations caused the immigrants significant anxiety.

In one instance, I was assisting a husband and wife from Laos, with their twelve-year-old child. When we came to part 7, I asked the question regarding Communist affiliation, and their son translated, as he had all day. For the first time since we had started, his parents looked at him with dismay and concern. They reflexively asked him to repeat the question. They looked at me (I was looking back in concern over the same point), and I immediately said to their son, "If they did ever belong or participate in the Communist Party, was it by choice? If not by choice, they can answer 'no'." The son quickly translated my follow-up, and the parents both firmly said no.[51] This question, more than any of the fifteen moral-character questions, seemed to cause applicants hesitation. Once I asked it, they became a bit warier of me.

In another typical instance, I was assisting a middle-aged ethnic Chinese woman from Vietnam who had come to the United States in 1985. She spoke fairly broken English, but was fluent for the purposes of our exchange. When we came to the Communist Party question, she became silent. Up until that point, we had been moving along fairly smoothly, and she would actually embellish the response, or provide more details about her children than their birthdates and locations of birth. But once we got to this question, she puzzled over the need to know this information, and said, "What do you need to know this for?" I dreaded to tell her that the U.S. government thought anyone who supported communism could not be a good U.S. citizen, but I informed her that applicants who were members of the Communist Party or supported communism would be denied naturalization. I further explained that the government only really cared about the previous ten years (even though the question reads "ever"), and that if joining the Party was not by free choice, she could answer no. She eventually did so—and I moved on, not wanting her to expand on that response.[52]

Among the hundreds of immigrants I assisted at citizenship drives and workshops, the responses illustrated here to the Communist Party question were typical. I could not determine the reason for this hesitation in relation to the respondees' actual political affiliations or beliefs, but rather I could speculate that the question itself raised a high level of discomfort, fear, and mistrust. It could be due to the person's own experiences leading to flight or immigration, or concern over particular events he or she had participated in for any reason. Through the frequency of similar responses, the vulnerability felt by Asian immigrants and refugees was starkly illuminated as the worthiness of their American citizenship was judged.

The second most difficult question for naturalization applicants was whether or not they had ever engaged in prostitution. To discuss sex with a stranger in such a public venue proved incredibly difficult for elderly Asian women applicants. In one particular uncomfortable moment, I was assisting a fifty-nine-year-old woman from Cambodia, who was accompanied by her teenage son. I was dreading this question from the moment they sat down. When I came to question 12c, which follows a question asking whether one is a habitual drunkard, and a question about polygamy, the son stopped and looked at me with questioning eyes, as if to ask did he really have to ask her this? I looked at him apologetically, but said we had to have a response for each question. He translated the question to his mother, who was already looking at him suspiciously, and she quickly shook her head, looking down at the table.[53]

When we consider the myriad ways that women survive displacement, refuge, and the pattern of sexual assault in refugee camps, questions like this seem rather cruel and disrespectful of the depth of people's experiences.

The nature of these two "good moral character" questions reflects the emphasis on American ideals of purity, chastity, and individualism. Aihwa Ong's notion of technologies of government proves helpful in understanding the particular characteristics used to define *good moral character* and how they are employed to discipline and shape the citizenry (or, in this case, potential citizenry). Ong defines technologies of government as the policies, programs, codes, and practices that attempt to instill in citizen-subjects particular values (such as self-reliance, freedom, individualism, calculation, or flexibility) in a variety of domains.[54] The immigrants who appeared at the citizenship drives ready to complete their N-400 were already well aware of the correct responses to the Communist and prostitution questions. The only major criminal background check was the FBI fingerprint scan; thus, by the time applicants approached "formal" procedures, they were already well aware (through their own tenacity as well as community channels and networks) that unless certain activities could be detected through FBI scan, they should not respond positively to the two moral-character questions. Thus, to demonstrate their good citizenship potential, immigrants are disciplined from their first initiation to demonstrate the ideals of American morality. Ong's notion of citizenship as a self-constituting practice (a practice in which immigrants strategically utilize microstrategies to negotiate the systems of power within public domains) applies here, as immigrants have consciously shaped themselves into what is culturally and governmentally defined as worthy, to acquire the resources they need or desire. In the case of legal citizenship status, a major hurdle to American belonging and entitlement, immigrants are forced to reformulate themselves into the *good moral citizen* with no regard to the trauma, atrocities, and poverty they have experienced.

Good Moral Character and Criminal Activity

This disciplining through state technologies was taken to more punitive levels with the convergence of immigration and welfare reform. The Illegal Immigration Reform and Immigrant Responsibility Act (IIRIRA) established new criteria affecting the naturalization process. Focusing on "good moral character," newly established criteria regarding past criminal activity and use of public benefits complicated the naturalization process and further prevented some immigrants from applying. Although, even before 1996, immigrants who had any criminal activity (arrests or convictions) in their background were immediately referred by community organizations to an immigration lawyer and heavily cautioned about applying for naturalization, once the 1996 laws passed the bar was raised. For certain criminal activity, regardless of when in the immigrant's life it occurred and regardless of what penalties had been served, submission of a naturalization application to the INS could lead to immediate deportation. Even before IIRIRA, applicants who had ever been arrested or convicted of a crime might automatically have their naturalization application denied, and deportation proceedings initiated against them. But until 1996, they were at least granted the right to have a hearing. The 1996 laws reduced judicial power to adjudicate immigrant proceedings, by mandating certain penalties entailing removal for a vastly broader array of aggravated felonies. Thus, if an applicant responded yes to the "good moral character questions" 15a or 15b, "Have you knowingly committed a crime or ever been arrested,"[55] he or she was stopped, and advised to go directly to an immigration attorney before filing the N-400. For such filing could result—and in many instances did—in immediate deportation.

Since 1996, then, immigrants are subject to forced detention and expedited removal as a result of past or newly committed crimes. Even where time has already been served, or where the noncitizen has lived in this country since early childhood, or even infancy, and has no memory of her or his country of origin, the subject is immediately funneled through a criminal removal system that defines an immigrant with a criminal record as a potential threat. With the broadening of criminal offenses subsumed under this law to include vices such as shoplifting, urinating in public, or others crime with only a one-year punishment, the ruling that two misdemeanors equals an aggravated felony means that a person who shoplifts twice is now treated as an aggravated felon and must be deported. Immigration judges have lost power to adjudicate discretionary penalties or to provide flexibility for cases with special circumstances. Rather, IIRIRA has laid out deportation guidelines for a broadened range of what can be considered criminal activity outside judicial discretion. As a result, removal rates have risen drastically since 1996, and more so since the 9/11 attacks of 2001. According to Park and Park, in post-9/11 immigration procedures, "good moral character" has become synonymous with absence of a criminal conviction. Since 1992, the rate of denial of naturalization grew dramatically, rising to 7 percent, then to 25 percent to 30 percent each year since 1998. Petitioners have been more likely to undergo a more thorough and extensive criminal background check, as well.[56]

The Fifth Amendment in such cases guarantees that no person shall be "deprived of life, liberty, or property, without due process of law." Further, the right to confront one's accusers and see the evidence against one is among the most basic elements of due process. IIRIRA, however, stripped all noncitizens of the right to due process. Essentially, the IIRIRA redefined the Fifth Amendment's notion of *person* to mean *citizen,* not *alien.* The anti-immigrant racial politics succeeded in stripping immigrants of equal person-hood; indeed, the anti-immigrant constructions of *criminals* and *terrorists* reduced suspected nonaliens' status to that of suspected enemies or threats to (economic) national security. This driving racialized nativism, legitimized in 1996, fundamentally altered noncitizens' relationship to equal protection under the law.

Public Charge and Public Assistance

In line with PRWORA, IIRIRA worked to exclude noncitizens from public assistance, through the Public Charge Provision, based on welfare receipt. Although the notion of *public charge* has been grounds for inadmissibility and deportation, in U.S. immigration law, for more than one hundred years, not until the implementation of specific guidelines based on receipt of public benefits was this provision used to systematically exclude poor immigrants.[57] According to the U.S. Department of Justice and the then-INS, a *public charge* is "an alien who has become [for deportation purposes] or is likely to become [for admission or adjustment-of-status purposes] primarily depend-ent on the government for subsistence, as demonstrated by either the receipt of public cash assistance for income maintenance, or institutionalization for long-term care at government expense."[58] Since its implementation, the Pub-lic Charge Provision has stirred enormous confusion for both immigrants and immigration officers overseeing determinations. The fear of being named a "public charge" as a mechanism for deportation resulted in a broad chilling effect that dissuaded immigrants from seeking public benefits they were due, and in some cases from applying for naturalization, from fear of repercus-sions. Stories of deportation cases ensuing from use of public assistance spread through immigrant communities.

With the passing of the IIRIRA, the Public Charge rule went into effect without initial guidelines or procedures. Thus, determinations were often left to the discretion of operating units within the INS, port-of-entry offices, or Department of Human Services. The system was plagued with inconsistent determinations and procedures by INS officials, resulting in a widespread panic over arbitrary deportation. In her research on the impact of the Public Charge Provision, Lisa Sun-Hee Park found that confusion regarding the use of California's Medicaid program, MediCal, resulted in the INS and California's Department of Human Services collaborating to make erroneous "public charge" determinations based on MediCal use alone.

Fearful of utilizing MediCal, legal permanent residents who remained qualified for such benefits chose not to receive emergency medical care. One community health care clinic director told of an incident in which a woman called for a family member who was having a heart attack, but was afraid to use the ambulance/paramedics for fear of the patient counting as a public charge.[59] In another case, an immigrant woman legally residing in the Bay Area scalded herself badly, but was afraid of getting herself or her family in trouble, and so hesitated for thirty days to receive emergency care. By the time she went to the emergency room, the infection was so advanced that she was beyond survival.[60]

In response to pressure from immigrant advocates and community-based organizations, the INS finally provided specific guidance and procedures for public charge criteria—three years after the law was passed. In May 1999 the INS produced and disseminated a "Field Guidance on Deportability and Inadmissibility on Public Charge Grounds." In this document, criteria for Public Charge determinations were narrowed to include use of Temporary Assistance to Needy Families (TANF), Supplemental Security Income (SSI), General Assistance (GA), and Medicaid specifically used for long-term care—that is, to cash-assistance programs. The INS also clarified that there was no "public charge" test for naturalization. However, although a Public Charge determination would not play out in naturalization determinations, it could intercede or impact the immigrant's status before she/he attempted to naturalize. Although, on the N-400, naturalization applicants were asked only if they had ever committed fraud to receive public assistance, at the time of intake they were asked to fill out an additional public benefits worksheet indicating all forms of public assistance they had ever received while residing in the United States.

The Public Charge Provision could be used against legal permanent residents to bar their reentry on returning from trips abroad. The food stamp program did not fall under this provision, but the INS inappropriately declared several legal immigrants who used this benefit "public charges" and immediately changed their immigration status. Even though these cases were overruled as inappropriate, and the INS had to pay restitution for subjecting immigrants to false fees and in some cases inappropriate deportation, fear persisted within immigrant communities. Immigrants who had or continued to use public assistance overwhelmingly expressed fear of being denied naturalization because they or their children benefited from some form of welfare. Even though we told the immigrants, as we were trained to, that their benefits would not be sole cause of denial of naturalization, their concerns were not easily appeased. In a typical example, a woman applicant looked upset when I asked her to fill out the public assistance information form. She asked whether she had to, and whether the form was going to the INS, and I told her it was for internal use within the immigrant program hosting the citizenship drive. She would not believe me and I had to get one of the immigrant attorney advocates to explain the reasoning behind the worksheet, as well as the process the INS would go through in regard to her history of public assistance. She eventually filled out the form, but was wary and nervous from that point on.[61]

From the moment an immigrant filed her N-400, she initiated a review process that allowed the state to scrutinize her public behavior and personal beliefs. As a primary system of determining who could become an American citizen, the naturalization process proved fraught with obstacles designed to ensure that supposed undesirables would remain outside the borders of legal entitlement. Whether disabeled, someone who had committed criminal activity (regardless of the contextual circumstances), or poor, an immigrant must fashion his or her self as an upstanding person of good morals to be judged by the INS officer making the determination of their citizen-worthiness.

NATURALIZATION PROCESS, CITIZENSHIP-MAKING, CREATION OF NEW VOTERS

For many immigrants the challenges proved too taxing. Naturalization among the elderly and disabled proved difficult even with the age and disability waivers for English requirements and U.S. history/civics exams. Nevertheless, the push for citizenship persisted and naturalization rates have shown the success of these efforts. One most impressive victory came after a year-long struggle for Hmong veterans and their families (described in chapter 3). Hmong community organizations fought simultaneously to retain food stamps for their veterans and to have their veterans' naturalization requirements altered, all on the basis of veteran status. The Hmong Veterans' Naturalization Act of 2000 instituted an exemption from the English language requirement and gave special consideration for civics testing for refugees from Laos who had served in support of U.S. military operations anytime from 1961 through 1978.

In spite of many obstacles, the many victories by immigrant advocates has led to an astounding increase in naturalization of Asian immigrants. The push to naturalize elderly and disabled immigrants has continued even though the harshest cuts to SSI were restored. Advocates have continued to encourage elderly and disabled immigrants to acquire full citizenship status, believing this the only way to guarantee that their noncitizen status cannot be used against them in the future. By 1998, the increase in naturalized Asian immigrants was already evident. On Thursday, March 19, 1998, "Celebrate Your Citizenship," an event co-organized by the Self Help for the Elderly and the Asian Law Caucus, celebrated four hundred newly naturalized elderly immigrants in San Francisco. In an article documenting the event, in *Asian Week*, March 26, 1998, seventy-one-year-old Lu Zhi Zhao emphatically declared that he decided to become a U.S. citizen because "I want to vote; it's my right."[62]

The increase in naturalized Asian immigrants immediately stirred commentary regarding the emerging potential of the Asian American swing vote. According to the Chinese American Voters Education Committee (CAVEC), by 1998 Asian Americans comprised nearly a third of the 724,000 people living in San Francisco. Of the legal permanent residents in the city, 67.5 percent were from Asia. The 79,000 Asian American registered voters constituted 16.4 percent of the city's voters. Of the nearly 16,000 newly registered Asian American voters in 1996, 75.6 percent were foreign born.[63] Thus, in San Francisco alone, the impact of naturalization was having a significant role in the creation of new voter pools. On a broader scale, Jeffey Passel of the Urban Institute found that the number of votes cast by whites in the U.S. presidential elections rose by only 4.3 percent between 1996 and 2000; the number of Asian votes rose by 22 percent. This increase is expected to continue through the next few decades as more Asians reach voting age or become citizens. Still, in the year 2000, 59 percent of Asians could not register to vote, though only 25 percent of whites could not register to vote.[64]

The emergence of new voter pools has had undisputed consequences for immigration politics. By the end of 1998, two years after the passing of PRWORA, several newspaper reports noticed the deemphasis of immigration in candidates' political platforms. Patrick McDonnel and Ken Ellingwood of the *Los Angeles Times* noted a popularly shared conclusion that "immigration has disappeared as an issue from the 1998 elections."[65] Citing the growing and active Latino voting block, McDonnel and Ellington reported that Republican politicians "don't want to touch immigration with a 10-foot pole," according to Allan Hoffenblum, a Los Angeles-based GOP political consultant. Likewise, Virta Ojito of the *New York Times* reiterated the point that "immigration, the source of much national angst in years past, has disappeared from the election debate."[66] Ojito further argued that legislators had attempted to undo most of the controversial harm done to legal immigrants, for fear of a retaliatory Latino/a vote. Both reporters ignore the increasing Asian vote, as Asians occupied a smaller overall voting bloc than a few years before, given their decreased relative demographic presence; however, their voting power was persuasively important in particular geographical regions.

Although organized and orchestrated anti-immigrant platforms thus waned for several years, between 1996 and 2000, the 9/11 terrorist attacks reescalated immigrant policies, again questioning civil and human rights. Noncitizens again found themselves subjected to a myriad of policy reforms and procedures that jeopardized their security and safety. Citizenship status as a legal framework has continued to shape the rights and security of those who reside in the United States legally, but who are still seen as a potential threat to the nation's well-being.

The details of this chapter demonstrate the highly subjective and ideological forces guiding the technology systems governing U.S. citizenship status. To naturalize successfully, immigrants were judged by higher standards than were birthright citizens. Noncitizenship status was singularly defined regardless of how long and from what age one had resided in the United States, how disabilities had been acquired, or what the conditions or reasons were for an immigrant's poverty. The state technologies that inserted "good moral character" into fifteen questions on the N-400 naturalization form have required immigrants to fashion themselves as unrealistically good citizens unmarked by life events or social conditions impacting their families' well-being.

The situation for Asian immigrants and refugees, who fewer than fifty years earlier lived the legacy of "aliens ineligible for citizenship" on a basis of "racial and cultural inassimilability," exposes the paradox of state-defined citizenship. The massive levels of immigration from Asia, and the increasing rates of U.S. naturalization since 1965, resulted in an anti-immigrant back-lash that during the 1990s reshaped this population's relationship to citizen-ship. The politics of belonging were taken to another level. The past was marked by a clear *foreigner* racialization that worked to exclude the physical presence of Asian immigrants. The contemporary nativist concern inserted the requirement to formalize *belonging,* as a means to sift out those who fail to meet certain standards of American citizenship, and as a means to force immigrants into a formal legal status for entitlement to public services.

The unexpected rise in creation of new citizens has resulted in a perhaps unplanned fortification of racial minority communities. In the words of one community organizer, the horrendous anti-immigrant policies of the 1990s, and the consequent push for citizenship, "[has been] one of the best things to happen to Asian Americans because it has prompted Asian Pacific Ameri-cans to become involved in the political process."[67] However, harsh anti-immigrant policies have not disappeared from political campaigns; rather, they have shifted venue from welfare and immigration fraud to potential terrorist affiliation. Nevertheless, organized immigrant communities have been prepared to challenge the plethora of anti-immigrant policies subsumed under broader antiterrorist policies. The concern over legal citizenship status clearly remains a prominent issue for contemporary racial politics.

5

On Not Making Ends Meet

Mothers without Citizenship

> When I came to the U.S., I thought life would be easier, but it wasn't. My husband left us. And I didn't have any money at all. On top of that they cut my welfare. We didn't have anything to eat. My neighbor had to give us food. I had no money to buy clothes for my children when school started. In the six months that my welfare was cut, my older kids had no money for school lunch. They cut my welfare because I don't speak English. They sent me left and right, I was confused. I was always missing some papers.
>
> —Mao Nang ("Borey's mom") from *Eating Welfare*

When the issue of welfare is raised, an immediate association arises with single mothers, reproduction, and what was formerly Aid to Families with Dependent Children (AFDC) and is now Temporary Assistance to Needy Families (TANF). In fact, the political preoccupation with welfare reform, as it encompassed drastic changes to multiple forms of public assistance, became synonymous in the arguments of avid reformers with assumptions about undeserving welfare mothers, deviant women's irresponsibility, and dependency. The racial gendered politics that surrounded the construction of the *welfare queen* conjured racist images of laziness and unworthiness to legitimize the complete undoing of a sixty-year safety net and entitlement program designed to keep families out of abject poverty.[1]

The case against immigrant women as burdens on the state had its more formal origins in localized anti-immigrant politics that scapegoated immigrants for economic crises, elevated levels of crime, and drug trafficking. As discussed in chapter 1, California's Proposition 187 codified anti-immigrant blame regarding immigrant women's reproduction, immigrant women's health care, and immigrants' children's use of the education system. Leo Chavez argues that reproduction played into anti-immigrant sentiment primarily regarding: the actual biological state of pregnancy and childbirth; the reproduction of the immigrant family; and the formation and reproduction of the immigrant community.[2] All three levels were simultaneously attacked through Proposition 187's attempt to eradicate the presence of undocumented immigrants by attacking the undocumented immigrant's family.

Consequently, the provisions of Proposition 187 would have banned public support for prenatal care of undocumented pregnant women. The oft-quoted claim that two out of three babies delivered in Los Angeles county hospitals were born to undocumented women was used by reformers as an "official statistic" to document the invasion of "illegal aliens" giving birth to American citizens.[3] To deplete resources for families headed by undocumented parents, Proposition 187 prohibited local and state agencies from providing publicly funded social services (such as WIC, a nutritional program for women, infants, and children), public education, and nonemergency health care without proof of U.S. citizenship or legal permanent residence status. And finally, Proposition 187 would have required all service providers to report undocumented persons to the state attorney general and the Immigration and Naturalization Service (INS). These provisions worked to create a state of terror for undocumented immigrants residing and working in California and indeed the nation.

Women immigrants and their families were centered as the carriers of reproductive threat to the racial and cultural complexion of California; the discourse of immigrant women's use of social services, prenatal care, and health care, and immigrant children's cost to the public school system carried over into welfare and immigration reform at the national level. That reform focused on reproduction issues was evident in the absence of proposed techniques that would target production or the immigrant worker.[4] The implicit message was thus that anti-immigrant reformers were going after the reproduction of the undocumented worker's family but not after the laborer or the employer (productive labor). In this vein, immigrant women's labor was left unpoliced, while their reproduction and family care suffered the taint of criminality.

Even in regard to otherwise qualified immigrants, PRWORA gave states the option to exclude noncitizens from TANF and Medicaid outright.[5] This immediately set immigrant families apart from citizens, as undeserving of public support. Giving states the option to exclude noncitizens from TANF programs left immigrants vulnerable to local state politics. Although all states except Alabama chose to include those noncitizens present in the United States before August 22, 1996, as eligible for TANF, more complex dilemmas emerged that demonstrated the particular challenges immigrants faced as they negotiated a more complicated and punitive welfare system. Poor English proficiency, low education level, cultural conflict, and fear left a great proportion of those immigrants previously on AFDC and still eligible for TANF, to fall from the rolls. The new system proved so confusing and difficult that immigrants had one of the greatest decreases in TANF participation.

Compounding the massive confusion over new eligibility requirements, PRWORA mandated a five-year bar from any federal means-tested public benefits for immigrants who entered the country after the law's enactment. Even after immigrants had resided in the country for five years, states could make a further distinction of eligibility for those who entered the country after the August 22, 1996, date. All these provisions complicated matters for poor immigrant women and families who needed to negotiate added barriers and requirements based on citizenship status. Immigrants who continued to contribute to the nation's economy, work force, tax base, and social fabric avoided the assistance they needed out of fear of jeopardizing their residence status, naturalization eligibility, or reentry rights should they take a trip abroad. Counties that had had high proportions of immigrant AFDC recipients experienced such drastic drops in the transition to TANF that these immigrant families were coined the "disappeared."

The situation for post–welfare reform immigrants became even more challenging with the further new guidelines imposed by the Illegal Immigration and Immigrant Responsibility Act (IIRIRA) of 1996. The two primary issues affecting immigrants needing public assistance were the addition of legally binding Affidavits of Support and the Public Charge Provision. As discussed in chapter 4, the Public Charge Provision seriously constricts immigrants' ability to enter the United States, reenter the United States, or become a legal permanent resident, should the INS evaluate that the immigrant might need to rely on public benefits in the future. Factors such as age, health, income, family size, education, and skills would of course influence the INS evaluations.[6] Thus, a lawful immigrant still needing to obtain legal permanent resident status would be at great risk should he or she receive any public benefits involving cash assistance (and thus indicating inability to support oneself and one's family).

The new Affidavit of Support guideline went into effect on December 17, 1997. Under the new rules for sponsorship requirements, an immigrant's sponsor had to demonstrate an income level at or above 125 percent of the federal poverty line.[7] Further, the sponsor had to submit the form INS I-864A, a binding legal contract in which the sponsor agreed to provide sufficient support to maintain the immigrant at 125 percent of the poverty line until the sponsor died, or until the immigrant became a U.S. citizen, worked for forty qualifying quarters, left the U.S. and gave up LPR status, or died. Thus, after the immigrant served her or his five-year bar from any federal means-tested benefits, any public benefits agency had to incorporate the income of the sponsor and the sponsor's spouse as part of the immigrant's income in determining eligibility to receive public benefits. If a sponsored immigrant received public assistance, the new law required that the Affidavit of Support be legally enforceable against the sponsor by the sponsored immigrant, as well as any federal, state, or local government or private agency providing a "means-tested public benefit" to the sponsored immigrant. Thus, sponsors would be liable to pay back any public assistance the immigrant received that failed to incorporate the sponsor's household income. The new affidavit has a prohibitive effect, not only on the ability of low-income individuals to sponsor family members, but also for low-income and working class immigrant families to receive any form of federal means-tested benefits, which include SSI, TANF, food stamps, and Medicaid. Restricting sponsorship through elevated income requirements prevents family reunification, which had been prioritized through the 1965 Immigration Act.

The immigrant provisions from both PRWORA and IIRIRA, and the hostile climate in which those laws were formulated, created a dilemma for poor immigrants and their families. Poor immigrant single mothers have been most devastated by the convergence of requirements set forth by the two laws. Approximately 41 percent of immigrant families receiving AFDC in San Francisco were headed by single mothers, and poor immigrant families had few options for supporting their families.[8] The mandatory work requirement, compounded with language barriers, low marketable skills, and overall unfamiliarity and fear surrounding the complicated immigration laws led many immigrant parents into a highly exploitable labor market. Community agencies became the primary buffer within the immigrant community, when time limits expired, to find sustainable employment for family support.

Looking specifically at the situation faced by immigrant women and families already receiving AFDC in the Bay Area at the time of TANF implementation, I found profound levels of confusion, fear, and mistrust with the newly devised welfare-to-work programs. Shortly after the first established sessions of intake appointments, county officials realized how difficult it was going to be to serve the immigrant clientele. TANF was touted as a great success as recipients left the rolls in the first few years of enactment, but county social service administrators soon realized that a major proportion of recipients were having a more difficult time than before in finding self-sustaining employment. Immigrants were quickly categorized as "hard to serve" or as clients with "multiple barriers" impeding ability to work.

The culture of the welfare-to-work program took on a professional service-oriented framework that did not account for the cultural, language, and educational needs of impoverished immigrants. My ethnographic research revealed the immediate crisis faced by immigrant families with poor English skills, lack of work experience, and many children to care for. Forced to work twenty to thirty-five documented hours per week to receive barely enough (and in many cases not enough) cash assistance to keep their families afloat, immigrants for the most part sought other avenues to make ends meet. In the first few years of TANF's enactment, community organizations encountered compounding problems of health care, child care, and domestic violence. The convergence of laws that overlapped punitive measures through gender and through citizenship biases left even fewer options, and distressing levels of panic, for poor immigrant and refugee women who had to choose to either negotiate the law under elevated levels of scrutiny, or succumb to exploitative working conditions and longer work hours.

The consequences of TANF policy for immigrant families reveal the impact of legal citizenship status on the well-being and livelihood of impoverished immigrants as they faced the additional obstacles of a more challenging system of assistance. The added difficulties of the new system itself, compounded by language issues, low education attainment, mental and physical health problems, and an intense fear of bringing themselves to the attention of immigration officials, played out in the avoidance by many immigrant families of TANF caseworkers and welfare-to-work program administrators. As a result, many immigrants were further trapped into low-skilled, low-wage employment with no health benefits and hyperexploitive conditions. The welfare-related effects of the Public Charge Provision and Affidavit of Support intensified existing levels of fear, leading eligible immigrants to make do without public assistance.

Just as structural adjustment policies in developing countries wreak a form of violence against the women who suffer most from economic and political dislocation (in terms of health care, child care, education, and income), PRWORA positioned all poor women into more economically vulnerable situations and exposed them to multiple forms of violence. For example, TANF regulated mothers utilizing assistance by enforcing cooperation with the biological fathers of their children. Issues of domestic violence, complicated by patriarchal structures within many Asian immigrant communities, deterred many immigrant women, fearing forced reconnection with abusive partners, from using TANF. Or, in cases where women were in abusive relationships, the restrictions of TANF left them no option but to stay in their situations. Given many immigrant mothers' unique legacy of global economic and political dislocation as well as of trauma experienced through war and flight, the economic abandonment of them made them particularly vulnerable to exploitative, abusive, and unregulated working conditions.

The culmination of these factors has resulted in immigrant households having fewer resources, higher poverty, and increased hunger. Nearly 75 percent of all children living in immigrant-headed households are U.S. citizens.[9] Thus, a significant proportion of these households contain U.S. citizen children who are denied their full citizenship entitlements because of their parents' immigration status; under TANF, citizen children of immigrant parents are shorn of their full rights and guarantees since the system further penalizes and discourages parents without citizenship status. To determine how to serve this invisible sector of recipients, county social service administrations relied on community-based organizations, county task force groups, and research groups to examine and report how immigrant families were faring following welfare reform. In the first few subsequent years, numerous research groups reported increased levels of food insecurity and high poverty levels. Unlike the highly visible movement to restore the harshest immigrant cuts from SSI and food stamps, the more gradual unfolding and implementation of state-devised programs for TANF recipients, and their impacts on immigrant communities, were gravely underrecognized.

INVISIBLE MOTHERHOOD

The implications of citizenship in relation to TANF and family well-being reveal another narrative of welfare reform, one that has generally remained invisible within broader examinations of PRWORA and the persistence of poverty. This narrative, embedded within preexisting constructions of *deviant motherhood, irresponsible reproduction,* and *racial pathologies,* indicates the persistent devaluation of immigrant families in the United States and the idea that recent immigrants are outsiders undeserving of American resources. In terms of immigrant families, the construction of *free-loading* moves beyond the notions of *irresponsibility* and *laziness,* to the idea of a parasitic foreign threat of impoverished Third World migrants unfairly taking advantage of an overgenerous welfare system. Given the mixed citizenship in immigrant households, the underlying assumptions that have shaped the lack of immigrant participation in TANF raise challenging questions regarding the rights of immigrant families and citizen children. The implementation of TANF legislation demonstrates the multilayered challenges to immigrant rights and equal citizenship that compound welfare reform's assault on mothers and families more generally.

TANF had many implications for Asian immigrant and refugee women as noncitizen mothers in the Bay Area of Northern California. In examining California's TANF plan, CalWORKs (California Work Opportunity and Responsibility to Kids), I have drawn on my extensive fieldwork to present the particular situations, barriers, and community supports that Asian immigrant and refugee women encountered in their negotiations with county agencies. Some key problem areas to arise as these women faced TANF programs were: language issues, child-care needs, medical crises, domestic violence, lack of appropriate job training and education, and an unconsciousness, at policy and personnel levels, of the impact of war, dislocation, and resettlement. I have pulled together the relevant provisions in both PRWORA and IIRIRA to show how immigrant and refugee women were simultaneously hit with two waves of policy changes, causing more vulnerability, insecurity, confusion, and mistrust of county officials. These women, many with a history of traumatic interactions with state authorities, have also been limited to low-wage, low-skilled economic niches. As TANF regulations and requirements further imposed the state into their lives, Asian immigrant and refugee mothers, in need of assistance for the survival of their families, were confronted with another form of terror.

In utilizing the state's cash assistance for family support, immigrant and refugee women were subjected to intensified state scrutiny concerning their immigration status. As legally defined noncitizens, subject to different policy requirements than were citizen women, these immigrant and refugee women's fear of doing something wrong led to fears of jeopardizing their immigration status. With the rights of noncitizens questionable, and additional requirements to achieve naturalization open to socially defined "personal" characteristics, the level of insecurity among these women transcended their negotiations with state agencies. In the anti-immigrant climate, fear of deportation took hold, even if specific welfare provisions would not result in forced removal. Thus, many immigrant and refugee women, unable to trust state agencies, instead looked for support through community groups or kin networks, friends, or family members. As most immigrants receiving assistance were already working in some capacity, many resorted to taking on multiple jobs, working well over forty hours a week; their minor children often had to find employment as well.

The political position of impoverished Asian immigrant and refugee women posed a counterintuitive logic to popular understandings of welfare use and necessity. The initial invisibility of Asian immigrants and refugees in relation to SSI and food stamp benefits was soon challenged through community mobilization and the exposure of harsh political agendas afflicting disabled and elderly Asian immigrant and refugee women. However, in the case of Asian immigrant and refugee women as mothers transitioning to TANF, the advocacy level remained stifled—as it was and has been for all poor women facing more stringent benefits requirements and the loss of a safety net.[10] Consequently, in the case for California, CalWORKs was slow and inadequate in addressing the particular needs and circumstances for immigrant and refugee women, who on the whole encountered doubly difficult barriers in fulfilling CalWORKs' requirements.

Approximately 90 percent of the Asian Pacific American CalWORKs caseload was Southeast Asian refugees.[11] Generally these participants had been traumatized by war and displacement, had greater health and mental health problems, and were in need of more assistance as they and their families resettled in the United States. But these Southeast Asian recipients again had the rules changed on them, in a country in which they were promised refuge. Resettlement and adjustment was given a tighter time limit, with fewer services and less understanding for their specific circumstances. The challenges they faced devolved from their citizenship status (correlating with the broader devaluation of immigrant families as foreigner outsiders, dispensable and overburdening the state, un-American, and inassimilable).

CALWORKS, CALIFORNIA'S WELFARE-TO-WORK PROGRAM

California's TANF plan, CalWORKs, officially began on January 1, 1998. The devolution imposed by PRWORA mandated that each state develop its own plan following basic federal guidelines. Thus, CalWORKs, one plan among fifty, could choose to develop welfare-to-work programs that accounted for the state's comparatively high proportion of immigrants. As shall be seen, California's poor immigrant families faced an incredible predicament when they had to transition to CalWORKs. This story speaks to the increasing vulnerability immigrant families faced, the persistent devaluation and demonization of immigrants in the nation, and the enormous amount of work that would be required to correct the erroneous mainstream belief that immigrants are a drain on public resources.

Federal guidelines for state-devised TANF programs mandate that a state's TANF plan must require that all parents and caretakers receiving assistance under the program engage in mandatory work or in state-defined work-related programs within twenty-four months.[12] Solo caretakers must work a minimum of thirty hours per week,[13] and two-parent families must have one adult engaged in at least thirty-five hours of work per week; however, if the family receives federally funded child care, then the spouse also must work at least twenty hours per week. Two-parent families had the option of allowing one parent to stay at home and provide care for their children, but single mothers had no choice but to be forced to work outside the home and leave their children in the care of others, or alone with no care.[14]

To ensure that individual work requirements are adhered to, states must also meet yearly increasing minimum work participation rates, to be eligible for full federal funds for the following fiscal year. If a recipient does not meet her mandatory work requirement, the state is required to reduce the amount of her family assistance or terminate assistance altogether. These punitive actions, referred to as sanctions/sanctioning, have been instrumental in reducing county caseloads. Several studies have already shown that women of color have higher sanctioning rates than have white recipients.[15] Sanctioning has been imposed for a range of infractions (tardiness to job training, lack of necessary work activity hours, or missing an appraisal appointment), and usually at the complete discretion of the case worker. Finally, PRWORA prohibits states from using federal TANF funds to provide assistance to parents and caretakers for more than five years (sixty months), whether or not consecutive.[16] According to PRWORA, this lifetime cap of five years can be lessened by the state should the state so wish.

The 1997 California legislature and the California governor, Pete Wilson, agreed to maintain immigrants' eligibility for the new CalWORKs program and for Medi-Cal regardless of when the immigrants entered the United States.[17] Once the California legislature passed the state law, AB 1542 (CalWORKs), implementing federally mandated TANF, the counties had to develop and begin implementing plans by January 1, 1998. Faced with the complete overhaul from AFDC to CalWORKs, county level departments of social services scrambled with local governments to develop plans to address the needs of their constituencies. As an observer to the Santa Clara County CalWORKs Implementation Advisory Committee, a participant in CalWORKs Workers' Rights and Impact of Welfare Reform on Immigrants trainings, and a volunteer in citizenship drives, I was able to observe the unfolding of local county plans to implement TANF programs. In getting CalWORKs operational, counties encountered unexpected challenges for immigrants, and social service offices relied on community organizations that were among the few established bodies able to liaison between immigrant constituencies and the welfare-to-work programs. Clearer profiles of immigrant families previously enrolled in AFDC emerged, as advocates worked to insert the needs of immigrants into county CalWORKs plans that originally failed to recognize the families' particular circumstances.

My diagram here represents a typical CalWORKs "participant flow chart," which maps the trajectory for a CalWORKs recipient from the time he or she enters the doorway for a first appraisal to the end of his or her five-year limit. The puzzle-like subject boxes and complicated arrow system demonstrate the convoluted bureaucratic appraisal system that a client must negotiate to receive cash assistance through CalWORKs. The participant flow chart shows a confusing labyrinth of services and regulations that social service providers were left to decipher for each individual client. This was particularly problematic since many offices and facilities listed as resources or services were not yet in place. For convenience and accessibility, county administrators attempted to provide these services in a "one-stop shopping" center so that recipients would not have to travel all over town for appraisal and intake interviews. In the counties that I studied, this one-stop shopping was referred to as *Job Club*. The participant flow chart was cumbersome for intake providers to follow; it was certainly more daunting for CalWORKs recipients. The system proved overly complicated, with myriad ways in which clients fell through the cracks. As TANF transformed an entitlement program for needy families into a temporary assistance program for minimal cash and scanty access to job skills and resources, the system took on a professionalizing commercial approach in which recipients were referred to as *clients*, or even, at times, *customers*. For immigrants, this system could not have been less accessible—in some cases, indeed, unfathomable enough to prevent their applying in the first place. It was not long before county officials realized that their immigrant constituencies had disappeared.

On January 1, 1998, the five-year time clocks began ticking.[18] In one Bay Area county with a high constituency of Southeast Asian AFDC recipients, the new system made its debut. CalWORKs letters had been sent to all previous AFDC recipients; initial interview appointment dates had been sent. But at this moment, the first phase of intake interviews, not one immigrant showed up. According to state rules, all of the immigrants failing to appear were to be officially sanctioned from the rolls. Realizing that something had gone wrong, and that better communication efforts were needed, county officials immediately extended the intake deadline and formed an Immigration Task Force to address the needs of its immigrant community. By July 1998, Alameda and Santa Clara Counties reported that nearly 60 percent of previous AFDC recipients did not appear for the CalWORKs contractual interviews. In Santa Clara County, where immigrants and their U.S.-born children made up 60 percent of the county's population, welfare reform had a chilling impact in immigrant communities. Nearly 42 percent of Santa Clara's immigrant recipients had withdrawn from CalWORKs participation. A remarkable level of confusion and fear prevented immigrants from using the public assistance they were eligible to receive.

CALWORKS AND BAY AREA IMMIGRANT FAMILIES ON WELFARE

In San Francisco and Santa Clara counties, where a large percentage of CalWORKs clients were Asian immigrants and refugees, community organizations were first to see the complications to emerge from the sudden and drastic set of changes in cash assistance for needy families.[19] In San Francisco, at the time of the welfare reform law's passing, 31 percent of AFDC immigrant

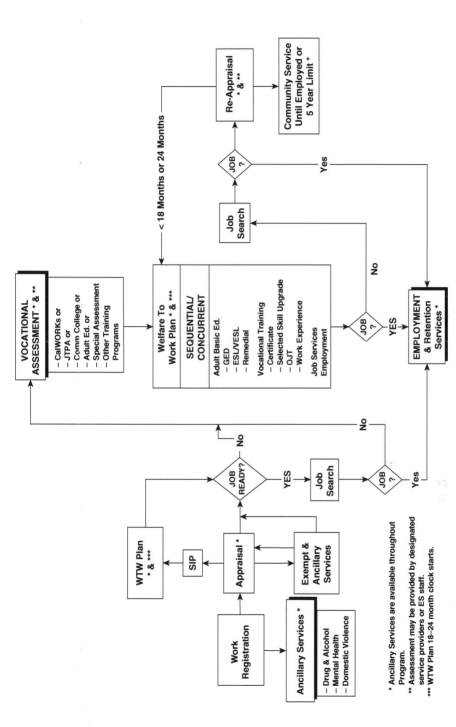

FIGURE 4. This participant flow chart reflects a common county-by-county approach to TANF programs. *Source:* Santa Clara County Department of Social Services.

VOCATIONAL ASSESSMENT * & *
- CalWORKs or
- JTPA or
- Comm College or
- Adult Ed. or
- Special Assessment
- Other Training Programs

Welfare To Work Plan * & *

SEQUENTIAL/ CONCURRENT

Adult Basic Ed.
- GED
- ESL/VESL
- Remedial

Vocational Training
- Certificate
- Selected Skill Upgrade
- OJT
- Work Experience

Job Services
Employment

< 18 Months or 24 Months

Re-Appraisal * & **

Community Service Until Employed or 5 Year Limit *

JOB ?

Job Search

Yes

No

JOB ?

YES

EMPLOYMENT & Retention Services *

WTW Plan * & ***

SIP

Appraisal *

Exempt & Ancillary Services

Work Registration

Ancillary Services *
- Drug & Alcohol
- Mental Health
- Domestic Violence

JOB READY?

YES

Job Search

JOB ?

Yes

No

No

* Ancillary Services are available throughout Program.

** Assessment may be provided by designated service providers or ES staff.

*** WTW Plan 18–24 month clock starts.

recipients were from China, 34 percent were from Southeast Asia. In Santa Clara County, 37 percent of AFDC recipients were Asian/Pacific Islander; approximately 37 percent of these were from Southeast Asia. (Santa Clara County is notable in regard to broader immigrant issues, given its high immigrant concentration. With one-third of its 1.7 million people being immigrants, Santa Clara has twice as many immigrants as any other county in the Bay Area, and in California is third only to Los Angeles and Orange Counties in number of immigrants.) Immediately, in Santa Clara County, sixteen immigrant groups were identified as the largest and neediest in relation to the changes in welfare.[20] The most immediate obstacle for immigrants was the need for translated CalWORKs Notices of Action (NOAs), the first formal letters explaining the transition from AFDC to CalWORKs.

Given the particularly high proportion of Asian and Southeast Asian recipients, language barriers were a continuing obstacle at almost every level of the CalWORKs program, including the search for employment. At a CalWORKs advisory board meeting, a social service administrator in Santa Clara County stated, "The only languages we can automatically print are Spanish and English, as is the case for all nineteen consortium counties. Bilingual workers are instructed to write handwritten notices on blank forms which are available."[21] The immediate solution to this problem was to attach a notice that provided a resource list of community organizations to which an immigrant could go for translation assistance in reading the letter. As a result, large percentages of CalWORKs recipients (non-English Vietnamese or Spanish speakers) received notices explaining the new requirements and advising them of their interview appointments in languages that they were unable to read. As 60 percent of adult CalWORKs recipients failed to show up for their contract interviews, many immigrant clients fell through the cracks, most likely because the notices were unreadable.[22]

The Department of Social Services of Santa Clara County immediately consulted with its Immigration Task Force to address specific needs and problems directly impacting the immigrant clientele. (The Immigration Task Force had been established as soon as PRWORA was signed into law, to deal with multiple impacts on noncitizens.) A list of immediate policy recommendations by the Immigration Task Force suggested more consistent translation of notices not only into Vietnamese and Spanish but also into Cambodian, Chinese, Cantonese, Farsi, Tagalog, Laotian, Hmong, and Russian. According to the state mandate set forth in AB 1542 (creating Cal-WORKs), county social service departments were required to translate notices only into Vietnamese and Spanish, and so it depended on the commitment of each county to make notices language-appropriate. Santa Clara County committed to translating all welfare forms (322 documents) into all ten languages suggested by the Immigration Task Force, and into Armenian. This process proved more daunting than expected; by the end of 1998, a majority of forms and notices had yet to be translated into languages in addition to Spanish and Vietnamese.

The Immigration Task Force stressed not only the dire need for appropriate language availability for all CalWORKs services, but also the need for cultural proficiency among CalWORKs personnel. Given the diverse histories of migration and refuge among the immigrant groups, it was important for social service workers, appraisers, and educators to understand the specific needs and issues of each group. Mental health issues, poor physical health, war trauma sequelae, and particular cultural customs greatly compounded the difficulties for many immigrants in communicating with translators. Community organizations reported that many immigrants were illiterate in their own language; to reach members of the community with limited reading skills, information needed to be provided in an accessible location in the community where changes in policy could be orally explained and understood.

The lack of accessible welfare-to-work programs led to underemployment. In a round-table discussion in San Francisco involving community service providers, immigrant rights advocates, and welfare rights activists, grave concern was expressed that most immigrant CalWORKs recipients would probably wind up in highly exploitative, dead-end, low-paying jobs. This seemed likely as, at the time, most General Assistance recipients already involved in workfare programs had been relegated to low-paying or community service janitorial work in public hospitals, public transportation, and city parks; welfare-to-work programs had yet to develop mass transitioning of recipients into unsubsidized labor. To shift federally mandated numbers of recipients into the labor force, counties struggled to get as many people off welfare and into work as quickly as possible. However, one community social service provider working with CalWORKs recipients in Alameda County noted that most clients she encountered were already working—in very low-paying menial jobs, work incapable of sustaining a family.[23]

The welfare-to-work programs operated under the assumption that job training and adult education would be sufficient in placing people in self-sustaining jobs. For immigrants, the role of English in job training was a crucial element that needed to be better integrated into vocational programs, as did the continuation of English as a Second Language (ESL) courses through welfare-to-work programs. According to the Immigration Task Force, "English is not only a skills preparation tool, but ... a job search, job retention, and survival skill, needed for successful transitioning to resettlement in the United States."[24] Vocational classes that did not provide instruction in the recipient's native language were relatively useless. At the time of implementation, integrated language and job training programs were very few, and they did not develop on a systematic scale for the thousands of immigrant CalWORKs recipients who began these programs in the first several years. Immigrant advocates pushed for TANF to allow ESL classes to count, like job training, toward mandatory work requirements—which, given how critical mastering English would be to finding sustainable employment, only made sense. One Vietnamese woman on CalWORKs expressed her frustration from lack of English skills: "I've applied to work in many companies but they didn't accept me because my English was not good. I wanted to take ESL but the people from CalWORKs made me go find a job first. After a while when I still couldn't find work then they let me go to school. It wasted my time."[25] The idea that immigrant CalWORKs clients with limited English would be able to find self-sustaining employment once they received very minimal training was certainly unrealistic, given the existing stratified job market. Immigrants continually stated that language barriers were a major obstacle in obtaining long-term employment adequate to support their families. It was clear that, given the highly competitive job market and lack of sufficient jobs, non–English speakers would be left without employment or adequate public assistance to support their families.

According to the California Budget Project, CalWORKs recipients had stiff competition. Unemployed persons not receiving public assistance, General Assistance recipients, college graduates, high school graduates, and underemployed individuals were among categories of people competing for the same jobs as CalWORKs recipients.[26] Although California was then currently experiencing strong economic growth, and unemployment had dropped to 6.5 percent in March of 1997, this relative growth was within the context of the state's worst economic recession since the 1930s. Many Californians had not benefited from the recent momentary surge of economic growth. Unemployment rates for segments of the population most affected by welfare reform were much higher than for the state as a whole. In 1996 the unemployment rate for women with less than a high school degree was 18.2 percent. The underemployed—defined as the official unemployed plus the discouraged (unemployed no longer on the rolls) plus involuntary part-time workers—numbered 30.9 percent of women with less than a high school degree.[27]

Estimated job growth at the time, based on the current economy, industry employment, and occupational patterns, revealed that the number of job seekers significantly outstripped the number of new jobs. Statewide, job seekers exceeded the number of projected new jobs, on an annual basis. According to the California Budget Project, job seekers exceeded available jobs in nearly every California county. Competition was particularly keen in those California communities where unemployment rates remained higher than the state average and welfare rolls were also high. In twenty-four California counties, during the first year of welfare reform, ten or more job seekers, not counting high school and college graduates and new arrivals to the state, competed for every projected new job.[28]

With nearly half of the projected jobs being low-skill positions requiring moderate on-the-job training, the most employable welfare-to-work recipients found employment to meet their mandatory work requirements, though not to generate enough income to support their families. Five out of fifteen of the fastest-growing jobs available to individuals leaving welfare for work paid wages below the poverty level. For many, the wages from full-time work failed to cover basic necessities. A full-time worker earning six dollars per hour, for example, could choose between spending 58 percent of her income on child care for two children, or 49 percent of the family's income for rent and utilities.[29] Moreover, many of the fastest-growing occupations and industries usually offered part-time or temporary work that often lacked basic benefits. Workers in retail trade expected to work an average of 30.7 hours per week at less than ten dollars per hour. Workers in the service sector, California's fastest-growing industry, worked an average of 32.4 hours per week, nationwide.[30]

Welfare-to-work time limits and work requirements had a devastating impact on poor Asian immigrant women and their families because of the women's limited English and low-level marketable skills. Not allowing ESL classes to count as welfare-to-work requirements proved illogical; English remained a necessary component of securing a job. In addition, 69 percent of foreign-born TANF recipients did not have a high school diploma or GED, compared to the 37 percent of citizen adult recipients without either credential.[31] Under TANF, however, education also did not count toward welfare-to-work activities. Already vulnerable to stereotyping in the service and manufacturing industry as a globally exploitable labor pool, immigrants who were forced into labor agreements as welfare-mandated workers further jeopardized their ability to expect fair and safe working conditions. Given the compounding barriers of language, poor education levels, lack of family-sustaining jobs, scarce child-care services, and sexual inequality and harassment in the workplace, Asian immigrant and refugee CalWORKs recipients could not find family-sustaining employment. The women were left with no other options but menial exploitative jobs, inadequate child care, and harsh subsistence. In the following section, I discuss the complex array of barriers, problems, and issues Asian immigrant and refugee women faced, as seen in the profiles I gathered of women who were receiving AFDC before the implementation of CalWORKs.

ASIAN IMMIGRANT AND REFUGEE WOMEN NEGOTIATING CalWORKs

The sweeping changes in immigration and welfare laws escalated the fears of sanctioning, even for legal permanent residents, who were vulnerable to new policies that made it more difficult to naturalize. As an intake provider and assistant with the N400 INS application form (see chapter 4), I met many women trying to naturalize whose situations were being drastically altered by the new rules and requirements. Food stamps were no longer available to them, and though they remained eligible for CalWORKs as noncitizens, the constant fear of losing provisions, and of having to, as legal permanent residents, rely solely on the job market exacerbated an already threatening set of circumstances.

What follows centers on the life circumstances of women I assisted through citizenship drives and information forums. At the time of my encounters with them, they were transitioned from AFDC to TANF. Given their economic situations and their family structure, they remained unquestionably eligible for CalWORKs, and were automatically shifted over once the policy was implemented on January 8, 1998. Their cases demonstrate the insurmountable challenges for women with language barriers, young children, few work skills, and low-paying jobs who lost the much-needed supplemental cash assistance AFDC had provided.

Nham Tran of Vietnam,[32] forty-three years of age, established legal permanent residence in the United States in 1991. She had four children, a tenth-grade education, and self-reported that her English was not good. She was receiving food stamps, which only her children under age eighteen could continue to receive, MediCal, and TANF (the intake report form had not yet shifted the cash assistance category to CalWORKs). She was not employed, and was taking ESL classes. At the time that I was assisting her with the application process, she was with two of her young children, who were approximately six and eight years of age. Her situation revealed a complex set of barriers and issues, given the new set of requirements under CalWORKs. She had a spouse, though it was not clear who would be the more able to fulfill the requirement of thirty-five hours of mandatory work. The type of vocational training SSA (the social service agency) offered to make her "job-ready" in a short time put her through an enormous amount of stress, and, given her level of education, English skills, and lack of work experience, finding full-time work at a livable wage seemed highly unlikely. Her family was already getting by on less food, and although her children remained eligible for CalWORKs assistance after their parents reached their five-year limit, the parents had to find any possible work in order to survive.

Another woman from Vietnam, Hong Le, established legal permanent residence in 1992. She had four children and a total household income of twenty thousand dollars per year. She had a twelfth-grade education, had been cut from food stamps, continued to receive MediCal and TANF, and had been able to find scattered employment for the previous four years. Although she had already pursued and maintained employment, with AFDC supplementing her low income, the amount of her aid had dropped as a result of her new income level. With TANF assistance, formulas were more stringent; thus, even though the cost of living increased, the amount of her cash assistance was on the whole reduced. Without a realistic safety net, especially in high-cost areas, the requirements necessary for the meager amount of assistance she would receive were not worth her time and energy. Rather, she was like thousands of other immigrants who found TANF too difficult to use, and who would opt to find another part-time job or additional low-paying job to pull together adequate income. At the time, she had been a legal permanent resident for six years, and was expected to obtain a full command of English and enough job skills to support her family. After relying on TANF for five years, she would have no other public resources to assist her should she find herself unemployed.

Another subject, a 60-year-old woman from Vietnam who filed for permanent legal residence in 1992, self-reported as having no English. She had a fifth-grade education and was living in a household with four other relatives. At the time, she was receiving General Assistance but no longer qualified for food stamps and would not be eligible for SSI unless she became disabled. In the United States a little over six years, without children under the age of eighteen, and not receiving SSI before the enactment of PRWORA, she was only eligible for General Assistance, which San Francisco had decided to reduce from $345 to $279 per month.[33] At sixty years of age, with no English skills, this woman found employment out of reach. Rather she had to continue to rely on her other household members, food banks, and support from other families to keep her from destitution and homelessness.

Mei Ho from China established legal permanent residence in 1990. She was fifty-one years of age, had a twelfth-grade education, had two children (aged fifteen and seventeen), and self-reported as not having good English. She was receiving TANF and MediCal, and her children still received food stamps. She was already working, but she said that she worked many hours at different places cleaning homes, schools, and businesses. All of her work was part-time, for very little money, but this was the only work she could find. She worked all hours of the day and night, depending on the nature of each job. Her children had to find employment to help the household economy, and must possibly forfeit college or have to attend part-time at a community college. Once Mei Ho's children turned 18, the family would no longer be eligible for food stamps or CalWORKs. CalWORKs does not guarantee sustainable employment, so once their CalWORKS eligibility ran out, they would only be eligible for General Assistance.

These scenarios were typical of hundreds of citizenship applicants who applied for naturalization in the first two years after welfare reform. I had the opportunity to look through the caseload files for 1998 at the Immigration and Citizenship Program, and found hundreds of intake forms of Asian immigrant and refugee women with profiles nearly identical to the ones here presented. Many of these women were already working part-time jobs that paid very little and did not generate enough income for family support. The monthly income they received from TANF was essential for basic necessities like rent, food, clothing, and utilities. Although a relatively large percentage of Asian immigrant and refugee families were two-parent households, both parents and older children tended to struggle to pull together enough part-time work for the household economy. Piecing work together has been the primary form of survival, and the CalWORKs requirements created a situation where recipients were forced to do a lot more work for minimal assistance.

Out of economic necessity, many immigrant and refugee families lived in very large households to share the expenses of rent, utilities, and food. Affordable housing was, and remains, a prominent issue for low-income and impoverished immigrants. Housing costs in the Bay Area were and are among the highest in the nation, and immigrants, like other poor Americans, have been forced to live in overcrowded living conditions. Children of noncitizen parents are more than twice as likely as children of citizens to live in families paying at least half their income in rent or mortgage.[34] Twenty-nine percent of these children live in crowded housing, a four-times greater percentage than for children of citizens.[35] With less support from CalWORKs and no additional housing assistance, immigrants have found their living conditions worsened.

A woman who arrived in the United States from Cambodia in the early 1980s had lived with eight others in her household. At thirty-six years of age, with a ninth-grade education, and with self-reported poor English skills, she relied on AFDC, food stamps, and Medi-Cal to support herself, her family, and the overall household economy. She lost her food stamp benefits, and was trying to decide how to participate in welfare-to-work activities. She said she had hoped by this time to have been able to afford a place of her own for herself and her child, but that hope had become even less likely to materialize. Given her level of education and job skills, she was most likely to be referred to vocational training and ESL classes. Finding self-sustaining employment with sufficient wages and benefits to support her child and live independently seemed unlikely; like others in her situation, she must cobble together forty-plus hours of work per week, at low wages with no benefits, to barely get by.

For young adult immigrants receiving AFDC, the new CalWORKs requirements were equally oppressive, and were particularly stressful for someone still officially a child. I worked with a 16-year-old girl who was in the eleventh grade. She was from Vietnam and gained her legal permanent resident status in 1990. Planning that by the time she received her INS interview she would be the required age of eighteen, she was applying for citizenship. Her English skills were self-reported as good. There were eight other people in her household; her parents had worked a total of two-and-a-half months during the past year. She was receiving food stamps and AFDC. Since CalWORKs went into effect, this young girl was required to stay in school full-time or lose her benefits. Already, on this level, she was policed by the state in a way that most of her classmates were not. Yet when she turned eighteen, two years later, she would no longer be eligible for CalWORKs assistance. Her benefits were undoubtedly a significant contribution to the overall family economy, with her parents unable to find steady work, and so she would have to seek work immediately upon graduation to help support the family. The reverberations from CalWORKs requirements on children of poor immigrant families have long-term impact on their college options, their future adult decisions, and the perpetuation of poverty.

In a similar situation, an 18-year-old woman originally from Laos, who was in the eleventh grade and living with her single mother, was no longer eligible for CalWORKs or food stamps. Despite strong English skills, this young woman still needed another year of secondary school to receive her high school diploma; however, without cash assistance and food stamps, she and her mother must both find work to maintain their household. The young woman's mother, only eligible for General Assistance, had to meet workfare requirements, and the daughter herself had to choose between finishing school while working part-time, or quitting to find full-time employment. Stripped of multiple forms of assistance at once, this daughter and mother were left in a desperate situation. Their status as refugees and victims of a war for which the United States bore substantial responsibility meant nothing to the Social Service Administration: their ages and citizenship status already excluded them from most benefits.

With the compounding loss of food stamps, and of SSI for those not receiving it as of August 22, 1996, households consisting of extended family members lost substantial portions of their incomes. For those within the household unable to work for reasons such as age, illness, or mental instability, public assistance was the only form of income. In these situations, all able and healthy adults had to work harder to support the same household with nothing to supplement low wages. The construction that single-mothered families would breed neglect and criminality was blindly based on stories that ignored the role of state policies hindering poor women and children from pulling themselves out of poverty.

EXPLOITABLE LABOR AND THE CONSEQUENCES OF CalWORKs

Although the Immigration Task Force advocated to the Santa Clara County Department of Social Services the need for greater flexibility and special consideration and planning for immigrant clientele with "limits on their language and cultural knowledge in this country, and/or . . . special needs in adjusting to work and to life,"[36] the new welfare-to-work requirements left little room for immigrant-directed assistance. Here as elsewhere, counties driven by federally mandated work participation requirements pushed those assisted for even quicker movement into the workforce, rather than offer language instruction and counseling for immigrants adjusting to work and life in a new nation. An example of this pipelining of services was (and is) SF Works, a San Francisco business-community-driven partnership that linked the Committee on Jobs, a coalition of several dozen of San Francisco's largest corporate employers; the San Francisco Chamber of Commerce, representing nearly two thousand San Francisco businesses of all sizes; and the United Way. Working with the San Francisco city government, SF Works had a primary goal of transitioning two thousand CalWORKs "caseheads" (recipients) into work by the end of the year 2000. This was just one avenue that the city of San Francisco added to their CalWORKs welfare-to-work program. Described as an innovative approach toward transition, linking community and business, SF Works posited that "classroom training is now a substitute for real-world work experience." The program offered efficient training that was supposed to teach the basic skills necessary to obtain and keep good jobs in the private sector. The likelihood, however, that any of the women here described could benefit from such a program was remote. Quick training for menial employment, without adequate language or skill development, resulted in a quick-to-work approach that left most immigrants still seeking other options to survive. Moreover, funneling welfare-to-work clientele into such programs established a large exploitable—and expendable—pool for participating corporations, industry, and businesses, with very few structural guarantees for fair and equitable employment for CalWORKs "employees."

In a survey study conducted by Equal Rights Advocates (ERA),[37] of seventy-five Vietnamese and seventy-five Mexican women immigrant Cal-WORKs recipients in Santa Clara County, similar profiles emerged. The women's limited level of English proficiency, low education levels (education primarily obtained in their native countries), and poor job skills led to poor utilization of CalWORKs services and programs. An important theme in the ERA study was the striking economic disparity faced by immigrant welfare mothers in the context of Silicon Valley's economic success and wealth. Located in this leading region of the microchip computer and electronics industry, poor immigrant women were paradoxically losing economic support for their families while being trained in menial assembly work. The majority of respondents reported that they had been channeled into temporary work without benefits or job security. Among the Vietnamese women in the study, the most commonly held job was assembly work.

In line with well-documented patterns of exploited women's labor in the global economy, CalWORKs recipients have suffered state-sanctioned labor exploitation as a condition to continue receiving cash assistance. Two women told ERA that they had received job training for electronics assembly and found temporary jobs that required them to work at home paid by the piece rate. When they added up their earnings, they earned less than California's minimum wage. The following profile from the ERA study demonstrates the covert collaboration between welfare reform and labor exploitation.

> At age 49, Mai lives with her 58-year-old husband and four children in an apartment in San Jose.... Over half of Mai's income must go to pay the rent, leaving her with few resources to care for her family. Mai is the sole breadwinner, as her husband's rheumatoid arthritis is compounded by the permanent effects of the beatings he received at a Vietnamese concentration camp.
>
> Her job as a subcontractor assembling electronics parts only yields about $200 per month at piece rates. Mai is forced to rely on food stamps, MediCal, and cash assistance for the rest of her family's needs. A local church is the last resort Mai often must turn to for free food.
>
> In addition, Mai said, her piecework has ruined her eyesight. "The pieces are very small. I can't concentrate, and then water starts to come out (of my eyes). I am about to have surgery on them.
>
> In addition to the problems of lack of childcare, transportation and English skills (Mai cannot read or write in English), she spoke of age discrimination against her. "No one wants to hire old people to work," she said. At 49 Mai has received only a few months of job training, ESL classes, and job search assistance through CalWORKs, but none of that led to a secure job.[38]

The ERA study found that women identified what may be considered gender-biased and ethnically stereotyped notions of their employment opportunities. When asked what type of employment they wanted, the majority of Vietnamese women said that they wanted electronics assembly jobs or work in nail/hair salons. Clearly these types of jobs represent an economic niche commonly occupied by Southeast Asian refugees and other Asian immigrants—and these are the types of jobs the women reported were open to them.[39] The benefit to corporate industry was obvious, as CalWORKs recipients could be used temporarily for low wages, without benefits, and with the constant threat of dismissal. When I spoke about CalWORKs work requirements with Gloria Tan of the Asian Women's Resource Center, Tan stated, "it is going to be very difficult for women to find jobs. The main kinds of jobs that they will be able to get are [in] sewing factories, waitressing, cashiers (if they have some English skills), and janitorial jobs; especially the ones in the hotels are good because they are unionized."[40]

One does not have to look far to see the implications of welfare-to-work restructuring. Although we often think that the vast inequities of exploited labor center on export-processing zones in developing countries, immigrant women's work in the United States continues to fulfill the labor needs of the manufacturing, electronic assembly, and apparel industries, as well as care work. PRWORA conveniently dismantled any forms of economic security that might have saved women immigrants from settling for hyperexploitable working conditions. The most unfortunate of the resultant circumstances is that the women were led to hope for work of any kind as long as they earned something to assist them in supporting their families. This arrangement suited corporate desires for expendable labor while denying immigrants their humanity as employees, parents, or community members struggling to raise their children. Although immigrant labor is still much desired by capitalist interests (as seen, for instance, in U.S. President George Bush's 2006 push to create a migrant worker visa program with Mexico), immigrants as members of American society have been effectively excluded.

NOWHERE TO TURN

The sweeping changes and punitive regulations established through TANF time limits and welfare-to-work requirements affected all poor women, yet they were experienced differently by Asian immigrant and refugee women.

The profiles of Asian immigrant/refugee CalWORKs recipients presented in this chapter reveal the overlapping and complicated ways that welfare-to-work requirements and welfare time limits drove immigrant and refugee mothers into highly exploitative and destitute situations. Commonly, even immigrant and refugee women with more than two children, an educational level of high school or below, and fair to poor English skills, were forced to work to receive their cash assistance, relying on unfamiliar child care, until they reached their five-year limit, then were left with no safety net. Even though Congress extended eligibility to seven years (instead of five) for refugees, the change had very little impact for most Asian refugees, who no longer resided under refugee status.

The multiple layers of welfare implementation reveal a group of women who, because of their citizenship status, were already politically disenfranchised from the system that they depended on for survival. Already in a state of insecurity, Asian immigrant and refugee mothers were working to pull money together from multiple sources to provide for their families. With work requirements that proved significantly complicated and difficult given the women's cultural, language, and educational obstacles, CalWORKs' assistance was more of a burden than a relief for some of the women. The intrusion of county agencies into their lives through mandatory eligibility interviews, periodic appraisals, and work requirement updates, only exacerbated the level of fear, terror, and vulnerability that Asian immigrant and refugee women endured through immigration protocol.

The scattered and complicated services of CalWORKs, and of TANF generally, have fallen short of serving a heterogeneous clientele that Congress did not consider in mandating welfare-to-work as a way to move women from alleged dependency to so-called self sufficiency. Transitioning recipients into work means that counties must establish and implement structural supports to deal with issues like inadequate and expensive child care, inaccessible transportation, domestic abuse, mental disabilities, and drug-and-alcohol-related issues. Since Congress did not establish a meaningful plan for states and counties to develop these necessary infrastructural supports for women and families in poverty, punitive measures against women and families needing assistance became simply the means to move people off public assistance. As a result, our public welfare system degenerated into disparate county-by-county "participant flow" plans consisting of one bureaucratic stage after another, with the ultimate goal of moving "caseheads" into unsubsidized labor.

To further complicate the economic security of immigrant families, other public assistance changes further jeopardized the health and well-being of immigrants and their children. In the first six years of TANF, several large-scale research groups examined the impact of welfare reform on immigrant families. Intersecting issues involving health care, nutrition, and child care together resulted in less food security and a health crisis among children of immigrants. The chilling effects from the Proposition 187 movement, leaving immigrants afraid to use public assistance for themselves and their children, has only been exacerbated by the increasing fear and insecurity among immigrants since 9/11. Consequently, immigrant families are worse off, and often it is the children who bear the burden of welfare reform the most.

6

The Devaluation of Immigrant Families

> Welfare reform has created two classes of citizen children. One class lives in households with noncitizens and suffers the disadvantage of losing benefits and the reduced overall household resources that may result; a second class of citizen children lives in households with only citizens and suffers no comparable disadvantage. The emergence of these two classes of citizen children begs the question whether their differing eligibility for benefits should be viewed as an example of constitutionally acceptable discrimination against aliens or as a more problematic instance of unacceptable discrimination between similarly situated citizens.
>
> —Michael Fix and Wendy Zimmerman, "All under One Roof," The Urban Institute

Confusion over TANF and its welfare-to-work requirements, far more complicated than the regulations of AFDC, resulted in a 53 percent enrollment drop among families headed by legal permanent residents, and a 79 percent drop by refugee-headed families.[1] Immigrant-headed families have more commonly been mixed-citizen families. Nationally, 78 percent of children of immigrants were U.S.-born citizens in 1992;[2] thus, any social policy directed at noncitizen parents would ultimately impact American citizen children. Changes in Medicaid, food stamps, and SSI have also resulted in reduced income and fewer resources for families headed by immigrants (through cuts, as noted in previous chapters, based on recipients' noncitizenship status). Given that nearly one-fourth of all children of immigrants live in poor families, welfare cuts directed at immigrant parents would obviously impact numerous children, a large proportion of whom are citizen children.

The move to use citizenship status to remove people from public assistance reflects an overall devaluation of immigrant families and their children. Even though a significant proportion of noncitizens and their children remain eligible for these benefits, fear and confusion have prohibited them from utilizing resources they need and to which they are entitled. The confusing distinction between those immigrants qualified before reform and those still qualified after (with those no longer qualified perhaps still eligible for certain benefits), has resulted in a purposeful deterrence with detrimental consequences for families. Similarly, given that the number of noncitizens arriving has continued to increase since August 22, 1996, a greater proportion of immigrant communities is currently ineligible for federal means-tested benefits and is held to unreasonable sponsorship-deeming rules. By 2002, approximately one-third of the lawful permanent resident population was admitted after the transition date and thus remains barred from federal public assistance.

The TANF reauthorization in 2001–2002 offered a brief opportunity to address the festering immigrant issues apparent to community-based organizations and local social service caseworkers. Unfortunately, rather than being adjusted so as to better assist poor immigrant families, the policies have gone unchanged at best, and even became more stringent toward noncitizens, given the political climate of fears about national security and foreign threat.

The present chapter shifts focus to include discussion of the children of immigrant parents who used public assistance *before* PRWORA made eligibility distinctions based on citizenship status. Given that immigrant mothers and parents have subsequently been less able to make ends meet, how have Asian immigrant and refugee women and their children been affected by these compounding policy changes? How has the health and well-being of children of immigrant parents changed since welfare reform? How have the harsher welfare-to-work requirements made the day-to-day circumstances for mothers and children more vulnerable to the injuries of poverty?

The devaluation of immigrant families and children has manifested in multiple ways. In an inhospitable host country, immigrant parents had to struggle with child care and health care, with language and cultural conflict. With the simultaneous cut to federal food stamp benefits in 1996, increased levels of food insecurity and hunger prevailed. Even after learning of the deterioration of health among immigrant children, Congress did not agree to reverse the eligibility requirements based on citizenship status. Meanwhile, health and hunger issues among immigrant children have continued to increase, and are reaching crisis level. This is a public health issue that remains invisible to many politicians. The cost to immigrant children has already been unacceptable, and, given the durability of anti-immigrant politics, positive change remains unlikely.

CHILD CARE AND THE INVISIBLE IMMIGRANT CHILDREN

Although TANF mandated child-care subsidies through the Child Care and Development Block Grant to states, the U.S. Department of Health and Human Services estimated that child-care block grant funding provided enough money to serve only 12 percent of eligible low-income children.[3] With the implementation of CalWORKs, county administrators quickly saw that allocations for child-care services were insufficient. Immigrant women from the Equal Rights Advocates (ERA) study stated that even when funds were available to assist with child care, funds alone were not enough. The issue of cultural and language-appropriate child care was a top concern and an inhibitor of immigrant women's participation in CalWORKs programs and/or employment. In addition, many women found evening or early-morning jobs when child care was, generally, unavailable.

If a woman was able to prove to the Social Service Administration's satisfaction that appropriate and suitable child care was unavailable to her and her children, she could receive a waiver for work requirements. However, much discretion remained in the hands of county welfare agencies. The Immigration Task Force of Santa Clara County stressed the problem this raised for immigrant and refugee families, who faced particular difficulties in finding suitable and appropriate child care. Immigrant rights advocates argued that the comfort level of monolingual or limited English-speaking immigrant CalWORKs recipients needed to be taken into greater consideration in granting exemptions. A survey of 434 child-care centers in San Francisco, Alameda, Merced, Los Angeles, and San Diego counties found that 77 percent of child-care centers served at least some children who either did not speak English or spoke very little English. However, only 55 percent of the centers had staff who could speak Spanish; further, the shortage of linguistically appropriate staff was greatest for Asian children.[4] Immigrant advocates argued to make home daycare licensing requirements and applications available in multiple languages.

The issue of child care was a major problem for recent immigrant women. Gloria Tan of the Asian Women's Resource Center, in the San Francisco Bay Area, said the Center encouraged women to pursue child-care licensing to provide child care for other Asian immigrant and refugee families, who would benefit from linguistically and culturally compatible child-care services. According to federal TANF guidelines, states had the option to exempt a single parent caring for a child under twelve months of age if the parent could demonstrate an "unavailability of appropriate and affordable formal child-care arrangements."[5] According to Tan, "the ironic element of CalWORKs recipients obtaining child-care licenses to fulfill their work requirements, in order to watch other CalWORKs recipients' children so they can fulfill their work requirements, means that TANF guidelines are fine if recipients watch other people's children, just as long as a recipient is not staying at home to watch her own children."[6]

As of this writing, most California counties have not been able to find the necessary amount and form of child-care assistance to serve the majority of immigrant CalWORKs recipients. Although CalWORKs pays the cost of child care in child-care centers or for, home-based providers or relative care, the process involved has proven particularly difficult for immigrant women. Women whose relatives watch their children often cannot receive subsidies because their relatives do not have Social Security numbers. Similarly, smaller community daycare sites or in-home daycare providers sometimes cannot take government payments. Yet these forms of care are the most frequent options, and the stringency of regulations thus prevents immigrant women with particular language and cultural needs from accessing their first choice of child care. In some cases, once women have found employment, even if barely over (or at) minimum-wage, their child care subsidies have been discontinued. Under AFDC, recipients who left welfare for work received a guaranteed entitlement of one year of subsidized child care; that entitlement was eliminated under TANF.[7] Immigrant families, particularly single mothers, have been forced to place their children in substandard child-care situations so as to fulfill welfare-to-work requirements, when they might otherwise have been home taking care of the children themselves. Since subsidized child care is paid by the state, a state could be paying the mother TANF benefits to care for her own children, rather than funding someone else to do so. As Tan noted, child-care licensing was suggested as one of the best employment options to women using the Asian Women's Resource Center.

DOMESTIC VIOLENCE

Issues of domestic violence have also emerged more publicly since welfare reform. According to Deeana Jang, the director of the Asian Pacific American Health Forum in San Francisco, studies show that, at the time welfare reform was passed, nearly one-third to one-half of the AFDC population were currently or had been victims of domestic violence.[8] AFDC had been one means of economic support allowing women to leave abusive relationships, but TANF did away with that guarantee. Rather, TANF established the Family Violence Option (FVO), allowing states to exempt battered women from welfare requirements, through waivers. In some cases, waivers of work requirement activities would only be allowed when actual participation in particular programs or services could lead to mortal threat or loss of safety for the domestic violence victim. A 1997 report on women and welfare found that high percentages of domestic violence victims reported conflicts with their intimate partners about such welfare-related issues as child support (30 percent), visitation rights (23 percent), and child custody (36 percent). Domestic violence victims also reported interference from the batterers with education, training, and work (15 percent to 49 percent).[9]

Under PRWORA regulations, the determinations of domestic violence, as well as the TANF protocols relating to it, are handled on a state-by-state basis. County welfare departments must then develop standards, procedures, and protocols for determining good cause to waive program requirements for victims of domestic violence. The presence of battery or extreme cruelty is evaluated on a case-by-case basis, and deferment of mandatory work requirements is granted only so long as deemed necessary. Counties are also required to develop a knowledgeable, designated staff to steer domestic violence victims to appropriate counseling, protective services, or work training. In most cases, according to immigrant advocates, these staff have failed to meet the diversity of immigrant women's needs. Asian immigrant women living in densely populated Asian immigrant areas are more likely to receive assistance than are those living in primarily white homogeneous areas. Generally, community activists in the Bay Area, therefore, remain concerned about the dearth of resources for Asian immigrant women and their children who need to escape abuse.

Although domestic violence cuts across all economic, cultural, and ethnic lines, immigrant women's limited access to information, services, and legal protection makes them particularly vulnerable to spousal abuse, and less able to leave abusive partners.[10] The options for immigrant women experiencing domestic violence are complicated by their citizenship status. Issues of sponsorship-deeming that make women dependent on their sponsor spouses, eligibility requirements for domestic violence services, and the general fear of interfacing with the criminal justice system before becoming naturalized further jeopardize the women's ability to leave abusive relationships. Too little information remains a problem for women who must negotiate particular patriarchal community structures, conflicting cultural values, and institutions incapable of addressing their specific needs.

In a telephone interview, Mei-sing of the Asian Women's Shelter expressed great concern over the new rules and regulations for cash assistance:

> At least 85 to 90 percent of our clientele are really low income, or [have] no income. Under the previous system, immigrants were subject to sponsorship-deeming for three years, in terms of their eligibility for public benefits. Many women who enter the shelter have been sponsored by their spouse, and in many situations women come to the shelter because they are trapped in a situation with an abusive spouse who is their sponsor, and by leaving the situation they lose everything.[11]

As Mei-sing notes, when a woman can show proof that she is experiencing abuse or extreme cruelty, through a police report or a restraining order, she may apply for public assistance without having to work with her spouse–sponsor and local welfare agency.

However, in situations where the level of abuse is not recognized as grounds for separation from the marital sponsor, a woman's options are greatly limited. Janice Kitano of the Legal Aid Society explained that domestic violence cases could be complicated and not always clearly definable. In Kitano's immediate caseload at the time (shortly before TANF replaced AFDC) was a woman who was experiencing extreme difficulties with her spouse's family. According to Kitano:

> The woman who came in only spoke Hakka and that dialect is very uncommon, so she had her child talk for her. She had recently come over. And was

still under sponsorship-deeming. Her husband's family kicked her out . . . and she needed assistance, but didn't qualify, because of sponsorship-deeming. Well, it turns out that her child is eligible, regardless, if the sponsor is not cooperating, but she is not eligible for AFDC so she was only eligible for General Assistance.[12]

The 1990 Immigration Act was the first legislation by Congress to address the specific problems faced by battered immigrant women. The problem was, and is, especially acute for those immigrant women petitioned to the United States through marriage by their spouses, and still in the process of gaining legal permanent residency. The Violence against Women Act (VAWA) of 1994 allowed women immigrants who were victims of abuse to complete the process of gaining permanent status without requiring the participation of their abusers. (Under previous conditions, a woman was forced to rely on the relative who petitioned her regardless of the conditions she faced, and if the petitioner threatened to discontinue his sponsorship before she became a legal permanent resident, she could face deportation.) VAWA allowed women victims of abuse to file their own petitions or to request suspension of deportation if the INS had instituted removal action against them. However, if a VAWA applicant received federal means-tested aid, the fact could be used against her in regard to public-charge provisions of the 1996 immigration reform law.

As for immigrant women already legal permanent residents, Congress made some exceptions, under IIRIRA, for battered women, in regard to IIRIRA's stricter rules concerning the Affidavit of Support. Under the new exceptions, if a woman or her child had been battered or subjected to extreme cruelty in the United States by a spouse, parent, or member of the spouse or parent's family residing in the same household, she could be exempt from the sponsor-deeming requirements.[13] To demonstrate or prove the existence of battery or extreme cruelty, the immigrant woman had to obtain official documentation from someone in criminal justice or health care—a stringent requirement that has been an obstacle, given that only in the most extreme cases would immigrant women seek documentation from such officials. Further, the woman had to demonstrate a connection of the battery or extreme cruelty to the need for public assistance; to receive benefits, the woman escaping abuse would have to no longer be residing within the house of the abuser. However, as Deanna Jang of the Asian Pacific Islander American

Health Forum stated, "this is going to create a great hardship on women who need the benefits in order to move out of the abusive household."[14]

Under CalWORKs, immigrant recipients determined to be victims of domestic violence are referred to ancillary programs if their situation is deemed a barrier to employment. Although the Immigration Task Force recommended that these programs offer services that are culturally, linguistically, and community appropriate, few immigrant women receive information about domestic violence waivers. In fact, 16 percent of the Vietnamese women (30 percent of single Vietnamese women) from the ERA study in Santa Clara County reported having experienced domestic violence; of these women, only one in four reported receiving any information regarding domestic violence services or waivers. At the time that CalWORKs was implemented, all social service staff in CalWORKS received instructions regarding the domestic violence waiver, and participated in a single day of training on domestic violence. Given that social service intake workers are usually not specifically trained to identify, counsel, or assist victims of domestic violence, welfare advocates immediately questioned the competence of CalWORKs' appraisers to provide the relevant information and assistance to women who had experienced or were currently experiencing abuse at the time of their appraisals.

Although Congress established exceptions for battered immigrant women in both PRWORA and IIRIRA, the overall situation for battered immigrant women remains bleak. The previous system, AFDC, though in many ways inadequate, did provide a guaranteed safety net for all poor women. The termination of poor women's entitlement to benefits (the five-year lifetime limit), and other severe cuts to welfare programs have deprived poor women trying to escape domestic abuse of a very important resource.[15] When an immigrant or refugee woman's five years of eligibility have expired, she will have no other options to financially support herself or her children, and will likely be forced to return to the abusive situation. With too few resources tailored to language and cultural needs, immigrant women are less likely to seek help until an abusive situation becomes extreme. Complicated by issues of sponsorship-deeming, public-charge sanctions, and the denial of other benefits such as food stamps or SSI, immigrant women's noncitizenship status jeopardizes their well-being and right to safety. This marginalizes not only poor immigrant women but also their children, whose ties to their mothers leave them fewer avenues out of the abusive home.

HEALTH CARE

Prevalence of Health Issues among Asian Immigrant Women

Although congressional findings concluded that out-of-wedlock births were responsible for the perpetuation of poverty, nearly every state has, since the implementation of TANF, conducted large-scale survey research to find out the real barriers to self-sustaining employment. Although legislators did acknowledge that mental and physical health issues and domestic violence would require ancillary programs to support transition from welfare to work, the level and depth of these issues were greatly underestimated. The constructions of *irresponsibility, laziness,* and *learned dependency* had become such presumed givens that politicians were blind to the near impossibility of maintaining self-sustaining employment for a person (or her/his children) chronically ill or dealing with mental health issues. For Asian CalWORKs recipients, of whom approximately 90 percent were Southeast Asian refugees, health and mental health problems emerged as prominent obstacles to maintaining self-sustaining employment. Immigrant rights advocates raised alarming concerns about the relatively high levels of post-traumatic stress disorder (PTSD) within the Southeast Asian refugee population. Concerns were raised over the lack of specialized, trained, and culturally sensitive CalWORKs intake workers to identify PTSD and understand the cultural views toward mental illness within immigrant and refugee communities, where fear of stigmatization usually prevented individuals from seeking treatment or hindered their ability to negotiate situations. Women refugees in particular needed specialized services to address rape and abuse that in some cases occurred during war, escape, or refugee camps,[16] or upon entering the United States as conditional migrants.

If there was concern that a mental disability existed that would impair the ability of a recipient to obtain employment, a CalWORKs recipient would be referred to the county mental health department. Under CalWORKs, each county welfare department possessed individual welfare-to-work plans for recipients with mental or emotional disorders, based on the mental health department's evaluation. For immigrants and refugees who had already endured trauma, the forced examination in county mental health facilities became a potentially dehumanizing scrutiny possibly detrimental to their health and well-being. The battery of tests put immigrants through frustration and intense fear in order to receive a tiny subsistence for five years at most. The logic of this format hardly would lead from welfare to work. In fact, the result was that more immigrants chose to avoid assistance, losing not only indispensable cash assistance, but also much-needed health care.

The overall mental and physical health of Asian immigrant CalWORKs recipients presented diverse maladies, given the experiences of war and displacement. The Santa Clara Social Service Administration, the Immigration Task Force, and the Community Health Alliance of Santa Clara conducted a mass survey of CalWORKs recipients in 1998 to gain a better idea of what "specific services clients need to help them gain self-sufficiency."[17] Of 550 participants (70 percent of them women), 58 percent of the Vietnamese respondents stated that they needed medical care for themselves, 46 percent that they needed medical care for their child(ren). Of the Cambodian respondents, 96 percent stated that they needed medical care for themselves; 100 percent said they needed medical care for their children.[18] Under the previous system, AFDC recipients were automatically "categorically linked" to Medi-Cal (California's version of Medicaid), but the procedures and regulations for Medi-Cal recipients were particularly confusing for immigrant communities. With PRWORA, confusion over immigrant eligibility for Medicaid resulted in a high unmet need for medical care for Vietnamese and Cambodian recipients and their children.

With minimal information regarding immigrant and refugee health and mental health status, social service providers knew very little about the particular health issues of Asian immigrant and refugee CalWORKs recipients. The Asian Pacific American Legal Center of Southern California (APALC) found, through focus groups conducted with Asian/Pacific Islander CalWORKs recipients (two-thirds of whom were refugees from Southeast Asia), that a bit more than half named mental health problems, such as PTSD, as a barrier to maintaining employment. Physical health problems also made it difficult to find and hold jobs. One respondent was quoted, "I tried to apply for a job, but I had two operations. I'm not healthy, so no one will hire me. Whenever I apply, they ask me about my health, and when they find out, they refuse to hire me." Participants with multiple health problems had difficulty in fulfilling their welfare-to-work requirements. One respondent stated, "Once I was working and I got sick, so I stayed home, and they told me that was a violation of the rules, so they cut me off of welfare." This latter example illustrates the way TANF further disciplines recipients beyond regular work expectations. Labor laws require a person to be allowed a sick day, but CalWORKs caseworkers sanction recipients for violations on the basis of welfare-to-work requirements.

County by county, health issues emerged as potential barriers to obtaining employment and to fulfilling work requirements. In Alameda County, an extensive study of CalWORKs recipients conducted by the Public Health Institute found that 51.1 percent of Vietnamese respondents reported having physical health problems within the previous twelve months that interfered with their ability to look for work, do job training, or fulfill responsibilities and commitments.[19] The same study noted the prevalence of mental health problems: on a scale of symptom frequency, the study found, 42.6 percent of Vietnamese respondents reported having a few symptoms and 19.1 percent reported having many symptoms.[20] The researchers argued that the recipients meeting the narrower measure of mental health barriers (having many symptoms) probably would experience problems finding and maintaining work. Because Asian Pacific Americans remain largely understudied in terms of physical and mental health, the impact of TANF on impoverished Asian immigrants unexpectedly caused trauma for many who would be unable to fulfill the welfare-to-work requirements or find steady employment. The loss of SSI for immigrants with physical and mental health disabilities further jeopardized the well-being of Asian immigrant families facing other cut-offs and sanctions.

Structural Changes in Immigrant Access to Health Care

To further complicate health-care accessibility for immigrants, changes to Medicaid and in health-care delivery through Medi-Cal left immigrants in California completely baffled about how to receive health insurance and medical care. Under PRWORA, states were given the choice to continue providing Medicaid benefits to current immigrant residents, and deny access to Medicaid for new arrivals until these immigrants had worked forty quarters or became citizens. Under the previous system, those eligible for AFDC and SSI were automatically eligible for Medicaid, but PRWORA severed this automatic federal link, and, for the first time, a bar was established on immigrant access to Medicaid. Immigrants who arrived after August 22, 1996, were barred from Medicaid for five years, with exceptions for refugees and veterans. After the five years, these immigrants would be subject to "deeming," with the income and resources of the sponsor and sponsor's spouse counted as available to the immigrant in determining his or her eligibility for Medicaid.

PRWORA indeed made significant changes to immigrants' eligibility for medical assistance and imposed new rules for states. States could not provide Medicaid to undocumented immigrants, and a state wishing to provide medical assistance to undocumented immigrants, other than emergency medical assistance, had to pass a law affirmatively providing such services, *after* the federal welfare law's enactment, even if the state already had such a law. (Emergency medical assistance must be provided to all immigrants, regardless of status.) Under PRWORA, eligibility for Medicaid was limited to: citizens; lawful permanent residents with forty qualifying quarters of work; refugees and asylees; veterans, active duty military, their spouses and dependents; lawful permanent residents in the United States on or before August 22, 1996 (at state option); and SSI recipients (this categorical link to Medicaid was retained through the Balanced Budget Act of 1997).[21] Battered spouses and children might receive benefits if there was "substantial" connection between the abuse and the needed benefit, and the immigrant no longer resided with the batterer.

California decided to maintain the link between Medi-Cal and Cal-WORKs, as well as to maintain immigrant eligibility for Medi-Cal regardless of when the immigrant entered the country. However, because many fewer families have received assistance under CalWORKs than under AFDC (primarily due to new income requirements), recipients have had to find other pathways to receive Medi-Cal benefits. California has also instituted a program called Healthy Families,[22] a health-care program for children under nineteen who have family incomes up to 200 percent of the poverty level, and who are not eligible for Medi-Cal. Under Healthy Families, parents pay premiums and copayments, with strict federally imposed limits on rates and fees. Although immigrants remain eligible for the Healthy Families program, immigrants who have entered the country after August 22, 1996, are still first barred for five years and subject to deeming.

In addition to the drastic changes in the overall Medicaid program, the move toward managed-care programs systematically altered the relationship of the client to her medical providers. This has created another obstacle for immigrant women to receive necessary and adequate health care for themselves and their children.[23] Health-care services organized through managed-care programs involve a primary care provider, who monitors and authorizes all visits to other doctors and specialists, hospital stays, and the use of tests and other procedures. Many Asian immigrant women find that the doctors they trust are not affiliated with the managed-care system, and the women are apprehensive about seeing a new doctor who may lack cultural sensitivity.

Subsequent to the drastic changes in procedures and requirements caused by welfare reform, and parallel with the move toward managed-care health organization in the Medi-Cal system, community organizations reported that confusion and apprehension among immigrants was leading to a health crisis. The myriad changes in federal and state policies resulted in such confusion that not only were immigrants unclear about what they remained eligible for, but so were service providers. In many instances, immigrants began avoiding medical care altogether. Amid growing fear and mistrust, immigrants were no longer certain that seeing a doctor would not result in a threat to their residency or naturalization process.

Community workers encountered numerous issues regarding health and health care after the reform implementation, and documented the impact on the health and well-being of Asian immigrant women and their families.

According to a policy report put out by the Asian and Pacific Islander American Health Forum (APIAHF), women and children were the majority of Medi-Cal consumers, and Asian and Pacific Islander American (APIA) immigrants were disproportionately impacted by the changes in health-care delivery systems. Community service providers ranked adequate health care as a major problem for Asian immigrant and refugee women.

Gloria Tan said that Medi-Cal accessibility is a major issue the Center confronts with its primarily immigrant women clientele: "Women don't know how to go about applying for Medi-Cal, and the system seems so overwhelming, we have to really assist them, and explain that they should apply for Medi-Cal, because otherwise they don't receive any non-emergency medical care at all, . . . which a lot of them don't." The lack of relevant information in appropriate languages leaves many Asian immigrant women completely unaware of available medical programs, clinics, and health-education services. According to Luella Penserga, the project coordinator of San Francisco–based APIAHF, "the need for information to be disseminated in all different A/PI [Asian and Pacific Island] languages is essential."[24] At the time of our discussion, Penserga's organization was compiling health materials from organizations all over the state, translating these into Asian languages, and redisseminating them to address the immediate language barriers faced by most Asian immigrant and refugee women. Janet Co, of the APIAHF, stated that very little was understood about the A/PI community and its health needs, because there had been so little tracking, or follow-up by social service agencies as to how Asian immigrants were receiving and using services. Her findings were based on a massive needs assessment by community-based organizations directly serving Asian immigrant communities on health-care issues.

Penserga stressed concern over the transitioning of Asian immigrant women to managed-care programs lacking compatible language facility or sufficiently knowledgeable service providers to explain procedures and process: "Preliminary information already indicates that, under Medi-Cal managed care, APIA beneficiaries have the highest default rate in choosing a plan."[25] These clients are confused about choosing a plan, and many want to continue with their traditional family doctor, and so are being reassigned to primary care providers without knowing who these providers are or where to go for care.

The primary care provider creates another level of discomfort and a potential barrier for Asian immigrant women. For example, managed-care plans require members to seek a referral from their (problematic) primary care providers before a visit to a gynecologist may be arranged.[26] Further, there is no guarantee that an assigned gynecologist will be a culturally preferred woman, or will be able to communicate with the client in her own language.

For Asian immigrants and refugee women struggling to nourish their families and to balance child care with minimum wage jobs (whether part-time or full-time), nonemergency health care is frequently the first need sacrificed. The leading cause of death for Asian immigrant and refugee women between the ages of twenty-five and forty-five is cancer. However, education efforts by social service providers with Asian immigrant women regarding cancer screenings, mammograms, breast self-examination, and pap smears remain minimal, even though such tests would begin to address the high rates of breast, cervical, and ovarian cancer among these women. In a study conducted by the Vietnamese Community Health Promotion Project, 45 percent of Chinese and 51 percent of Vietnamese women had never received a pap smear; 47 percent of Vietnamese women had never had a breast examination.[27] The relatively high incidence of cervical cancer in this group corresponds, too, with the high rate of Asian Pacific Islander women in America who have not received a pap smear.[28]

Reproductive health remains a critical issue for Asian immigrant and refugee women. Approximately 51 percent of Asian Pacific Islander women in the United States are of reproductive age (fifteen to forty-four years old).[29]

In California, a high percentage of births to Laotian and Cambodian women were not attended by a physician, midwife, or nurse assistant; Laotian women were least likely (34.7 percent) to receive prenatal care in their first trimester.[30] Low birth weights and high rates of infant mortality among Asian immigrant women's babies attest to the systemic need for health care in the clients' primary language and for cultural sensitivity to women needing reproductive care. Managed-care programs could enhance plans for Asian immigrant and refugee women by considering: language capabilities of the primary care physician, community accessibility to health care, and gender/ethnic compatibility.

Although California decided to maintain medical eligibility for immigrant recipients, the political discourse surrounding Proposition 187 successfully developed a construction of immigrants as overusing health-care services. This hostile climate instilled major confusion, fear, and apprehension for immigrant women needing health care. A year after the president signed PRWORA into law, California's then-governor, Pete Wilson, aggressively pressed to further deny undocumented women access to prenatal care. Since 1988, California's Medi-Cal program had provided state funds for checkups and other prenatal aid for pregnant women with family incomes up to 200 percent of the federal poverty level, without regard to immigration status; Wilson planned to impose a ban on prenatal care for undocumented pregnant women by January 1, 1998. Although at least three court rulings blocked Wilson's planned implementation of the ban, the attempt reflected the racialized hostility toward immigrant women as reproducers—coexisting with a willingness to benefit from their labor. The movement, central to immigration and welfare reform, to discourage third-world immigrant women's access to health care terrorized many and left them fearful of accessing health care at all. Rules established by IIRIRA that hospitals and health-care services needed to report the immigration status of clients left many undocumented immigrants (as well as legal permanent residents who did not understand these rules) fearful of deportation should they use public health facilities. Community organizations reported that undocumented immigrants were avoiding public health-care services even in emergency situations.

Crisis in Health Care for Children of Immigrant Parents

Speakers at the 1997 immigrant health symposium cosponsored by the New York Academy of Medicine and the New York Task Force on Immigrant Health reported considerable misinformation in immigrant communities;[31]

according to panelists, legal permanent immigrants feared that using public health services would make reunification with family still overseas more difficult.[32] Upon reentry to the United States, they feared, they could be deemed a public charge, refused entry, and deported immediately. Yet if immigrants turn away from preventive care, the estimated long-term costs will extend far beyond immigrant communities. From a public health standpoint, maintaining the health of immigrants protects the health of all U.S. residents. However, not only are many immigrants afraid to use public health services, but, as already discussed, many indigent immigrant populations have been disqualified from preventive services critical to their future health.[33]

As a result of the drastic decline in health services, immigrant advocates argue, the health status of children in immigrant families has reached crisis proportions. Nationally, 22 percent of children of immigrants are uninsured, more than twice the rate for children of citizens.[34] Although California has continued to provide state health insurance for immigrants regardless of when they entered the country, the uninsured rate of immigrants in that state remains at the national level. This is probably due to the chilling effects of unclear eligibility and of sponsorship-deeming rules that have prevented immigrants from using public services more generally. High uninsured rates accompany poor access to health care. Nationally, 14 percent of children of immigrants lack a usual source of health care, and 9 percent are in only fair or poor health.[35] The five-year bar to Medicaid has had reverberating consequences, as immigrants believe they are ineligible for public health care altogether, even if states continue to consider them eligible. Some believed that they would be deported if they sought assistance.[36]

Thus, too many children in immigrant families were not getting the health care they needed. In spite of a strengthening economy, the already fragile health status of children in immigrant families significantly declined following welfare reform, as immigrants' use of public health insurance diminished and medical care followed suit. From the perspective of equal rights, the exclusions to public health insurance mandated for noncitizens further isolated immigrants and their children from fair access to health care. Such an attack on health care for immigrants not only went against good public health logic, but also further weakened immigrant families. The long-term effects of poor health care continue to manifest as these children grow into adulthood. The "work first" mantra of TANF has proven illogical, when health resources are denied to those attempting to raise healthy workers.

RISE IN HUNGER AND THE LOSS OF FOOD STAMPS[37]

The struggles that immigrants faced with TANF were exacerbated by the cut to food stamps, resulting in less household economic support for basic necessities, on September 1, 1997, when most legal immigrants were terminated from federal food stamp benefits, as mandated through PRWORA. Between 1994 and 1998, 1.2 million noncitizens were dropped from food stamps, a decline in noncitizen enrollment of more than 80 percent. During the same period there was a decline of one million U.S. citizen children of lawfully present immigrant parents from the food stamp program; this was a 75 percent drop of those citizen children who remained eligible.[38] The complicated nature of welfare-to-work requirements compounded the general loss of food stamps and SSI. Among legal immigrant recipients, between 1994 and 1999, TANF use declined by 60 percent, food stamps by 48 percent, SSI by 32 percent, and Medicaid by 15 percent. For refugees (anyone who had entered under refugee status as of 1980, regardless of current immigration status), declines were at 78 percent for TANF, 53 percent for food stamps, 36 percent for Medicaid.[39] The drastic drops of immigrant participation in public benefits (even among immigrants who remained eligible) reflects the success—or, as it is often called, chilling effect—of welfare reform in creating a state of paralysis among eligible immigrants and their children.

The convergence of multiple policy changes resulted in the documented rise in food insecurity[40] and hunger within poor immigrant households. Since the passing of PRWORA, several large-scale research groups have examined the well-being of immigrant families directly impacted by PRWORA. The first, the California Food Security Monitoring Project,[41] looked specifically at the impact of the cut to food stamps, in interviews from November 1997 to March 1998 in San Francisco and Los Angeles, California. In November, 40 percent of the impacted group experienced moderate or severe hunger, compared to 33 percent of the control group. By March, 50 percent of the impacted households experienced moderate or severe hunger, compared to 38 percent of the nonimpacted group. In San Francisco, 33 percent of the impacted households with children were experiencing moderate or severe hunger; persons in these households were 35 percent more likely to experience this level of hunger than were those living in nonimpacted households. The study concluded that the alarmingly high rates of food insecurity and hunger among legal permanent residents demonstrated that the mandated immigrant food stamp cuts were generating hunger and harming children and adults alike.[42]

In March 2001, the report "Hardship among Children of Immigrants," based on a nationally representative sample from the 1999 National Survey of America's Families, documented the above-average hardship among children of immigrant parents. Nationwide, 37 percent of all children of immigrants lived in families that worried about or encountered difficulties affording food, compared with 27 percent of children of nonimmigrants.[43] In March 2002, the report "How Are Immigrants Faring after Welfare Reform?" presented findings from an extensive survey of immigrants in Los Angeles and New York, made from 1999 to 2000. The study found that, in Los Angeles and in New York, 38 percent of all immigrant families with children experienced food insecurity, and that about 12 percent of all immigrant households with children experienced moderate hunger. In Los Angeles the rate of food insecurity was twice as high among families having limited English proficiency than among English-proficient families (40 percent versus 21 percent). Among single-parent immigrant families in New York, 50 percent were food insecure; in Los Angeles, 45 percent were food insecure.[44]

The findings from these large-scale reports paint a harrowing picture of the effects of PRWORA on immigrant households. In places such as the Bay Area, the amounts provided by CalWORKs assistance did not, and still do not, cover the regionally high cost of living, and families struggled (and struggle) with insufficient benefits for housing, food, clothing, and other daily expenses. In addition to uncovering the aggregate data that revealed the increased levels of hunger and food insecurity, community organizations and immigrant advocates worked to expose the specific circumstances women faced as they were forced to rely more on food banks to nourish their children. The Equal Rights Advocates (ERA) study of Vietnamese and Mexican immigrant women on CalWORKs presented profiles of women trying to make ends meet with less monthly cash than before. The following profile reflects the harsh circumstances immigrant women faced when they could not afford the food to feed their children.

> Born in Vietnam, Elizabeth made her way to the [United States] through the Amerasian Homecoming Act of 1988. In her late 20s, Elizabeth had never received formal education or job training. She was living with her two children with five friends in a crowded apartment. Yet her portion of the rent

consumed over half of her income. When the rent increased and her food stamps and cash assistance greatly decreased, she was forced to forego her family's nutritional needs to pay for her children's school clothes. Elizabeth stated, "I [now] buy less good food and look for free food at the local church."[45]

As these situations surfaced, newspapers began to print the stories. A series titled "Making Welfare Work" in the *San Jose Mercury News* followed the lives of six families on welfare for eight months.[46] One family, the Huynhs, exemplified the plight of immigrants and refugees unable to obtain enough food. The Huynhs were from Vietnam. The parents had five children, ages nine to fourteen; one child was learning-disabled due to brain damage from a high fever. The family had been in the United States for only eleven months, so they were eligible for benefits as refugees. The husband, Huynh Hoang Hai, suffered from chest pains; his wife, Lam Thi Trinh, suffered from arthritis. They were renting a two-bedroom apartment for which the monthly rent was four dollars more than their monthly benefits check. The newspaper reported, two months into the series, that the Huynhs were not doing well. With little English, the husband was unable to find employment and could not afford enough food to nourish them all. Hai and Trinh skimped on meals so their children might have more food. The neighbors, worried that the children were not getting enough to eat, tried to help out with food and clothing. Three months later, the newspaper reported on the new hope that had buoyed the Huynh family:

> Hai worries constantly about how to pay rent and feed their five children. . . . One day, the family of seven shared a small bowl of rice topped with tofu, lotus root and soy sauce. Trinh and Hai ate only rice, giving the protein to the children.
>
> Recently things began to look up. Second Harvest delivered three boxes of food, and the Huynhs will be able to pick up fresh fruits and vegetables once a month from another program.[47]

The need to rely on food banks and food distribution programs reflected the dire circumstances imposed by the loss of benefits, benefits that could realistically assist a family as the adults seek tools for more gainful employment. In an *Asian Week* article, the increasingly common need for food banks was conveyed by the comment of a recent immigrant from China who had run out of options.

> Clasping a notice from the Department of Human Services terminating her food stamp benefits, Ling Chen gently pushed her son's stroller as she lined

up for free food being distributed at Cameron House in Chinatown. Ling
Chen, a 32-year-old immigrant woman from China, has two children, ages 2
and 5. Ms. Chen and her husband are currently unemployed, and both remain
ineligible for naturalization for another 2 years. They used to receive $200 in
food stamps, until September 1, 1997, when that amount was cut in half. "It's
so hard because of the children," said Chen, speaking through an interpreter.
"My husband and I don't mind, but what can you say to your children when
they ask for food?"[48]

Although food banks were historically considered the very last resort to
prevent starvation, since PRWORA they have become a primary governmental means to keep immigrants and their families from starvation. However, parallel with the documentation of a rise in hunger and food insecurity
among immigrants came the observation that food banks were underuti-
lized. County social service offices and community organizations realized
that acquiring free provisions from food banks was not so simple a task for
immigrants. A volunteer from Bread, Jobs, and Justice expressed, at a food
distribution site (Food Pantry) in San Jose, the complicated, confusing, and
intimidating matrix a person must go through to receive free food:

> People have to show residency and may be at the wrong food bank location.
> The location requirements need to be made more clear. Some people can't
> show their residency, or have to experience more humiliating procedures when
> they come to pick up food. Ethnic food needs to be made available. There is
> an underutilization by Asian immigrants at the food banks, possibly because
> the food is incompatible, or the food bank is not close enough to their homes.
> Also, transportation is a big problem for many who have a hard time getting
> around.[49]

To better understand why immigrants were not using food banks, the Santa
Clara County Social Services Food Safety Net Project conducted a telephone survey of 376 randomly selected immigrants recently cut from food
stamps. The main barriers cited were: lack of awareness about the existence
of the food banks; the location; the language; and the hours of the day that
the food banks were open. More than half of the immigrant families needing food did not have their own vehicle and relied on other means of transportation; thus, proximity to the distribution sites was critical.

Almost half of the participants in the study indicated that they did not
have enough food. The study reported that the primary ways that families
made up for their food stamp loss were to work more hours, to purchase less
food, or to rely on relatives. The most common types of food needed by the

immigrant respondents included meat, rice, milk, vegetables, and fish, which are all foods unavailable through the food banks. Similarly, as immigrants had to increase their work hours or take on more part-time employment, they were unable to get to the food distribution sites during the sites' hours of operation. Finally, even though the need for language and culturally appropriate outreach and information had been understood, and several interpreters hired, this was still insufficient for the language needs of a vastly diverse group of immigrants with varying literacy levels.

The mission of the USDA states that the "Food Stamp Program represents the pledge that hunger will not be tolerated in America. It is the tangible expression of the principle that everyone has a right to food for themselves and their families."[50] Congress originally intended the program to "safeguard the health and well-being of the Nation's population by raising levels of nutrition among low-income households."[51] Nevertheless, the 1996 reform laws determined that hunger could be tolerated among families headed by immigrant parents. Several studies have documented that low-income parents need the increased food-buying power afforded by food stamps so as to provide adequate nutrition in the home. It is generally recognized that the food stamp program is the nation's most important and effective nutrition safety-net program. The Tufts University Center on Hunger and Poverty, in a 1995 study, showed that poor children in families receiving food stamps were significantly better nourished than poor children in families that did not receive food stamps.[52] Children receiving inadequate nutrition had greater health problems, lower academic performance, and heightened anxiety and stress. As of this writing, some food stamp cuts have been restored, but immigrants remain unaware of their eligibility or too frightened to take advantage of it.

ADDRESSING IMMIGRANT NEEDS IN THE REAUTHORIZATION OF TANF

By September 30, 2002, TANF was up for reauthorization. Congress needed to decide whether to continue TANF as it was, modify it, or end it. Along with welfare rights and feminist activists, community-based organizations and immigrant advocates took the opportunity to expose the problems and hardships caused by TANF. In the hope of altering TANF to actually address issues of poverty and family welfare within Asian immigrant households, several prominent organizations participated in a campaign to pressure Congress to address issues of food insecurity, hunger, and lack of health care. The National Asian Pacific American Legal Consortium and the Southeast Asia Resource Action Center, both based in Washington, D.C., were prominent in promoting and supporting pro-immigrant proposals in the reauthorization, in a move to restore lost benefits.

At the most fundamental level, immigrant advocates argued for restoring equal access to public benefits for legal permanent residents. The multilayered restrictions differently affecting immigrants arriving before August 22, 1996, than those arriving afterward had, as already described, decimated benefit use by all immigrants, leading to poorer health and greater hunger and malnutrition. Advocates argued that not only was this bad for immigrants and their children, but it posed risks for the larger public as well. And the advocates pointed out that, given that immigrants were taxpayers and helped pay for the costs of education, roads, national defense, and public benefits, they should be allowed to receive the services they in fact helped pay for.[53]

Second, policy analysts recommended limiting sponsorship-deeming responsibility from the "lifetime" mandated through IIRIRA to more reasonable expectations. The 1996 sponsorship-deeming rules made it impossible for post-1996 immigrants to receive any means-based assistance, and caused undue hardship on sponsoring families—with detrimental economic effects for the broader immigrant community, and threatening family reunification and stability.

A third major area of pressure in the reauthorization debate was to allow English as a Second Language (ESL) instruction and other language acquisition activities to be counted as separate work activities earning credit for welfare-to-work requirements. Without more opportunities and better support for English language courses, immigrants would remain in economically vulnerable employment sectors. Language was a primary advocacy point for immigrants within the reauthorization debate.

To address the decline in health status among immigrants and their children, the bipartisan set of bills *Healthy Solutions for America's Hardworking Families 2001* (S. 583, HR 2142) included three pieces of legislation. These acts would have: reestablished eligibility for all immigrant children to federally funded health care; restored food stamps to immigrants; and allowed noncitizen domestic violence victims to obtain the same services available to other Americans. Unfortunately, the bills did not pass. And Congress failed to pass TANF reauthorization legislation by the September 2002 deadline. Stymied, and unable to agree on the scope and degree of alterations, Congress passed a series of shorter reauthorization extensions. After a series of numerous short-term extensions, Congress enacted the Deficit Reduction Act in 2006 that formally reauthorized TANF. Efforts by immigrant rights organizations to expose the hardships on immigrant families dwindled after the brief window of opportunity in 2001.

Although undeniable evidence demonstrated that immigrant families, immigrant children, and citizen children of immigrants have suffered tremendously under PRWORA and IIRIRA legislation, concern by policy makers for the well-being of immigrants appears to have diminished. Subsequent House and Senate reauthorization proposals have been indifferent to the obstacles that welfare rights advocates have been citing since PRWORA was implemented. Rather, stricter work requirements, longer hours of employment for women with children under the age of six, clearer sanctioning guidelines, and a host of marriage and fatherhood projects with hefty budget allocations have reigned. In reauthorization attempts in 2003, neither Senate nor House bills lifted restrictions on legal immigrants' eligibility for TANF, health care, and other benefits. In the post-9/11 climate of "antiterror" policy and its enforcement, concern for restoration of immigrant rights has given way to complacency over continued erosion of these rights. To date, poor immigrants remain fearful of using public services, for fear that any exposure to government agencies leads to tighter surveillance and suspicion. Thus, although immigrants have fallen from welfare assistance, they have not moved out of poverty. With greater poverty, poorer health, and fewer opportunities for immigrants' children, immigrant communities must continue to struggle with unequal access to the resources they support as residents.

SURVIVING ON LESS

The racial gendered politics permeating the anti-immigrant movement in California that led to the passing of Proposition 187 constructed immigrant women and children as an invasive threat to the well-being of U.S.-born Americans and their children. The stories that supposedly overgenerous welfare programs and free medical care lured poor women to the nation were based on racialized assumptions of who belongs and who does not. The presence of brown women as migrant workers—cleaning the homes, businesses, and places of leisure for affluent Americans, or filling electronic factories around the clock to build the products elevating the nation's wealth, or caring for the children and elderly of middle-class Americans—this presence was off the radar during the crisis that led to these women's exclusion from welfare. The presence of these women to serve labor needs at exploitive wages remained unchallenged; rather, it was the fact that these women dared to have children, raise families, and establish communities that formed the core of nativist hostility. The children of these women were also doomed to outsider status, as their citizenship status was deemed less legitimate than it was by the Constitution.

In both PRWORA and IIRIRA, Congress ignored the fact that most women receiving public assistance were already engaged in some form of labor, including the care of their own children. Immigrant women had participated in the labor force throughout U.S. history, often in exploitative conditions and work sites as a result of their immigration, racial, and educational status. Advocates have raised many concerns about unfair labor practices for workfare workers, about the absence of sustainable wages for their families, about their loss of health-care benefits, and about the repercussions of five-year eligibility limits. Subjected to highly exploitative working conditions, Asian immigrant and refugee women have been placed at greater risk for state-sanctioned abuse and harassment, given that probably few extremely exploitative employers adequately inform their employees of workers' rights, sexual harassment policies, or wage laws. In the name of "work not welfare," these women, many already working in multiple capacities, are left to fend for themselves.

With cash assistance and health care for needy families more complicated and more difficult to obtain, Asian immigrant and refugee women scrambled to support their families, and found the new system required too much work for a tiny payment. Imposed punitive measures directed at all poor women injured the stability and security of poor Asian immigrant and refugee families, as their means for security and self-sufficiency were further stripped away. Likewise, the implementation of welfare-to-work programs showed complete disregard of the need for culturally sensitive services. The emphasis on "assimilability" that grounded the anti-immigrant resentment of "foreigners receiving public benefits" allowed this negligence over the need for linguistic and culturally appropriate programs. Rather, the rubric of *personal responsibility* assumed full cultural and linguistic assimilation as requisite for survival.

The systematic removal from public support of immigrant women and their children has been based on, and has rendered, them as less valued guests within the nation. Although one can point to a persistent societal devaluation of women and families across the board, immigrants have been differentiated through the recent social policies as unentitled due to citizenship status. The blade of *citizenship* presents itself at every turn since the trio of 1996 policies enacted state differentiation of eligibility for public assistance. With the further loss of due process, and increased surveillance, immigrants and their children have suffered a tremendous erosion of rights and entitlements. Citizen children of immigrant parents pay dearly for their parents' devalued citizenship status. The brief possibility of humane reform for immigrants has waned in the shadows of increasing threat and suspicion of "foreigners." The first attempts at reauthorization in the garish light of 9/11 have left poor immigrants and their children even more disenfranchised from state responsibility.

Conclusion
The Continuing Significance of Racialized Citizenship

It feels like I'm sitting in a pot of boiling water every day. I'm sorry I had to bring you to this country and then leave you behind.

—Chia Yang, October 1997

I consider myself an honest American who responds to the call for help from a wounded nation. I am someone who will halt my private life to answer the silent plea from those who have no voice.

I cannot stand by passively watching an inequity manifest itself in the future of a people whose only hope is the hopeless despair offered by a disintegrating Constitution.

I must once again stand forward and bear arms for my country, not with the conventional weapons of war, but with words and civil action.

Therefore, I am a Minuteman instantly ready to protect that which I hold dear. On this basis I pledge my life, my liberty, and my sacred honor. To do any less is treason.

—Jim Gilchrist, founder of the Minuteman Project,
"Why Am I a Minuteman?"

When I think back to the words left behind by Chia Yang, I remain so perplexed at how government officials can boast that "welfare reform was a great success." For some, suicide was seen as the only way out. Millions of others continue to experience higher levels of poverty and hunger; and their children now have less parental supervision, contact, and nurturing because either their mothers are struggling to fulfill thirty hours of work requirements, or they are engaged in long hours of exploitative labor to make ends meet. The boiling pot that Yang described reflects the social, political, and economic conditions shaped by the hostile anti-immigrant movement she had to negotiate as a political refugee in poor health. Fear of having to watch her children starve and suffer, as she had once before, was more than she could bear. I believe the message she left behind is for us to realize how potent social policies are in directly affecting people's lives. The overwhelming public sentiment that supported the immigrant and welfare reform movements was based upon racialized constructions that demonized poor women, immigrants, and their children. Almost a decade later, we see an even more fervent galvanization of anti-immigrant politics. One decade after the devastating wave of 1996 anti-immigrant policies, the "enemy immigrant" continues to occupy contemporary nativist constructions of national threat and inassimilability.

In the immediate aftermath of PRWORA, with the rash of suicides by distraught immigrants and corresponding community mobilization efforts, some restorations to life-threatening cuts to immigrants were achieved. Several prominent political leaders publicly decried the wrongful cuts to disabled and elderly immigrants, recognizing that Congress had gone too far. Whether appealing to new voting constituencies (as discussed in chapter 4), or negotiating the continuing need for immigrant labor, this very short stint of regret disintegrated into an even sharper downturn for immigrant rights with September 11, 2001. Jacqui Alexander's conceptualization of the *citizen patriot* and the *civilian soldier* accurately characterizes the heightened levels of distrust and suspicion that have come to occupy immigration politics in the new millennium. The scapegoating of immigrants in the 1990s established and codified into law the precedent of differentiating access to public services by citizenship status. In addition, the association of immigrants with criminality and terrorism resulted in the loss of due process and in mandatory rules for deportation, which, with more draconian laws like the USA Patriot Act, have led to a *politics of removal* through heightened enforcement and surveillance.

The passing of PRWORA was embedded in a public preoccupation with "welfare mothers" as a threat to family values, and in the increasing visibility of third world immigrant families challenging the imaginary cultural homogeneity of an idealized American nation. Through this book I have shown how the *foreigner* racialization of Asian immigrants reinforced an ignited politics of citizenship that operated at multiple and hierarchical levels. In the context of increasing human displacement resulting from global economic restructuring and war, a new nativism has reshaped a contemporary racial politics in which the new civilian soldier heeds a mission to protect his [sic] nation from undeserving foreigners who threaten the stability of the country by their use of public resources. As in earlier times of nation-building, this concern over a changing American cultural citizenship focused attention on women's reproduction and the reproductive costs of "undeserving" families. Previously thought of as future citizens, immigrants and their families used to be on a par with citizens, as members of the country, members whose families might face economic hardship just as might any American family, and who might then need government assistance. Although the resentment over welfare in general involved a multilayered attack on both citizens and noncitizens, the differentiation by citizenship status clearly demarcated noncitizens and their children as even less entitled to receive enough food, adequate medical care, and cash assistance for other necessities. It is true that too many citizens also face these conditions, and it is probable that the current welfare system has treated inhumanely those deemed "the hard to serve" and seen as individually responsible for the persistence of their poverty. However, the use of citizenship status as a category to instantaneously exclude hundreds of thousands of participants has allowed racial bias to be expressed and legitimized through a seemingly neutral category.

In what sociologist Avery Gordon refers to as "complex personhood," the testimonies of poor Asian immigrant and refugee women confronting the general abandonment of immigrant support have revealed the converging layers of history and politics that encapsulated some forms of violence sanctioned by the state. To make sense of this new nativist immigration control in dialogue with histories of exclusion, Gordon's construction of *haunting* as a social analysis of state domination lends a valuable language for articulating the perplexing complexities that emerge when one centers on the depth of distress of poor Asian immigrant and refugee women negotiating welfare reform.[1] As in the testimony left by Chia Yang, the traumas of war, economic dislocation, sexual terror, and gender-based violence are entities that inhabit the complex personhood of Asian immigrant and refugee women as they face state agents with little or no understanding of existing levels of panic and cultural unfamiliarity.

The tragic levels of despair inflicted on poor, disabled, and elderly immigrant women posed a challenge to human rights principles that questioned the morality of legislators who favored PRWORA. Primary tenets in the

Declaration of Human Rights assert that all people have the right to life, dignity, and security regardless of citizenship status. Yet the implementation of PRWORA's immigrant provisions immediately cut life-sustaining benefits to nearly five hundred thousand immigrants who had received those benefits as recognition that they could not work because of age, disability, or blindness. The politics of their inassimilability suddenly positioned them outside the borders of American entitlement, and their noncitizenship status was used to encode their ineligibility. The testimonies of despair and betrayal by Southeast Asian refugees have reflected the cruelty and trauma that social policy wreaked on a completely vulnerable group of noncitizens.

This study has shown the ways that immigrants have responded to the loss of benefits. Out of despair, a few chose to end their lives, but the vast majority have rushed for citizenship through a naturalization process that, however, left many incapable of naturalizing. Immigrant mothers with young children have predominantly dropped from TANF, since the only federal program designed to support poor families with children became too difficult and inaccessible for immigrant parents. In general, affected immigrant families have suffered from the drastic cut in food stamps, and now experience higher levels than before of food insecurity and poor nutrition. The same disaster has occurred in their levels of health care.

However, the discrimination by citizenship status in determining benefits was an effective wake-up call, and thousands of immigrants successfully naturalized. Despite the extreme manner in which anti-immigrant politics has been actualized through federal and state policies, immigrants have continued to naturalize at record levels. One may hope that in the future this phenomenon will have a more concrete impact in balancing out the anti-immigrant politics that continues to dominate the national agenda. With more immigrants achieving political enfranchisement, legislators will be less likely to appease extreme anti-immigrant nativist groups and their agendas to further marginalize immigrants from social and economic protections.

The multiple constituencies affected by the 1996 policies reveal a complex notion of entitlement that was shaped by the politics of both social citizenship and legal citizenship. The drive to dismantle AFDC was led by a war on the poor that utilized existing racist and gendered constructions of *welfare queens* and *pathological cycles of dependency, irresponsibility,* and *laziness,* constructions that charged poor women, especially poor women of color, with not fulfilling their citizenship responsibilities. With these assumptions, the punitive measures established through welfare-to-work programs devalued the women's constitutional rights to privacy and reproduction, thus devaluing their citizenship status. The movement to exclude noncitizens targeted immigrants of color, as it was their presumed racial difference and cultural inassimilability that drove the arguments to deny them public assistance even though they contributed to the national economy. Given the varied constituencies affected by such a comprehensive dismantling, the tendency to differentiate the welfare rights movement from the immigrant rights movement has had lasting consequences. The immediate immigrant cuts from SSI and food stamps led to a dire situation that required immediate mobilization and public awareness long before TANF was fully implemented. However, the tendency to view the different constituencies as involving separate issues underestimated the groups' commonalities, as well as the potential force that could be galvanized to reframe the welfare agenda as a right for those who face poverty in a hyperglobalized economy. With this consideration in mind, it is clear that a new citizenship politics must restore rights and belonging to all residents within the nation-state, and to reassert the responsibilities of the state to adjudicate fairly among all inhabitants, without prejudice or malice.

WELFARE VICTIMS, WELFARE MOTHERS, AND CITIZENSHIP RESPONSIBILITY

The convergence of welfare reform and immigration control revealed a disconnected discourse between wronged immigrants and the racial-gendered politics of motherhood. The "end of welfare" was characterized by the loss of AFDC and the implementation of TANF, along with the devolution of welfare that left immigrants vulnerable to local politics and newly established limitations for American citizens. The vital mobilization efforts among immigrant communities that exposed the new laws' injustices toward the elderly, disabled, and veterans did not gain the same level of attention for immigrant women as mothers and workers generally. Modes of sympathy that made Asian immigrant and refugee women visible operated, in many respects, around the construction of the *victim*. First victims of economic dislocation or war, and then victims of social policy, the elderly, disabled, and veteran immigrants became a focus of the welfare immigrant rights movement that resulted in substantial restorations from the original cuts. However, able-bodied adult mothers who had to negotiate the same political and economic system did not acquire the same broad level of community attention.

The issues that poor Asian immigrants and refugees faced as mothers with inaccessible and demeaning welfare-to-work activities, issues that resulted in these women's higher sanctioning rate, proved the most challenging for a broad-based immigrant mobilization effort. The ending of welfare and the racialized social constructions permeating the debates around unemployment and so-called overdependency and fraud proved more complex as the scope of involvement was broadened. The counterintuitiveness that embodied Asian immigrant and refugee women as welfare subjects challenged not only limited models of state politics, but also dominant discussions around the racial politics and feminization of poverty. Regardless of the multifaceted involvement and presence of Asian immigrant and refugee women within these immigrant communities, gender as a mode of oppression and exclusion was not named directly. Looking at two different levels of welfare policy reform that involved distinct and different communities of women, the question becomes: how do we incorporate the women's multiple levels of belonging, citizenship, and exclusion? Gwendolyn Mink has pointed to the missing feminist voices, voices that failed to effectively challenge Congress and President Clinton in their misinformed work-not-welfare campaign.[2] The absence of gender-conscious advocacy on the part of immigrant rights voices within post–welfare reform efforts left a particular group of Asian immigrant and refugee women invisible and unable to articulate why welfare-to-work was indeed state-sanctioned violence against women.

The reason for the disconnect between "victims" of SSI and food-stamp cuts and the broad-based mobilization efforts for AFDC/TANF recipients derives from a complicated notion of gendered responsibilities of motherhood, as well as from the resounding racialized arguments that poor mothers of color were irresponsible and pathological. Thus, the relatively fewer welfare rights advocates remained detached from the immigrant rights campaigns, and the immigrant rights campaigns saw little integration of the campaigns against the loss of AFDC and the emerging problems with TANF. The "ending of welfare as we know it" connoted a loss of liberty and justice for women in poverty, framed by welfare rights advocates in terms of civil rights, equal access, and discriminatory politics. The loss of benefits for noncitizens evolved into a human rights platform that focused on the loss of equal protection and on the general abuses that immigrants face in an exploitative economy that casts them as unwelcome outsiders. The persistence of these two advocacies as differentiated efforts obscured the possibility of viewing social citizenship and legal citizenship as involving two interconnected constituencies.

In terms of the dismantling of AFDC, political commentary noted the eerie absence of a welfare rights movement like the one that had been so crucial to the equalizing of welfare benefits in the 1960s. The government responsiveness to the African American uprising against political and economic disenfranchisement, and the threat of a growing bloc of economically disenfranchised voters, was contrasted with a sense of complacency in response to the welfare devolution of the 1990s. An article in the *New York Times Magazine* of December 20, 1988 (the cover image: a brick wall with the washed-out painted white letters WELFARE WAS HERE) discussed the general resignation and acceptance of welfare reform in New York City, once the center of the welfare rights movement. Author Jason DeParle, after following New York Welfare Commissioner Jason Turner through "job centers" newly transitioned from previous welfare centers in Harlem, noted the loss of the struggle that had been the heart of the welfare rights movement three decades previously. De Parle described Turner's response to concerns about clients lacking the money to meet their needs, one year after the ending of AFDC: Turner explained to welfare caseworkers in Central Harlem that the real way their clients could learn how to manage money was "to live on what you get, and if you run out, figure out what to do until your next paycheck." Then, De Parle notes, "For a moment, the room fell silent. The city's new Welfare Commissioner—this Ivy League-educated, Republican white man—had just traveled to the heart of Harlem and proclaimed it morally instructive for the poor to face empty cupboards. Once upon a time, there might have been a riot. In the end-welfare age, the stunned silence leads to applause."[3] DeParle attributes this latter-day conservativeness to the many welfare caseworkers who have managed to find an occupational niche in social services. However, DeParle also pays special attention to juxtaposing the welfare complacency of today with the welfare rights movements of the 1960s. That broad-based mobilization was not present to combat the welfare devolution of the 1990s.

However, to construct the activism of the past as a ghostly essence no longer present to challenge right-wing ruthlessness negates the many local sites of activism that have been critical in shaping local agencies since the passing of the law on August 22, 1996.

An example of this emerged out of a local struggle by predominantly Southeast Asian youth in the Bronx, New York, opposing the degradation and humiliation their mothers were enduring through workfare and insensitive welfare office agents. The Youth Leadership Project of the Committee against Anti-Asian Violence (CAAAV) organized the occupation of the local welfare office in the Bronx, insisting on a meeting with the director to demand adequate translation services for the area's large population of Cambodians and Vietnamese, to make assistance more accessible, and to find meaningful work for their mothers in place of the degrading jobs of picking up trash at local parks and playgrounds around the city.

The video *Eating Welfare* tracks the efforts of these youth organizers and activists, while educating audiences about the refugee experience of those residing in the Bronx and the refugees' struggle to survive following welfare reform. The film eloquently and painfully documents the depth of their poverty and the day-to-day humiliations their parents deal with as they struggle to get assistance under the new rules and conditions. The youth themselves have become intermediaries and translators at very young ages to help their parents communicate with impatient welfare agents. They are forced to miss school, are put into embarrassing positions with invasive questions, and must deal with their own parents' shame when forced into menial workfare wageless jobs to receive their assistance. The video presents the youth project's work of educating the community on members' rights, and of organizing an occupation of the local welfare office, where the youth persist until they receive their meeting with the office's director.

Eating Welfare demonstrates the commonalities between what have typically been treated as two separate platforms, immigrant rights and welfare rights. The youth in this film brilliantly weave a narrative of war, dislocation, trauma, and the history of welfare assistance as a racialized and gendered system of discipline and control by bureaucratic agencies. In one scene, they use a phone list, provided by the welfare office, of available translating services from local organizations. Call after call, they encounter rude, puzzled, and dismissive county agents who have no idea why they are being called or why they are on a list from the welfare office. This list was the only form of translating services that the welfare-to-work program provided.

A narrative that weaves throughout the video is a daughter's quest to see what her mother does all day to earn her welfare check. As someone who has not found employment, the mother participates in the city's workfare program (a program "serving" three hundred thousand people). The daughter follows the mother from very early in the morning as the mother opens the gates to a small community playground and begins picking up trash. Hour after hour, the mother picks up trash with a stick with a nail on the end. She has no contact with anybody, and at first did not have the gloves or the poker stick to do her job. The mother, who appears to be in her mid-fifties, tells the camera, with her daughter translating, how humiliating and dirty the work is, and how it is not providing any training for finding a better job. With her lack of English skills or work skills, and her poor education, this mother will be unable to find employment when she reaches her five-year lifetime TANF limit, thus will be shuffled onto General Assistance and remain part of the largest workfare program in the country. In the end, the youth group succeeded in their demands that children not be relied upon in place of other translators, and they managed to persuade the director to discontinue some of the worst workfare conditions.

Eating Welfare appeared in 2000, four years after welfare reform and two years before the first attempt at reauthorization of TANF. This film, like numerous other scholarly and community-based projects, has overwhelmingly demonstrated that welfare reform has not reduced poverty. Yet the dominant official government narrative is "welfare reform has been a huge success." That could only be so were the system merely measured by the drastic drop in welfare participants. Ronald Reagan's statement, "We should measure welfare's success by how many people leave welfare, not by how many are added,"[4] continues to haunt a system once designed with the understanding that welfare was needed because of poverty, rather than the perverted illogic that welfare is the cause of poverty. PRWORA was successful in pushing people from welfare, but did not lead the majority of recipients to secure jobs with living wages and adequate health care or other benefits. With each consecutive reauthorization opportunity to make substantial changes to a policy that has increased food insecurity, hunger, ill health, and unjust working conditions for women, the appeal to restore benefits for immigrants on an equal footing with citizens has moved farther and farther from the debate. In the 2002 reauthorization attempt, immigrant provisions were still a prominent issue with advocates and policy research groups. In the 2006 attempt at reauthorization, little to no challenging discourse existed, let alone concern over the specific circumstances for immigrants.

To grapple with the comprehensive sweep of welfare reform, a multilayered approach must consider how citizenship reshaped entitlement for all poor mothers and made further distinctions for immigrant women. The implementation of PRWORA as a form of domestic economic restructuring demonstrated the further dismantling of social economic supports for women in particular. Like the structural adjustment policies imposed upon developing countries, the ending of welfare in the United States was an economic calculation and social abandonment of women that denied the existence of a racialized gendered labor force and of income stratification. Likewise, not only did the particular exclusions for immigrants force more women into highly exploitive and unprotected labor conditions, but the compounding provisions in the IIRIRA have fundamentally reshaped which people could immigrate at all. Once understood as a necessary and healthy form of migration, family reunification no longer holds the same priority if the family is poor. The more stringent sponsorship-deeming rules and minimal income requirements, as well as harsher public-charge provisions, have narrowed the invitation to migrants with higher capital and standing in the transnational marketplace. Yet, for all immigrants, political conditions have only worsened. Since 9/11, significant questions over civil and human rights violations have arisen regarding unlawful detentions, deportations, and surveillance of immigrants. Immigrant rights have in many ways reached an all-time low. The loss of political ground initiated by the fundamental shifts in welfare, immigration, and antiterrorist policies in 1996 paved the way for even more legislation and enforcement practices hostile to civil rights (in particular, the USA Patriot Act and the creation of ICE, or Immigration and Customs Enforcement).

MULTILAYERED AND HIERARCHICAL CITIZENSHIP POLITICS REVISITED

As I set out to examine the citizenship politics embedded in the convergence of immigration and welfare reform, I reasoned that this discussion needed to be conceptualized within a multilayered construct, in which one's citizenship, or noncitizenship, always occupies different layers—local, ethnic, national, state, cross- or trans-state and suprastate—and is affected and often at least partly constructed by the relationships and positionings of each layer in a specific historical context.[5] I proposed that to more critically analyze the multilayers of inclusion and exclusion, we must think of immigration policies as a logic of encompassment[6] that is always dialectical in nature to the politics of citizenship. The logic of encompassment allowed me to examine citizenship as a dialogical and relational process embedded in cultural and associational life[7] revealing the hierarchical and dialectical nature of belonging and exclusion.

Upon first look, the demarcation of eligibility based on citizenship status clearly indicated a multilayered differentiation of entitlement based on citizenship status. I have shown, throughout this book, the multitude and complex layers of citizenship politics that have instrumentally established hierarchies of entitlement and disenfranchisement. With Proposition 187 and again with PRWORA and IIRIRA, undocumented immigrants were not only set outside the parameters of public participation (as "impossible subjects"),[8] but, even more, were recriminalized as illegal agents of cultural contamination, rather than recognized for their invited and needed labor and contributions to the economy. With a refortification against an assumed threat, and resultant exclusion, undocumented immigrants were pushed further into hiding and invisibility, a situation that would only worsen with the increasing vilification of "illegal aliens" in the post-9/11 climate.

Among legally residing immigrants, new differentiations were established, based on more specious grounds. The establishment of date of entry as a criterion on which to determine eligibility for public assistance established new ideological assumptions about immigrants in this country. Those who entered after August 22, 1996, face different rules for participation than did those who preceded them. As a result, eleven years later, we are faced with an ever-growing proportion of immigrants, who have entered post-enactment, who find themselves in need. Subjected to more stringent and constricting sponsorship-deeming rules, public-charge concerns, and income requirements, these immigrants reside outside the boundaries of public participation regardless of the contributions they bring to the nation or the fact that they may be future citizens.

Welfare and immigration reform further stratified U.S. cultural notions of veteran status. The orientalist, racist, and xenophobic narratives of "the enemy" pervading mainstream U.S. collective memory of the memorialized Vietnam War continued to shape an inability to see Southeast Asian refugees as American veterans. George Lipsitz argues that, with the neoconservative agenda that took hold in the 1980s, a *new patriotism* emerged that would refortify the nation as a country strong and powerful and that relied on patriarchal protection for the purity of the American family.[9] This new patriotism worked to redemonize Vietnam—to fight the war all over again, not only to win but to undo the cultural changes it generated.[10] These re-demonizations were present in the plethora of Vietnam movies, such as the *Rambo* trilogy, in the 1980s.

The cultural violence waged toward Vietnam and Southeast Asia was also demonstrated in the 1989 Cleveland Elementary School shooting in Stockton, California. A white man wearing combat fatigues fired more than one hundred rounds of ammunition from an AK-47 assault rifle into a crowd of mostly Asian American students, killing four Cambodian children and one Vietnamese child. State officials commented that it was highly probable he chose that particular school from animosity toward "Southeast Asians," whom the gunman described as people who received "benefits" without having to work.[11] The association of Southeast Asians and welfare proved an accessible condemnation to continue the demonization of the enemy to whom America lost the war; the horrific killings of these school children must be seen in relation to the ongoing unresolved politics of the Vietnam War. By 1996, Southeast Asians were so firmly seen as un-American that racist and gendered constructions of protector, provider, and hero denied them the sacrifices and contributions they made to U.S. military campaigns in Southeast Asia: denied them their veteran status, denied them access to veteran's benefits and, subsequently, to public resources. Thus they have been left destitute and fearful, when they believed their acts of loyalty would guarantee their livelihood.

The layers and complexities of citizenship politics raise more alarming questions when we consider the disparate circumstances for children with immigrant parents. The converging provisions of welfare and immigration reform refortified existing systems of inaccessibility for children in immigrant households. For citizen children of undocumented parents, legal citizenship status is particularly questionable: under PRWORA, state agencies are required to obtain the immigration status of all applicants, and thus undocumented immigrants are deterred from applying for assistance for their eligible citizen children. These social service workers are also encouraged to report any applicants suspected of illegal status to the Bureau of Immigration and Naturalization Services. Basically, these citizen children are thus not granted citizenship in any real way, for the risk of becoming visible themselves could mean the deportation of their parent or parents, and their own forced removal to remain with their parents.

Given the large number of citizen children in immigrant-headed households, these mixed-status families pose challenges for understanding immigration provisions that impose a calculated benefits cut that must unquestionably hurt both citizen and noncitizen children. The myriad of requirements, confusing eligibility exceptions, time-of-entry delineations, and penalties form an equation by which the purposeful technocratic system of inaccessibility leaves citizen children of legal noncitizens without the financial and health assistance to which they are entitled. The subsequent fear of deportation, of adjustment of their residence status, or of possibly becoming a future public charge has fundamentally reshaped the meaning of support for immigrant families facing poverty.

Perhaps the most complex form of multilayered citizenship appears from the perspective of the advocate. The differentiation of characterization to emerge between elderly and disabled immigrant women losing SSI, and immigrant mothers of young children struggling to support their families through TANF, offered possibilities for counter-struggles utilizing what Aiwha Ong refers to as *citizenship-making*. Refugees losing SSI and food stamps could rely on moral condemnation that demanded for them the rights of citizenship and entitlement. Meanwhile, for poor mothers of families facing insurmountable hardship while trying to raise their families, the fundamental constructions of *responsibility* and *independence* pervaded; thus, advocacy efforts for them usually took the form of needed culturally and linguistically appropriate services, rather than a demand for economic security and a safety-net for all families facing hardship in an increasing deindustrialized society. Thus, both the immigrant movement and the welfare rights movement in confronting PRWORA forgot the hundreds of thousands of immigrant mothers soon to face additional challenges associated with their citizenship status. As a result, these immigrant families dropped from assistance, with a noted increase in food insecurity and poorer health.

The multiplicity of these layers and hierarchies demonstrates the potential for competing concerns and interests among welfare rights and immigrant rights constituencies. The multitude of differentiation established through the policy reforms indicates a new citizenship politics beyond the mere citizen–noncitizen dichotomy. Just as citizens of different social locations face different levels of civil rights and civil liberties from perpetuated systems of inequality, so today noncitizens must negotiate newly established state technologies intended to keep immigrants outside the reach of public resources. In my elaboration of multilayered citizenship (chapter 2) to frame the levels of differentiation and encompassment for immigrants under PRWORA, I asked the questions: how are noncitizens protected by the laws within nation-states, and what social rights to services should immigrants claim? From the details and circumstances presented throughout this book, it is clear that immigrants have lost protections by the new law and have been stripped of social rights to public services.

The logic of encompassment has significantly narrowed, so that poor noncitizens and their children (citizen and noncitizen) remain outside the boundaries of entitlement of the American community. Often overlooked, however, is the possibility that the very specific demarcation that restricted benefits for noncitizens softened the dismantling and restriction of welfare for all citizens. This book's focused look at the specific provisions of welfare and immigration policies, the consequential circumstances that Asian immigrant and refugee women faced, the response from the affected communities, and the possibilities for change through making visible and publicizing the trauma, despair, and injustice involved, all demonstrate the increasing need for vigilance against the peeling-away of basic rights for differently positioned immigrants. Even where certain gains or restorations have been made as a result of the mobilization efforts of immigrant rights groups, legislative concessions have not come with a systematic grappling with basic civil or human rights. Rather, restorations of benefits have been achieved in a piecemeal manner, with specific immigrant groups having to appeal to tenets of morality or to some particular historical grievance. Since 1996, immigrants have actually made little ground in the recovery of basic rights or entitlements, and if anything the few rights available have continued to erode. The losses incurred through the 1996 policies have, ten years later, been severely exacerbated by an even more fervent anti-immigrant movement.

NEW POLITICS OF CITIZENSHIP: NEW VOTING BLOCKS VS. TERRORIST CELLS

As discussed in chapter 4, by the 1998 elections the issue of immigration had waned from political agendas. Concerned with the growing presence of an active Latina/o voting block in such places as Orange County in Southern California, where unexpected winner Loretta Sanchez beat out Republican Bob Dornan for the House of Representatives. Sanchez appealed to the growing constituency of Latina/o and Asian voters, and Dornan, insistent that "illegal aliens" had voted, demanded an investigation of voting fraud that lasted fourteen months. Dornan's loss, in heavily conservative Orange County, sent a strong message to politicians that the new voting pool was shifting the political agendas.

Although the politics around immigration as an urgent issue did subside in the 1998 election, the harm certainly was not reversed. New nativist policy reform continued to operate as, after 1996, new immigrants continued ineligible for nearly all forms of social support. Further, though new nativist discourse surrounding public resources was not central to subsequent political campaigns, the 1996 comprehensive immigration reforms nevertheless resulted in more deaths along the border and increased poverty and hunger in immigrant homes. The nativist direction in immigration policy was only further compounded by the war politics of 9/11 that further entrenched nativist assumptions of immigrant threat as national enemy.

In the past ten years, we have witnessed a transition from an anti-immigrant politics of exclusion to a racial profiling under Homeland Security, a politics moving beyond exclusion to removal. Until 1996, immigrants were at least granted the right to due process, but the 1996 laws reduced judicial power to adjudicate immigrant proceedings by mandating certain penalties, whether detention or removal, for a far broader array of what are constituted as aggravated felonies. Of course, this process has racial implications. With the broadening of criminal offenses subsumed under the law, more immigrants who could not afford legal representation for misdemeanors committed long before these laws were created, now find themselves branded as suspected terrorists and at risk of deportation.

Fortifying provisions in the IIRIRA and the Anti-Terrorist Act of 1996, the USA Patriot Act, signed into law on October 26, 2001, allows a committee consisting of the attorney general, defense secretary, and CIA director to label citizens and noncitizens *enemy combatants.* This *enemy combatant* designation puts in motion the mandatory detention of suspected terrorists in military custody, where they can be held indefinitely, subject to so-called harsh interrogation, and not granted either judicial review or communication with outsiders. The Patriot Act grants the attorney general broad powers to certify an immigrant as a *risk,* who then may be certified a *suspected terrorist.* As a result, expedited removals have been initiated and institutionalized, and incarceration without hearings or legal representation has become commonplace.

Subsequently, the net around immigrants has closed tighter. On November 22, 2002, President Bush signed the Homeland Security Act, which created the Department of Homeland Security and dissolved the Immigration and Naturalization Service (INS). The newly created U.S. Citizenship and Immigration Services (USCIS) replaced the INS and was placed under the Department of Homeland Security. The restructuring of the INS as the USCIS resulted in a more elaborate structure of services, patrol, and enforcement. The Immigration and Customs Enforcement (ICE) is a new bureau within the USCIS, overseeing the enforcement and investigation components, such as investigations, intelligence, special registration, detention, and removal. The drastic increase in forced removals speaks to the new anti-immigrant climate, the "enemy immigrant" having matriculated from "welfare cheat" to "suspected terrorist." In 1996, 69,680 aliens were expelled; in 1997, the figure was 114,432; and by 2003, 186,151 aliens were expelled. Across two decades, the numbers of expelled aliens jumped fourfold, from 233,000 (1981–1990) to 940,000 (1991–2000).

In light of this fundamental restructuring of immigration policies and the general setback to the ongoing immigrant rights movement, immigrant and labor rights organizations engaged in a large-scale Immigrant Workers Freedom Ride, from September 20 to October 4, 2003. Inspired by the Freedom Rides of the 1960s civil rights movement, Freedom Riders were deployed from ten different cities across the country, and altogether stopped at over eighty-five cities along their routes to Washington, D.C., for a day of lobbying federal legislators, followed by a massive demonstration in New York City that included over one-hundred thousand protestors. Despite the great success and boost to morale created by the massive outpouring of support seen in the immigrant Freedom Rides, only two years later major policies were proposed to further restructure immigration, illegal immigration in particular.

As discussed in chapter 1, anti-immigration politics again erupted as a national political problem. In April 2005, hundreds of "American" volunteers with the newly founded Minuteman Project set out to the Arizona–Mexico border to "patrol" undocumented border crossings. This month-long display of citizen initiative claimed to be protecting the nation from "illegal immigration [that] is bankrupting states along the border . . . and placing our national security at risk."[12] The Minuteman Project declared itself defender of the country from "drug lords and violent gangs streaming into the U.S. from Mexico, and terrorists who are walking in unopposed," claiming that the United States' southwestern border is littered with Arabic papers and

Islamic prayer rugs.[13] Otto Santa Ana's discourse analysis of Proposition 187 proves relevant, more than ten years later, in this regard, as the Minuteman members believed themselves to be serving a *patriotic duty* to stop a *flood* of illegal border-crossers from Mexico. With the organized vigilante dramatization of the Minuteman Project, and the Republican-backed Sensenbrenner bill that would drastically criminalize undocumented immigrants, the notion of immigrant threat again brought in familiar ideological assumptions of immigrant corruptibility and inassimilability.

The call to arms by Jim Gilchrist in the epigraph of this chapter clearly demonstrates feminist scholar Jacqui Alexander's notion of the citizen patriots or civilian soldiers who see themselves as the country's noble gatekeepers from those who have become enemy invaders. To dispel this myth, immigrants demonstrated and protested proposed legislative changes on a massive scale. In 2005, the country witnessed a massive politicized immigration presence, with undocumented immigrants, legal permanent residents, and citizens, along with supporters, taking to the streets to make their presence and support known. Protestors worked to remind the public that most undocumented immigrants are in the United States working, supporting families, and contributing to the nation. The insult of assumed criminality denies the fact that the labor of undocumented immigrants is essential to the nation's economy. Without access to legalization, undocumented immigrants are forced to live in the shadows of American society without access to laws and protections, making them hypervulnerable to labor exploitation and abuse.

On May 1, 2006, a day declared the "National Day without Immigrants," an organized nationwide boycott succeeded in slowing or shutting down many farms, factories, markets, and restaurants.[14] To demonstrate the essential role immigrants, whether documented or undocumented, play in the nation's economy, over a million immigrants boycotted work, school, and businesses and marched in massive demonstrations in cities and towns across the country. Most noted about these marches was the unapologetic and fearless presence of undocumented immigrants marching with families, children, and even their employers. Immigrants voiced opposition to the criminalization of the undocumented—demanding, instead, fair labor laws to reduce rampant exploitation, more efficient and expedited procedures for family reunification, and avenues to legalization and citizenship.

In response to the intense pressure to enact harsh legislation that would basically turn 11.5 million undocumented immigrants into felons, and the subsequent response by undocumented immigrants demanding recognition for their multiple contributions to the nation through access to legalization, citizenship, and labor protections, President Bush took a somewhat surprising reconciliatory position in the polarized immigration reform debate. Through a televised statement made fifteen days after the nationwide boycott, Bush attempted to validate the nativist concerns over economic and national security while also recognizing the essential labor supplied to the country by undocumented immigrants. In attempts to maintain good relations with the immigrant population and its supporters, as well as with Mexico, Bush stated that "the vast majority of illegal immigrants are decent people who work hard, support their families, practice their faith, and lead responsible lives. They are a part of American life, but they are beyond the reach and protection of the American law."[15]

This move—promising comprehensive immigration reform that would not turn undocumented immigrants into criminals, but rather would provide pathways for legalization—surprised immigrant advocates and, with its proposed amnesty program, stung anti-immigrant foes. On the other hand, in attempts to appease conservative anti-immigrant voters, Bush mandated the immediate deployment of the National Guard to the U.S.-Mexican border, and the building of seven hundred miles of fortified fence there. As in the Proposition 187 campaign more than ten years earlier, anti-immigrant politicians focused on the threat of invasion from Mexico. The result was a recommitment to increasing the militarization of the U.S.-Mexico border, making conditions harsher and deadlier for migrants crossing to work in a country needing and using their labor.

These most immediate immigration debates aimed to move beyond the terrain of existing legislation created through the USA Patriot Act, and beyond the practices set forth through ICE under Homeland Security. These policy debates reflected an embedded immigration discourse and policy movement established nearly ten years before, a discourse and movement that more firmly established differentiations of rights between citizens and noncitizens, thus making these post-9/11 policies possible. These earlier immigration debates are critical to understanding the anti-immigrant movements that continue to shape discursive politics and policy enactments. Asian immigrants, although deeply impacted by immigration policies, are typically miscounted as insignificant or unconcerned. The 1.5 million undocumented immigrants from Asia have a direct stake in how future immigration policies may impact their lives. My examination of the policy movement of the 1990s demonstrates both the profound impact of a hostile anti-immigrant climate on the well-being of immigrants and their families, and the direct policy implications gravely affecting Asian immigrant communities.

The anti-immigrant climate since 9/11 reflects the dire circumstances that immigrants now face as automatically suspected terrorists or enemy combatants. The level of anti-immigrant hostility has led to the formation of overt racially biased groups such as the Minuteman Project. The state-sanctioned vigilantism speaks to probable reasons for the near silence regarding persistent immigrant concerns in the latest round of TANF reauthorization. Asian immigrant advocacy groups have been overwhelmed with deportation cases, removals, and detentions. Within Asian Pacific Islander communities, the drastic increase of deportations among Cambodians and Filipinos has alarmed communities as families are separated, and as people are deported back to a country they do not know and/or where they will face persecution. Thus, even though new voting blocs have emerged and reshaped local politics with high immigrant constituencies, the pervasive "terrorist" threat has subjugated political consciousness of immigrant rights. Immigrant families continue to struggle with higher rates of poverty, hunger, and poorer health, yet to rise up and protest amid the ongoing post-9/11 hysteria is more dangerous, under the current "war on terrorism" administration, than before. For this reason, the obligation for this necessary task lies with citizens who can afford the visibility to reengage in an immigrant and welfare rights campaign that redefines the notion of belonging, that champions the government's responsibility to address poverty, and that protects the poor from being punished for their poverty.

Notes

Introduction

1. Melissa Healy, "Gingrich Lays Out Rigid GOP Agenda," *Los Angeles Times,* November 12, 1994.

2. U.S. Commission on Civil Rights, *Civil Rights Issues Facing Asian Americans in the 1990s,* report of the United States Commission on Civil Rights, Washington, D.C., February 1992, ch. 1.

3. Larry Shinagawa, "The Impact of Immigration on the Demography of Asian Pacific Americans," in *Reframing the Immigration Debate,* ed. Bill Ong Hing (Los Angeles: LEAP Asian Pacific American Public Policy Institute and University of California Los Angeles [UCLA] Asian American Studies Center, 1996). Among individuals, the figure rose from 14.1 percent in 1990 to 15.3 percent in 1994; 66.8 percent of the Asian Pacific American population was foreign born.

4. Southeast Asian Resource Action Center, "Welfare and Benefits Restoration Policies," Washington, D.C., September, 2002, http://www.searac.org/aawelfareben .html.

5. I recognize the problematic of the term *Southeast Asian* given that this encompasses people beyond Vietnam, Cambodia, and Laos; however, the other widely used term, *Indochinese,* reflects the colonial naming of French colonies.

6. The term *refugee* is also complex when discussing Asian immigrants and refugees. Those who entered as Asian refugees or asylees at any time are referred to as *refugees* because of their experiences of war, political persecution, need to flee, and resettlement, even after their residency status had changed to legal permanent resident once their official refugee status of five years ended. Some refugees from Southeast Asia may actually enter through immigration procedures, such as family reunification, but still be referred to as refugees though they never acquired formal refugee status. Throughout this book, I utilize the term *refugee/s* to indicate a person or group who came to the United States as a result of displacement or political persecution.

7. A recent example can demonstrate this ongoing dilemma. On June 4, 1998, the American Sociological Association (ASA) held the Hill Briefing on Immigration

on Capitol Hill before sixty-five staffpersons from congressional offices, executive branch agencies, and nongovernmental agencies, as well as the media. Presenters representing the ASA were Ruben Rumbaut, Richard Alba, Douglas Massey, Felice J. Levine, and Lisandro Perez. Primary issues discussed were the causes and consequences of immigration from Mexico; the role and fluidity of the U.S.–Mexico border; bilingualism; "immigrant stock"; and locations where immigrants settle. The main discussion that covered Asian immigration concerned the population of Asian immigrants settling in suburban ethnic enclaves. Richard Alba noted that "the evidence for assimilation often overstates the reality, although Asian and light-skinned Latinos with middle-class incomes show assimilation in the suburbs." See "ASA Holds Hill Briefing on Immigration," in the American Sociological Association's *Footnotes* 26, no. 6 (July/August 1998).

8. See for example Angelo Ancheta, "Introduction: Neither Black nor White," in *Race, Rights, and the Asian American Experience* (New Brunswick, N.J.: Rutgers University Press, 1998); Robert S. Chang, *Disoriented: Asian Americans, Law, and the Nation-State,* (New York: New York University Press, 1999); Frank H. Wu, *Yellow: Race in America beyond Black and White* (New York: Basic Books, 2002).

9. Lisa Lowe, *Immigrant Acts: On Asian American Cultural Politics* (Durham, N.C.: Duke University Press, 1996); Ancheta, *Race, Rights, and the Asian American Experience.*

10. See Diane L. Wolf, "Situating Feminist Dilemmas in Fieldwork," in *Feminist Dilemmas in Fieldwork,* ed Diane L. Wolf (Boulder, Colo.: Westview Press, 1996), 1–55.

11. Pierrette Hondagneu-Sotelo, "Why Advocacy Research? Reflections on Research and Activism with Immigrant Women," *American Sociologist* 1993, no. 24: 56–68.

12. See Hondagneu-Sotelo, "Why Advocacy Research?" and Francesca M. Cancian, "Participatory Research and Alternative Strategies for Activist Sociology," in *Feminism and Social Change: Bridging Theory and Practice,* ed. Heidi Gottfried (Chicago: University of Illinois Press, 1996), 187–205.

1. New Nativism and Welfare Reform

1. All statistics in this section were derived from the U.S. Census 1980, 1990, and 2000. The compilations of data on Asian Pacific Americans were taken from *The New Face of Asian Pacific America: Numbers, Diversity, and Change in the Twenty-first Century,* ed. Eric Lai and Dennis Arguelles (Los Angeles: UCLA Asian American Studies Press, 2003).

2. U.S. Census Bureau, "1-in-5 U.S. Residents either Foreign-Born or First Generation," Census Bureau Reports, http://www.census.gov/Press-Release/www/2002/cb02–18.html.

3. Lisa Lowe, *Immigrant Acts: On Asian American Cultural Politics* (Durham, N.C.: Duke University Press, 1996), 4.

4. Ibid., 8.

5. Ibid., 6. See also Angelo Ancheta, *Race, Rights, and the Asian American Experience* (New Brunswick, N.J.: Rutgers University Press, 1998); and Robert S. Chang, *Disoriented: Asian Americans, Law, and the Nation-State* (New York: New York University Press, 1999).

6. Lowe, *Immigrant Acts,* 5. I draw from Lowe's conceptualization of U.S. national culture, in which "the collectively forged images, histories, and narratives that place, displace, and replace individuals in relation to the national polity. . . powerfully shapes who the citizenry is, where they dwell, what they remember, and what they forget."

7. Ancheta, *Asian American Experience,* 64.

8. Frank H. Wu, *Yellow: Race in America beyond Black and White* (New York: Basic Books, 2002), 184.

9. Chang, *Disoriented.* Chang provides a critical discussion regarding the notion of nativistic racism "where nativism and racism are mutually constitutive of the other."

10. Néstor P. Rodríguez, "Social Construction of the U.S.–Mexico Border," in *Immigrants Out: The New Nativism and the Anti-Immigrant Impulse in the United States,* ed. Juan F. Perea (New York: New York University Press, 1997), 225.

11. U.S. Census 1990, U.S. Census 2000; California Policy Research Center, *The California Latino Demographic Data Book* (Berkeley, Calif., 1998), http://ucdata.berkeley.edu/new_web/ldb/ldbintro.html; Rubén G. Rumbaut, "Origins and Destinies: Immigration to the United States since World War II," in *New American Destinies: A Reader in Contemporary Asian and Latino Immigration,* ed. Darrell Y. Hamamoto and Rodolfo D. Torres (New York: Routledge, 1997).

12. Rumbaut, "Origins and Destinies," 16.

13. Patricia Zavella, "The Tables Are Turned: Immigration, Poverty, and Social Conflict in California Communities," in *Immigrants Out,* 141. For poverty statistics, Zavella cites: Linda Neuhauser, Doris Disbrow, and Sheldon Margen, "Hunger and Food Insecurity in California," California Policy Seminar Brief 7, no. 4 (April 1995): 3.

14. Zavella, "Tables Are Turned," 141.

15. Ibid.

16. Rumbaut, "Origins and Destinies," 16.

17. Leo Chavez, "Immigration Reform and Nativism: The Nationalist Response to the Transnational Challenge," in *Immigrants Out,* 62.

18. The National Council for Research on Women, "The Feminization of Immigration: Give Us Your Tired, Your Hungry, Your Poor, No More," *Issues Quarterly* 1, no. 3: 6.

19. See Miriam Ching Louie, "Breaking the Cycle: Women Workers Confront Corporate Greed Globally," in *Dragon Ladies: Asian American Feminists Breathe Fire,* ed. Sonia Shah (Boston: South End Press, 1997); Grace Chang, "The Global Trade in Filipina Workers," in *Dragon Ladies;* Pierrette Hondagneu-Sotelo, *Domestica: Immigrant Workers Cleaning and Caring in the Shadow of Affluence* (Berkeley and Los Angeles: University of California Press, 2001).

20. Chavez, "Immigration Reform and Nativism," 71; Syd Lindsley, "The Gendered Assault on Immigrants," in *Policing the National Body: Race, Gender, and Criminalization,* ed. Jael Silliman and Anannya Bhattacharjee (Boston: South End Press, 2002).

21. Lindsley, "Gendered Assault," 182; Dorothy Roberts, "Who May Give Birth to Citizens? Reproduction, Eugenics, and Immigration," in *Immigrants Out,* 207.

22. Proposition 187 consists of five major sections: (1) illegal aliens are barred from the state's public education system, and educational institutions are required to verify the legal status of students and their parents; (2) providers of publicly paid, nonemergency health services are required to verify the legal status of persons seeking services; 3) persons seeking cash assistance and other benefits are required to verify their legal status before receiving services; 4) service providers are required to report suspected illegal aliens to the state attorney general and the Immigration and Naturalization Service (INS); 5) it is a state felony to make, distribute, and use false documents that conceal one's legal status to obtain public benefits or employment. See Adalberto Aguirre Jr., "Nativism, Mexican Immigrant Workers, and Proposition 187 in California," in *California's Social Problems,* ed. Charles F. Hohm (New York: Addison Wesley Longman, 1997), 143.

23. Otto Santa Ana, *Brown Tide Rising: Metaphors of Latinos in Contemporary American Public Discourse* (Austin: University of Texas Press, 2002).

24. Ibid., 77.

25. Ibid., 77.

26. Kevin R. Johnson, "The New Nativism: Something Old, Something New, Something Borrowed, Something Blue," in *Immigrants Out,* 179.

27. Ibid., 179.

28. Kitty Calavita, "The New Politics of Immigration: "Balanced-Budget Conservatism" and the Symbolism of Proposition 187," *Social Problems* 43, no. 3 (August 1996).

29. Ibid., 295. Calavita draws from Sidney Plotkin and William E. Scheuerman, *Private Interest, Public Spending: Balanced-Budget Conservatism and the Fiscal Crisis* (Boston: South End Press, 1994), who argue that the "deficit becomes the central ideological prop in the long-term conservative attack on the public sector, and frustration among taxpayers whose attention is focused on the inability of government to balance the budget." This "deficit mania" and disdain for a government unable to balance its books are the source of what Plotkin and Scheurerman call "balanced-budget conservatism."

30. Ibid., 295.

31. Ibid., 296.

32. Berta Esperanza Hernandes-Truyol, "Reconciling Rights in Collision: An International Human Rights Strategy," in *Immigrants Out,* 254.

33. See, for example, Roberts, "Who May Give Birth," in *Immigrants Out;* Kenneth J. Neubeck and Noel A. Cazenave, *Welfare Racism: Playing the Race Card against America's Poor* (New York: Routledge, 2001); Peter Brimelow, *Alien Nation:*

Common Sense about America's Immigration Disaster (New York: Harper Perennial, 1995).

34. Lynn Schnailberg. "Judge Rejects Prop. 187 Bans on California Services," *Education Week,* November 29, 1995.

35. Brimelow, *Alien Nation,* 264.

36. Ibid., 59.

37. Ibid., 265.

38. Wu, *Yellow,* 91. Also, Jonathan P. Decker, "Congress Debates Jus Soli," *Migration News,* http://migration.ucdavis.edu/mn/comments.php?id=844_0_2_0 (retrieved August 27, 2005).

39. Chavez, "Immigration Reform and Nativism," 65.

40. Ibid., 69; Lindsley, "Gendered Assault," 184.

41. William Wong, "Asian-Americans and Welfare Reform: The Mainstream Press Perpetuates Images but Fails to Report on Real Experiences," *Nieman Foundation for Journalism at Harvard University* 53, no. 2 (Summer 1999).

42. Norm Matloff, "Welfare Use among Elderly Chinese Immigrants," testimony to the Subcommittee on Immigration, U.S. Senate Judiciary Committee, 104th Congress, February 6, 1996.

43. Much of Matloff's anecdotal evidence comes from his interviews. He states that he conducted "numerous" interviews, but does not provide a direct count of the community center workers, immigrants, welfare officials, or immigration attorneys interviewed.

44. Matloff, "Welfare Use," 31.

45. George Borjas, "Immigration," in *The Concise Encyclopedia of Economics,* http://www.econlib.org/library/Enc/Immigration.html.

46. George J. Borjas and Stephen J. Trejo, "Immigrant Participation in the Welfare System," in *Industrial and Labor Relations Review* 44, no. 2 (1991): 210.

47. Michael E. Fix, Jeffrey S. Passel, and Wendy Zimmerman, "Summary of Facts about Immigrants' Use of Welfare," Urban Institute, http://www.urban.org/url.cfm?ID=410345.

48. P.L. 104–193, Title IV—Restricting Welfare and Public Benefits for Aliens. A more detailed discussion of the new categories of qualifications is in chapter 2.

49. Ibid., Section 400.

50. See Angie Wei and Sasha Khokha, "Devolution's Drastic Consequences: Welfare Reform Devastating to Immigrants," *Network News* (Washington, D.C.: National Network for Immigrant and Refugee Rights, 1997).

51. Bill Ong Hing, "Don't Give Me Your Tired, Your Poor: Conflicted Immigrant Stories and Welfare Reform," *Harvard Civil Rights–Civil Liberties Law Review* 33, no. 1 (Winter 1998): 159.

52. Louis Freedberg, "Immigrants' Peril—'One Strike and You're Out,'" *San Francisco Chronicle,* September 3, 1996.

53. Public Law 104–208 includes major immigration and welfare provisions: (1) doubling the size of the Border Patrol and stiffening penalties for "alien smuggling"

and document fraud; (2) tightening penalties on undocumented immigrants caught in the United States; (3) barring undocumented immigrants from qualifying for Social Security benefits or public housing; (4) giving states the right to deny driver's licenses to undocumented immigrants; (5) allowing welfare workers to verify immigrants' legal status before giving them welfare checks; (6) increasing the earnings requirement for U.S. residents wanting to sponsor immigrant family members to 125 percent of the poverty level, an increase from the previous 100 percent of the poverty level; and (7) making the affidavits of support signed by sponsors legal and binding documents, thus enforceable by the sponsored immigrant, the federal government, or any state or local government providing any means-tested public benefits. The law also includes "public charge" factors determining whether an immigrant is excludable at the time of application for a visa, based minimally on such characteristics as age, health, family status, financial status, and education and skills (see P.L. 104–208, Title V).

54. Elizabeth (Betita) Martinez, "Latinos Create a New Political Climate: The War on Immigrants Sparks a Massive Movement," *Z Magazine*, June 2006.

55. "Many Illegal Immigrants Shun Protest: Non-Hispanics Fear Notice, Say Congress Ignores Their Needs," *Associated Press*, April 17, 2006, http://www .baltimoresun.com/news/nationworld/bal-te.immigration17apr17,0,2549426 .story?coll=bal-home-headlines (retrieved October 13, 2006). This article reported that a Korean drum band led about seven thousand protesters through the streets of Los Angeles.

56. K. Oanh Ha, "Asian Illegal Immigrants Keep Low Profile in Debate," *San Jose Mercury News*, Sunday, May 7, 2006.

57. Works centered on contemporary forces shaping Asian immigration in the 1990s tended to focus on Asian immigrant workers in the context of economic restructuring at the labor site. Analyses of Asian immigrants in the context of global labor remain essential, especially given existing patterns of displacement and global economic restructuring in Asia. In *Mothers without Citizenship*, I center on the process of outsider racialization that involved Asian immigrants in regard to social policy.

2. Welfare Reform and the Politics of Citizenship

1. Gwendolyn Mink, "Aren't Poor Single Mothers Women? Feminists, Welfare Reform, and Welfare Justice," in *Whose Welfare?* ed. Gwendolyn Mink (Ithaca, N.Y.: Cornell University Press, 1992), 172. Beyond the epigraph at the beginning of this chapter, Mink argues "The law continues to injure poor single mothers' rights even after time limits end their access to benefits, for it directs them to forsake child raising for full-time wage earning. Both while they receive benefits and after they lose them, the Personal Responsibility Act (PRA) taxes poor women who have chosen motherhood and endangers their care and custody of children."

2. M. Jacqui Alexander, "Not Just Anybody Can Be a Patriot," lecture, University of Oregon, April 13, 2005.

3. See Will Kymlicka and Wayne Norman, "Return of the Citizen: A Survey of

Recent Work on Citizenship Theory," *Ethics* 104 (January 1994): 252–381. Kymlicka and Norman describe the increase as an "explosion of interest in the concept of citizenship among political theorists," such that in 1978 it could be confidently stated that "the concept of citizenship has gone out of fashion among political thinkers" (Herman van Gunsteren, "Notes toward a Theory of Citizenship," in *From Contract to Community*, ed. F. Dallmayr [New York: Marcel Decker, 1978], 9). "Fifteen years later, citizenship became the 'buzz word' among thinkers on all points of the political spectrum" (Derek Heater, *Citizenship: The Civic Ideal in World History, Politics, and Education* [London: Longman, 1990], 293; Ursula Vogel and Michael Moran, *The Frontiers of Citizenship* [New York: St. Martin's Press, 1991]).

4. The recent expansion of social citizenship has encompassed emphases of political rights, as well as social/cultural inclusion in the face of multiculturalism. Prominent frameworks that have entered citizenship scholarship include: *cultural citizenship*, see Renato Rosaldo, "Cultural Citizenship, Inequality, and Multiculturalism," and Renato Rosaldo and William V. Flores, "Identity, Conflict, and Evolving Latino Communities: Cultural Citizenship in San Jose, California," both in William V. Flores and Rina Benmayor, *Latino Cultural Citizenship: Claiming Identity, Space, and Rights* (Boston: Beacon Press, 1997); *flexible citizenship*, see Aihwa Ong, *Flexible Citizenship: The Cultural Logics of Transnationality* (Durham, N.C.: Duke University Press, 1999); *multilayered citizenship*, see Nira Yuval-Davis, "The 'Multi-Layered Citizen' Citizenship in the Age of 'Globalization,'" *International Feminist Journal of Politics* 1 (June 1, 1999); *global citizenship*, see Jan Jindy Pettman, "Globalisation and the Gendered Politics of Citizenship," in *Women: Citizenship and Difference*, ed. Nira Yuval-Davis and Pnina Werbner (London: Zed Books, 1999); and *multicultural citizenship*, see Will Kymlicka, *Multicultural Citizenship: A Liberal Theory of Minority Rights* (Oxford: Oxford University Press, 1995).

5. Stuart Hall and David Held, "Citizens and Citizenship," in *New Times: The Changing Face of Politics in the 1990s*, ed. Stuart Hall and Martin Jacques (London: Verso, 1990), 175.

6. Ibid., 175.

7. See Yuval-Davis, "'Multi-Layered Citizen.'"

8. T. H. Marshall, *Citizenship and Social Class, and Other Essays by T. H. Marshall* (Cambridge: Cambridge University Press, 1950).

9. Kymlicka and Norman, "Return of the Citizen," 354.

10. Ibid., 354–55.

11. Ibid., 352.

12. Ibid., 354.

13. Kymlicka, *Multicultural Citizenship*, 193.

14. Benedict Anderson, *Imagined Communities: Reflections on the Origin and Spread of Nationalism* (London: Verso, 1991), 101.

15. Anderson, *Imagined Communities*, 149.

16. Evelyn Nakano Glenn, "Citizenship and Inequality: Historical and Global Perspectives," from *Social Problems* 47, no. 1: 10.

17. Christian Joppke, *Immigration and the Nation-State: The United States, Germany, and Great Britain* (New York: Oxford University Press, 1999), 6.

18. David Theo Goldberg, *Racist Culture: Philosophy and the Politics of Meaning* (Oxford: Blackwell, 1993), 78–79.

19. Howard Winant, *The New Politics of Race: Globalism, Difference, Justice* (Minneapolis: University of Minnesota Press, 2004), 144.

20. Ibid., 145.

21. For example, Saskia Sassen, *The Global City: New York, London, Tokyo* (Princeton, N.J.: Princeton University Press, 2001); *Globalization and Its Discontents: Essays on the New Mobility of People and Money* (New York: New Press, 1998); *Losing Control? Sovereignty in an Age of Globalization* (New York: Columbia University Press, 1996).

22. Saskia Sassen, "Transnationalizing Immigration Policy," from *Challenge to the Nation-State: Immigration in Western Europe and the United States,* ed. Christian Joppke (New York: Oxford University Press, 1998), 49–85.

23. Ange-Marie Hancock, *The Politics of Disgust: The Public Identity of the Welfare Queen* (New York: New York University Press, 2004), 16. According to Hancock, public identities involve moral explanations for established stereotypical behavior. Public identities also function dynamically in goal-oriented contexts of politics, as ideological justifications for public policy.

24. Ibid., 6.

25. This depiction begins an article by Nathalie A. Augustin, "Learnfare and Black Motherhood: The Social Construction of Deviance," in *Critical Race Feminism: A Reader, First Edition,* ed. Adrien Katherine Wing (New York: New York University Press, 1997), 144.

26. P.L. 104–193, Title I, section 101(1)–(2).

27. Ibid., section 101(10).

28. Ibid., section 401(a)(1)–(4).

29. Gwendolyn Mink, *Welfare's End* (Ithaca, N.Y.: Cornell University Press, 1998), 104. According to PRWORA, states have the option to not require mandatory work of the single parent of a child less than one year of age. Also, states are required to continue support for single parents caring for children less than six years of age if the parent can prove an inability to obtain child care.

30. Linda Gordon, *Pitied but Not Entitled: Single Mothers and the History of Welfare, 1890–1935* (New York: Free Press, 1994), 19.

31. Ibid., 44.

32. Ibid., 45.

33. Gwendolyn Mink, "The Lady and the Tramp: Gender, Race, and the Origins of the American Welfare State," in *Women, the State, and Welfare,* ed. Linda Gordon (Madison: University of Wisconsin Press, 1990), 102.

34. Gwendolyn Mink, *The Wages of Motherhood: Inequality in the Welfare State, 1917–1942* (Ithaca, N.Y.: Cornell University Press, 1995), 5.

35. Ibid., 31.

36. Ibid., 127.

37. Jill Quadagno, *The Color of Welfare: How Racism Undermined the War on Poverty* (New York: Oxford University Press, 1994), 21.

38. See Frances Fox Piven and Richard A. Cloward, *Regulating the Poor: The Functions of Public Welfare* (New York: Random House, 1971), 245.

39. Quadagno, *Color of Welfare*, 120.

40. *King v. Smith*, 88 S.Ct. 842 U.S. (1968).

41. *Shapiro v. Thompson, Reynolds v. Smith*, 394 U.S. 618 (1969).

42. Quadagno, *Color of Welfare*, 121.

43. Wahneema Lubiano, "Black Ladies, Welfare Queens, and State Minstrels: Ideological War by Narrative Means," *in Race-ing Justice, En-gendering Power: Essays on Anita Hill, Clarence Thomas, and the Construction of Social Reality*, ed. Toni Morrison (New York: Pantheon Books, 1992), 338.

44. Teresa L. Amott, "Black Women and AFDC: Making Entitlement out of Necessity," in *Women, the State, and Welfare*, ed. Linda Gordon (Madison: University of Wisconsin Press, 1990), 290.

45. Ibid., 290; White House Working Group on the Family, *The Family: Preserving America's Future: A Report to the President*, November 13, 1986.

46. Martha Fineman, "Images of Mothers in Poverty Discourses," in *Duke Law Journal*, no. 2 (April [1991]): 277.

47. Ibid., 283.

48. Nancy Fraser, *Unruly Practices: Power, Discourse, and Gender in Contemporary Social Theory* (Minneapolis: University of Minnesota Press, 1989), 152.

49. Ibid., 151–53.

50. Martha Minow, "The Welfare of Single Mothers and Their Children," in *Connecticut Law Review* 26, no. 3 (Spring 1994): 818.

51. A much more elaborate discussion and examination of Temporary Assistance for Needy Families is presented in chapters 5 and 6.

52. Eileen Boris, "When Work Is Slavery," in *Disdained Mothers and Despised Others: The Politics and Impact of Welfare Reform, Social Justice* 25, no.1 (1998): 29.

53. Mink, *Welfare's End*, 98.

54. Judith Shklar, *American Citizenship: The Quest for Inclusion* (Cambridge, Mass.: Harvard University Press, 1991), 67.

55. Nancy Naples. "From Feasible Participation to Disenfranchisement," in *Disdained Mothers*.

56. See Mink, *Welfare's End*, 62–63. According to Mink, "so far New York City, Massachusetts, California, Florida, Tennessee, Texas, and Wisconsin compel mothers to work outside the home immediately upon receiving benefits; Wisconsin requires recipients to work longer hours than required by the federal law. Michigan reduces benefits by 25 percent if people do not meet work requirements within two months. Alabama, South Carolina, and Wyoming will not provide benefits to noncitizen immigrants."

57. Boris, "When Work Is Slavery," 28. Boris quotes from a woman who participated in New York's Work Experience Program (WEP), one of the state-level workfare initiatives; the woman states, "I don't mind doing the work. But we are just like a piece of waste material the way the state program treats us. They feel like we're slaves or something, having to work off our check."

58. Nancy Naples, "Participation to Disenfranchisement," 51. Naples cites Michelle Billies et al., *Welfare, Workfare, and Jobs: An Educator's Guidebook* (New York: Urban Justice Center Organizing Project, 1997). Michelle Billies and collaborators report, "over 9,000 students on welfare have been forced to leave the City University of New York to participate in workfare" since New York City began implementation of PRWORA.

59. Frances Fox Piven, "Welfare and Work," in *Disdained Mothers:* 71.

60. Mink, *Welfare's End,* 93.

61. Ibid., 75.

62. Ibid., 77.

63. Dorothy Roberts, *Killing the Black Body: Race, Reproduction, and the Meaning of Liberty* (New York: Vintage Books, 1997), 209.

64. Ibid., 245. This broader argument of white resistance to Black "inclusion" and the prescriptions for racial justice are further developed by Roberts.

65. Ibid., 244.

66. Pierette Hondagneu-Sotelo, public talk for the Center for the Study of Women in Society, University of Oregon, 1993.

67. P.L. 104–193, Title IV, Section 400(5).

68. Charles B. Keely, "The Immigration Act of 1965," in *Asian Americans and Congress: A Documentary History,* ed. Hyung-Chan Kim (Westport, Conn: Greenwood, 1995), 538.

69. P.L. 89–236, Section 201(b), "The immediate relatives' referred to in subsection (a) of this section shall mean the children, spouses, and parents of a citizen of the United States. . . . The immediate relatives specified in this subsection who are otherwise qualified for admissions as immigrants shall be admitted as such, without regard to the numerical limitations in this act."

70. Yen Le Espiritu, *Asian American Women and Men* (Thousand Oaks, Calif.: Sage Publications, 1997), 63.

71. Frank H. Wu, *Yellow: Race in America beyond Black and White* (New York: Basic Books, 2002), 91.

72. See Michael E. Fix and Karen Tumlin, "Welfare Reform and the Devolution of Immigrant Policy," Urban Institute, New Federalism Issues and Options for States, Series A, No. A-15 (Washington, D.C., October 1997).

73. Bill Ong Hing, "Don't Give Me Your Tired, Your Poor: Conflicted Immigrant Stories and Welfare Reform," *Harvard Civil Rights Law Review* 33, no.1 (Winter, 1998): 162.

74. Fix and Tumlin, "Welfare Reform and the Devolution of Immigrant Policy," 45.

75. Wendy Zimmerman and Karen C. Tumlin, "Patchwork Policies: State Assistance for Immigrants under Welfare Reform," *Assessing the New Federalism,* no. 24 (Washington, D.C.: Urban Institute, 1999).

76. Peter H. Schuck, "The Re-Evaluation of American Citizenship," *Georgetown Immigration Law Journal* 12; *Georgetown Immigration Law Journal* 1. 1997.

77. Benedict Anderson, *Imagined Communities,* 6.

78. Glenn, "Citizenship and Inequality," 16.

79. Jan Jindy Pettman, "Globalisation and the Gendered Politics of Citizenship," in *Women, Citizenship, and Difference,* eds. Nira Yuval-Davis and Pnina Werbner (London: Zed Books, 1999), 215.

80. Pnina Werbner and Nira Yuval-Davis, "Women and the New Discourse of Citizenship," in *Women, Citizenship, and Difference,* 23.

81. Ibid., 23.

82. See Pettman, "Globalisation and the Gendered Politics of Citizenship," 1999; see Miriam Ching Louie, "Breaking the Cycle: Women Workers Confront Corporate Greed Globally," in *Dragon Ladies: Asian American Feminists Breathe Fire,* ed. Sonia Shah (Boston: South End Press, 1997); Grace Chang, "The Global Trade in Filipina Workers," in *Dragon Ladies;* Pierrette Hondagneu-Sotelo, *Domestica: Immigrant Workers Cleaning and Caring in the Shadow of Affluence* (Berkeley and Los Angeles: University of California Press, 2001).

83. Sassen, *Globalization and Its Discontents,* 95.

84. Ibid., 7.

85. Joanathan Xavier Inda, *Targeting Immigrants: Government, Technology, and Ethics* (Malden, Mass.: Blackwell Publishing, 2006), 18. Inda argues that a postsocial politics of responsibilization has emerged with a highly racialized technology of citizenship that imposes individual responsibility as central to citizenship, and deems those imprudent or dependent on the state to be anticitizens in need of containment/punishment.

86. Ibid., 46–52. See Inda's elaborate discussion of TANF and the logic of work-first programs to discipline recipients into so-called responsible citizenship.

87. Mae M. Ngai, *Impossible Subjects: Illegal Aliens and the Making of Modern America* (Princeton, N.J.: Princeton University Press, 2004), 6.

88. Ibid., 7.

89. Victor C. Romero, *Alienated: Immigrant Rights, the Constitution, and Equality in America* (New York: New York University Press, 2005), 162.

90. Ibid., 191.

91. Leti Volpp, "Critical Race Studies: The Citizen and the Terrorist," *UCLA Law Review* 49 (June 2002): 1575 .

92. Ibid.: 1593.

93. Ibid.: 1578.

94. Yuval-Davis, "'Multi-Layered Citizen'": 122.

95. Werbner and Yuval-Davis, "Women and the New Discourse," 10.

96. Ibid., 10.

97. The feminization of migration reflects the increasing migration of women resulting from forces of globalization. See Cynthia Enloe, *Bananas, Beaches, and Bases: Making Feminist Sense of International Politics*, 2nd edition (Berkeley and Los Angeles: University of California Press, 2001); Grace Chang, *Disposable Domestics: Immigrant Women Workers in the Global Economy* (Cambridge, Mass.: South End Press, 2000); Miriam Ching Yoon Louie, *Sweatshop Warriors: Immigrant Women Workers Take On the Global Factory* (Cambridge, Mass.: South End Press, 2001), Pierette Hondagneu-Sotelo, *Doméstica: Immigrant Workers Cleaning and Caring in the Shadows of Affluence* (Berkeley and Los Angeles: University of California Press, 2001).

98. Pettman, "Globalisation and the Gendered Politics of Citizenship," 214.

99. Evelyn Nakano Glenn, *Unequal Freedom: How Race and Gender Shaped American Citizenship and Labor* (Cambridge, Mass.: Harvard University Press, 2002), 53.

100. Lisa Lowe, *Immigrant Acts: On Asian American Cultural Politics* (Durham, N.C.: Duke University Press, 1996), 4.

101. See Aihwa Ong, *Buddha Is Hiding: Refugees, Citizenship, the New America* (Berkeley and Los Angeles: University of California Press, 2003).

102. Ibid., 276.

103. I will discuss Aiwha Ong's more specific analysis of citizenship in relation to refugees in chapter 3, where I examine the notion of betrayal through social policy meant to exclude noncitizens regardless of government obligation.

3. Refugees Betrayed

1. Deborah Hastings, "Reform Hits Hard among Refugees," *Asian Week 19*, February 10–25, 8.

2. Ibid., 10.

3. Stephen Magagnini, "Suicide Illustrates Welfare Reform's Toll among Hmong," *Sacramento Bee*, November 9, 1997, A1.

4. Ibid.

5. Bert Eljera, "Hmong Desperate on Welfare Reform," *Asian Week*, December 4, 1997, 13–14.

6. SSI was restored to noncitizens who resided in the United States as of August 22, 1996, and were either then receiving SSI or became disabled at a later time.

7. Magagnini, "Suicide," A1.

8. Ibid., A1.

9. Eljera, "Hmong Desperate," 14.

10. Lisa Lowe, *Immigrant Acts*, 156–57. Lowe states: "To consider testimony and testimonial as constituting a 'genre' of cultural production is significant for Asian immigrant women, for it extends the scope of what constitutes legitimate knowledges to include other forms and practices that have been traditionally excluded from both empirical and aesthetic modes of evaluation."

11. Lowe, *Immigrant Acts*, 157. Here, Lowe is citing Chandra Mohanty, "Cartographies of Struggle," *Introduction to Third World Women and the Politics of Feminism* (Bloomington: Indiana University Press, 1991, 34).

12. Eduardo Bonilla-Silva, *Racism without Racists: Color-Blind Racism and the Persistence of Racial Inequality in the United States* (New York: Rowman and Littlefield, 2003) 76. Here, Bonilla-Silva is citing Norman K. Denzin, *The Research Act* (Englewood Cliffs, N.J.: Prentice Hall, 1989).

13. Bonilla-Silva, *Racism without Racists*, 76.

14. See "Number of World's Migrants Reaches 175 Million Mark," press release from United Nations Populations Publications, October 2, 2002, http://www.un.org/esa/population/publications/ittmig2002/press-release.

15. See the International Rescue Committee, "Humanitarian and Emergency Aid to Refugees and Other Victims of Persecution," October 28, 2004, http//www.theirc.org.

16. Convention Relating to the Status of Refugees. Adopted on July 28, 1951, by the United Nations Conference of Plenipotentiaries on the Status of Refugees and Stateless Persons Convened under General Assembly Resolution 429 (V) of December 14, 1950, entry into force April 22, 1954, in accordance with Article 43, http://www.unhchr.ch/html/menu3/b/o_c_ref.htm.

17. This section draws from Sucheng Chan, *Asian Americans: An Interpretive History* (Boston: Twayne Publishers, 1991), 153–54. Chapter 8 provides one of the most concise timelines of politics and events during the war in Southeast Asia.

18. Aihwa Ong, *Buddha Is Hiding Refugees, Citizenship: The New America* (Berkeley and Los Angeles: University of California Press, 2003), 28.

19. Sucheng Chan, *Asian Americans*, 154.

20. Ibid., 154–55.

21. Anne Fadiman, *The Spirit Catches You and You Fall Down* (New York: Farrar, Straus, and Giroux, 1998), 138–39.

22. Bill Ong Hing, *Defining America through Immigration Policy* (Philadelphia: Temple University Press, 2004), 237.

23. Ibid., 237.

24. Ibid., 237.

25. Ong, *Buddha Is Hiding*, 81.

26. Aihwa Ong, "Cultural Citizenship as Subject-Making," in *Current Anthropology* 37, no. 5 (1996): 742.

27. Christian Joppke, *Immigration and the Nation-State: The United States, Germany, and Great Britain* (New York: Oxford University Press, 1999), 50.

28. Ibid., 50.

29. Ong, *Buddha Is Hiding*, 81.

30. Hing, *Defining America*, 236.

31. P.L. 94–23, May 23, 1975, Section 2(a).

32. Chan, *Asian Americans*, 156.

33. Ong, *Buddha Is Hiding*, 81.

34. Charles B. Keely, "The Immigration Act of 1965," in *Asian Americans and Congress: A Documentary History*, ed. Hyung-Chan Kim (Westport, Conn.: Greenwood Press, 1995), 537.

35. Edward J. W. Park and John S. W. Park, *Probationary Americans: Contemporary Immigration Policies and the Shaping of Asian American Communities* (New York: Routledge, 2005).

36. Ibid., 38–39.

37. See Mary Elizabeth Kelsey, *Negotiating Poverty: Welfare Regimes and Economic Mobility,* dissertation, University of California, Berkeley, 1994, 84. Also see P.L. 96–212, March 17, 1980, Title I.

38. P.L. 96–212, March 17, 1980, Title I: "In providing assistance under this section, the Director shall make available sufficient resources for employment training and placement in order to achieve economic self-sufficiency among refugees as quickly as possible."

39. P.L. 96–212, CH 2, Section 412(e), Cash Assistance and Medical Assistance to Refugees.

40. Hing, *Defining America,* 137.

41. U.S. Commission on Civil Rights, *Civil Rights Issues Facing Asian Americans in the 1990s,* Washington, D.C., February 1992, 17.

42. Bill Ong Hing, *Making and Remaking Asian America through Immigration Policy, 1850–1990,* 137.

43. Eric Tang, "Collateral Damage: Southeast Asian Poverty in the United States," *Social Text* 18, no. 1 (Spring 2000).

44. Hing, *Defining America,* 137.

45. Ibid., 137.

46. Elizabeth Gong-Guy. *California Southeast Asian Mental Health Needs Assessment* (Oakland, Calif.: Asian Community Mental Health Services, 1987).

47. Laura Uba, *Asian Americans: Personality Patterns, Identity, and Mental Health* (New York: Guilford Press, 1994), 146.

48. See Jeremy Hein, *From Vietnam, Laos, and Cambodia: A Refugee Experience in the United States* (New York: Twayne Publishers, 1995), 72–73.

49. This middle-American resentment can be seen through Jeremy Hein's research, as well as in a video documentary created in 1981, *Becoming American,* by Ken Levine, New Day Films, about a Hmong family's resettlement in the United States, a video that contains explicit comments by white Americans expressing their resentment for the war in Vietnam and the influx of refugees into "their" communities.

50. Ong, "Cultural Citizenship," 742.

51. See the Southeast Asian American Statistical Profile, by the Southeast Asia Resource Action Center (SEARAC), Washington, D.C., 2004. All tables are based upon the U.S. Census for 2000.

52. Ibid.

53. Marjorie A. Muecke, "Trust, Abuse of Trust, and Mistrust among Cambodian Refugee Women: A Cultural Interpretation," in *Mistrusting Refugees,* ed. E. Valentine Daniel and John Knudsen (Berkeley and Los Angeles: University of California Press, 1995), 38.

54. See Sucheng Chan, *Asian Americans*, ch. 8; *Passages: An Anthology of the Southeast Asian Refugee Experience*, compiled by Katsuyo K. Howard, Southeast Asian Student Services, California State University, Fresno, 1990; *The Far East Comes Near: Autobiographical Accounts of Southeast Asian Students in America*, ed. Lucy Nguyen-Hong-Nhiem and Joel Martin Halpern, Amherst: University of Massachusetts Press, 1989.

55. Hein, *From Vietnam, Laos, and Cambodia*, 35.

56. Ibid., 36.

57. See Ong, *Buddha Is Hiding*, ch. 2; Muecke, 1995.

58. The problem of sexual violence against refugee women remains unaddressed, primarily because the perpetrators of sexual atrocities are not always the named enemy. In addition to rape and sexual torture used as persecution by wartime enemies, sexual violations by security officers, refugee camp officials, and male fellow refugees are rampant forms of such violence; all continue to occur, for lack of adequate international sanction.

59. See Hein, *From Vietnam, Laos, and Cambodia*; David Haines, *Refugees as Immigrants* (Totowa, N.J.: Rowman and Littlefield Publishers, 1989); Nancy D. Donnelly, *Changing Lives of Refugee Hmong Women* (Seattle: University of Washington Press, 1994); Judy Chu, *In America and In Need: Immigrant, Refugee, and Entrant Women* (Washington, D.C.: U.S. Department of Labor Women's Bureau, 1985); Ngoan Le, "The Case of Southeast Asian Refugees: Policy for a Community 'At-Risk,'" in *The State of Asian Pacific America: Policy Issues to the Year 2020* (Los Angeles, Calif.: LEAP Asian Pacific America: A Public Policy Report, 1993).

60. Hein, *From Vietnam, Laos, and Cambodia*, 140–41.

61. Ibid., 119.

62. Cindy Thuy Phan, *Comparing the Success in Cultural Adaptation of Vietnamese Refugee Women and Men*, dissertation, United States International University, 1994, UMI Dissertation Abstracts Database.

63. Judy Chu, "Southeast Asian Women in Transition," in *In America and in Need: Immigrant, Refugee, and Entrant Women*, ed. Abby Spero (Washington, D.C.: American Association of Community and Junior Colleges and U.S. Department of Labor Women's Bureau, January 1985).

64. David W. Haines, "Vietnamese Refugee Women in the U.S. Labor Force: Continuity or Change?" in *International Migration: The Female Experience*, ed. Rita Simon and Caroline Brettell (Totowa, N.J.: Rowman and Allenheld, 1986), 62–75.

65. Ibid., 62–75.

66. Yen Le Espiritu, *Asian American Women and Men* (Thousand Oaks, Calif.: Sage Publications, 1997), 71–72.

67. "Asian Workers Breaking the Model Minority Myth," in *Network News* (National Network for Immigrant and Refugee Rights, Oakland, Calif.), Winter 1997–98, 6–7.

68. "Not the Model Minority: 2000 Census Reveals Achievement Gaps and Signs of Hope for Americans from Cambodia, Laos, and Vietnam," press release,

Southeast Asian Resource Action Center, May 4, 2003, http://www.searac.org/pr-2000-census.html.

69. Anne Anlin Cheng, *The Melancholy of Race: Psychoanalysis, Assimilation, and Hidden Grief* (New York: Oxford University Press, 2001), 3.

70. Ibid., 20–21; Paul Gilroy, *The Black Atlantic: Modernity and Double Consciousness* (Cambridge, Mass.: Harvard University Press, 1993), 63.

71. For a more elaborate discussion from a social-movements perspective, and an analysis of the community mobilization efforts of the immigrant rights movement to restore SSI, see Lynn Fujiwara, "Immigrant Rights Are Human Rights: The Reframing of Immigrant Entitlement and Welfare," *Social Problems* 52, no. 1.

72. Deeana Jang, "Welfare Reform Targets Immigrant Women," in *Network News* (National Network for Immigrant and Refugee Rights, Oakland, Calif.), Fall 1997.

73. Eljera, "Hmong Desperate."

74. Karen McAllister, "No Welfare, No Hope, Immigrant Takes Life Fearing Loss of Check," *Fresno Bee*, October 26, 1997, A1.

75. Stephen Magagnini, "Hmong Experts Gather to Offer Help: National Conference Includes Look at Mental Health Issues," *Sacramento Bee*, March 29, 2001.

76. Eljera, "Hmong Desperate." These perspectives were provided by a Hmong spokesperson of the California Statewide Lao Hmong Coalition.

77. See Fujiwara, "Immigrant Rights Are Human Rights."

78. Magagnini, "Suicide."

79. Ibid.

80. Robert Pear, "Administration Welfare Plea Is Scorned in Congress," *New York Times*, February 14, 1997, A30.

81. Field notes, May 28, 1997.

82. Angelo Ancheta, "A Costly Victory but More Battles to Come: A Message from the Executive Director," *The Reporter*, Asian Law Caucus 19, no. 2 (November 1997).

83. Laura Hyun Yi Kang, *Compositional Subjects: Enfiguring Asian/American Women* (Durham, N.C.: Duke University Press, 2002), 197.

84. Lowe, *Immigrant Acts*, 9.

85. Deborah Hastings, "Hmong Woman's Suicide Puts Spotlight on Welfare Problems," *Los Angeles Times*, February 22, 1998, B1.

86. Department of Veteran Affairs, http://www1.va.gov/about_va/page.cfm?pg=1.

87. Ibid.

88. See David L. Eng, *Racial Castration: Managing Masculinity in Asian America* (Durham, N.C.: Duke University Press, 2001).

89. Magagnini, "Suicide."

90. Ibid.

91. Bert Eljera, "Last Lines of Defense," *Asian Week*, November 13, 1997, 13–14.

92. Deborah Hastings, "Hmong Woman's Suicide."

93. P.L. 105–33, Section 5561.

94. Tim Weiner, "To Many Laotians, U.S. Is Land of False Promises," *New York Times,* December 27, 1997, A-1.

95. *Yang v. California Department of Social Services,* 183 F.3d 953 (1999).

96. Eljera, "Hmong Desperate," 13–14.

97. Ibid.

98. Ibid.

99. Ibid.

100. Weiner, "Laotians."

101. Ibid., A-1.

102. Ibid., A-1.

103. Eljera, "Hmong Desperate," 13–14.

104. Virginia Ellis, "Hmong Seek Exemption from Food Stamp Cuts," *Los Angeles Times,* November 2, 1997, A3.

105. John Howard, "Out Front—Hmong Food Stamps," *Associated Press,* http://home.vicnet.net.au/~lao/laonews/old/laos1102.txt.

106. Andrew Blasko, "Laotians Honored for War Service," *Asian Week,* October 3, 1997, 8.

107. *Yang v. California Department of Social Services.*

108. Bill Ong Hing, "Don't Give Me Your Tired, Your Poor: Conflicted Immigrant Stories and Welfare Reform," *Harvard Civil Rights–Civil Liberties Law Review* 33 (1998): 159; Michael E. Fix, Jeffrey Passel, Wendy Zimmerman, "Facts about Immigrants' Use of Welfare" (Urban Institute, Washington, D.C., 1996), http://www.urban.org/url.cfm?ID=410345.

4. The Rush for Citizenship

1. Mae M. Ngai, *Impossible Subjects: Illegal Aliens and the Making of Modern America* (Princeton, N.J.: Princeton University Press, 2004), 5.

2. Aihwa Ong, *Buddha Is Hiding: Refugees, Citizenship, The New America* (Berkeley and Los Angeles: University of California Press, 2003), 6.

3. Ibid., 12.

4. Stuart Hall and David Held, "Citizens and Citizenship," in *New Times: The Changing Face of Politics in the 1990s,* ed. Stuart Hall and Martin Jacques (London: Verso, 1990), 175.

5. Hyung-Chan Kim, "American Naturalization and Immigration Policy: Asian American Perspective," in *Asian Americans and Congress: A Documentary History,* ed. Hyung-Chan Kim (Westport, Conn.: Greenwood, 1995), 2. Congress was given exclusive power over immigration, by virtue of the Supreme Court's decision in *Chy Lung v. U.S.* in 1876; however, "The practice of favoring certain classes of people for immigration had been so entrenched in the machinery of immigration that subsequent federal legislation on immigration did not depart radically from these patterns."

6. Angelo Ancheta, *Race Rights, and the Asian American Experience* (New Brunswick, N.J.: Rutgers University Press, 1998), 24.

7. John Hayadawa Torok, "Asians and the Reconstruction Era, Constitutional Amendments and Civil Rights Laws," in *Asian Americans and Congress*, ed. Kim, 22.

8. Ibid. Torok draws his analysis directly from the *Congress Globe*, 39th Congress, 1st Session, 813, 1034 (1866).

9. Ngai, *Impossible Subjects*, 42.

10. See *Ozawa v. United States*, 160 U.S. 178 (1922).

11. Tomas Almaguer, *Racial Fault Lines: The Historical Origins of White Supremacy in California* (Berkeley and Los Angeles: University of California Press, 1994), 177–78.

12. Chinese Exclusion Act, U.S. Congress, 47th Congress, 1st Session, May 6, 1882, ch. 126, preamble.

13. Raymond Leslie Buell, "The Development of the Anti-Japanese Agitation in the United States," in *Asian Americans and the Law: Japanese Immigrants and American Law*, ed. Charles McClain (New York: Garland Publishing, 1994), 43. (Reprinted in *Political Science Quarterly* 37 [1922], 605–83. Courtesy of Yale University Law Library.)

14. Buell, "Development of the Anti-Japanese Agitation," 42–43.

15. Bill Ong Hing, *Making and Remaking Asian America through Immigration Policy, 1850–1990* (Stanford, Calif.: Stanford University Press, 1993), 29.

16. Filipinos were still able to immigrate as nationals after the annexation of the Philippines in 1898. This eventually halted, in 1934, with the Tydings McDuffie Act that would grant the Philippines independence on July 4, 1946, when Filipinos would lose their status as nationals of the United States and become aliens not automatically eligible for citizenship.

17. Neil Gotanda, "Towards Repeal of Asian Exclusion: The Magnuson Act of 1943; The Act of July 2, 1946; The Presidential Proclamation of July 4, 1946; The Act of August 9, 1946; and The Act of August 1, 1950," in *Asian Americans and Congress: A Documentary History*. ed. Hyung-Chan Kim, (Westport, Conn: Greenwood, 1995), 310.

18. The preference system established by the Immigration Act of 1965, ranked in descending order of preference: (1) unmarried sons and daughters of U.S. citizens; (2) spouse and unmarried sons and daughters of an alien lawfully admitted for permanent residence; (3) members of the professions, and scientists and artists of exceptional ability; (4) married sons and daughters of U.S. citizens; (5) brothers and sisters of U.S. citizens; (6) skilled and unskilled workers in occupations for which labor is in short supply in the United States; (7) refugees to whom conditional entry or adjustment of status might be granted; (8) (without preference) any applicant not entitled to one of these preferences.

19. P.L. 89–236, October 3, 1965, Sect. 201(a), which states, "No person shall receive any preference or priority or be discriminated against in the issuance of an immigrant visa because of his race, sex, nationality, place of birth, or place of residence."

20. Ancheta, *Race Rights, and the Asian American Experience*, 35.

21. Charles B. Keely, "The Immigration Act of 1965," in *Asian Americans and Congress*, 531. See also Sucheng Chan, *Asian Americans: An Interpretive History* (Boston: Twayne Publishers, 1991).

22. Hing, *Making and Remaking Asian America*, 79.

23. Larry Shinagawa, "The Impact of Immigration on Demography," in *Reframing the Immigration Debate*, ed. Bill Ong Hing and Ronald Lee (Los Angeles LEAP Asian Pacific American Public Policy Institute and UCLA Asian American Studies Center, 1996), 60.

24. Paul Ong and Don Nakanishi, "Becoming Citizens, Becoming Voters" from *Asian American Politics: Law, Participation, and Policy*, ed. Don T. Nakanishi and James S. Lai (New York: Rowman and Littlefield, 2003), 114.

25. See Shinagawa, "Impact of Immigration on Demography," 87. Data source for figures is the U.S. Immigration and Naturalization Service.

26. Ong and Nakanishi, "Becoming Citizens, Becoming Voters," 115 and table 3.2a.

27. Ibid., 117.

28. Don T. Nakanishi, "Beyond Electoral Politics: Renewing a Search for a Paradigm of Asian Pacific American Politics," in *Asian Americans and Politics*, ed. Gordon H. Chang (Stanford, Calif.: Stanford University Press, 2001), 110.

29. Michael E. Fix, Jeffrey Pasel, Kenneth Sucher, "Trends in Naturalization," Urban Institute, Policy Briefs/Immigrant Families and Workers, Washington, D.C., 2003, http://www.urban.org/urlprint.cfm?ID=8580.

30. Nancy F. Rytina and Chumong Saeger, "Naturalizations in the United States: 2004," *Annual Flow Report* (Washington, D.C.: U.S. Department of Homeland Security, June 2005).

31. "Statistical Portrait of the Asian American and Pacific Islander populations produced by the US Census Bureau for Asian Pacific American Heritage Month in 2004," http://www.census.gov/Press-Release/www/releases/archives/foreignborn_population/000815.html.

32. U.S. Department of Homeland Security, United States Citizenship and Immigration Services Bureau, http://uscis.gov/graphics/services/natz/index.htm, accesssed on July 31, 2004.

33. With the prompting and input of community organizations, the N-400 was revised to make it clearer and easier for applicants to fill out.

34. Interview and observation of the Immigration Program of Catholic Charities, San Jose, California, March 25, 1997; discussions with volunteer coordinator.

35. Field notes, March 25, 1997.

36. See Tara Shioya, "Immigrants Desperately Seeking Citizenship," *SF Weekly*, February 12–18, 1997, 12–15.

37. Ibid.

38. Ibid.

39. Ibid.

40. P. C. Sheela Murthy, "Overview of the Citizenship Process and Disability Waivers," http://www.muthry.com/arc_news/a_overcp.html, posted November 20, 1999, retrieved on August 2, 2005.

41. Interview with legal assistant of the Asian Law Caucus, San Francisco, California, November 17, 1996.

42. The Asian Women's Shelter is a shelter program for abused Asian women and their children. Located in San Francisco, the shelter housed fifty-three women and their children in 1993. The Asian-Pacific Islander American Health Forum (APIAHF) is a national advocacy organization dedicated to promoting policy, program, and research efforts for the improvement of the health status of all Asian and Pacific Islander Americans. APIAHF is based in San Francisco, California, with a branch office in Washington, D.C.

43. Interview with Deeana Jang, October 21, 1996.

44. The Southeast Asian Community Center was first established in 1975 in response to refugee influx, and was originally called the Center for Southeast Asian Refugee Resettlement. As an incorporated organization since 1978, the SEACC operates through projects including language assistance and job assistance, and through business development, health education, family services, and other community services.

45. Interview with Loretta Kruger, Southeast Asian Community Center, February 24, 1997.

46. Catholic Charities USA is the nation's largest private network of independent social service agencies. The goal of Catholic Charities USA is to reduce poverty, support families, and empower communities in the United States. In California, most Catholic Charities branches have an immigration and refugee assistance program that includes advocacy, citizenship, and resettlement services.

47. Interview, Duron Le, Catholic Charities, San Raphael, March 5, 1997.

48. See U.S. Department of Justice, "Memorandum Opinion for the General Counsel, Immigration and Naturalization Service," February 5, 1997, http://www.usdoj.gov/olc/oathltr3.htm, retrieved on August 1, 2005.

49. U.S. Department of Homeland Security, Bureau of Citizenship and Immigration Services, "Procedures for Implementing the Waiving of the Oath of Renunciation and Allegiance for the Naturalization of Aliens Having Certain Disabilities," June 30, 2003.

50. Form N-400, Part 7, Immigration and Naturalization Service. This was the form that preceded the 2002 revised version. The question about Communist affiliation or support of communism still remains, although as a different segment and reading differently: Part 10, Section B, Question 9, "Have you ever been a member of or in any way associated (either directly or indirectly) with: a. The Communist Party? b. Any other totalitarian party? c. A terrorist organization?" Boxes to check yes or no follow each option.

51. Field notes, citizenship drive, San Jose, California, through the Immigration and Citizenship Program, Center for Employment Training, September 20, 1997.

52. Field notes, citizenship workshop, Asian Women's Resource Center, San Francisco, California, October 18, 1997.

53. Field notes, citizenship drive, San Jose, California, through the Immigration and Citizenship Program, Center for Employment Training, November 15, 1997.

54. Ong, *Buddha Is Hiding*, 6

55. "15a. Have you ever knowingly committed any crime for which you have not been arrested? 15b. Have you ever been arrested, cited, charged, indicted, convicted, fined or imprisoned for breaking or violating any law or ordinance, excluding traffic regulations?"

56. Edward J. W. Park and John S. W. Park, *Probationary Americans: Contemporary Immigration Policies and the Shaping of Asian American Communities* (New York: Routledge, 2005), 113.

57. See Lisa Sun-Hee Park, "Perpetuation of Poverty through 'Public Charge,'" in *Denver University Law Review* 78, no. 1161 (2001): 1161–77.

58. U.S. Department of Justice, Immigration, and Naturalization Service, fact sheet: "Public Charge," http://www.rapidimmigration.com/www/news/news_237.html, retrieved August 9, 2005.

59. Lisa Sun-Hee Park, "Perpetuation of Poverty."

60. Ibid.

61. Field notes, citizenship drive, San Jose, California, through the Immigration Program, Center for Employment Training, September 20, 1997.

62. Bert Eljera, "I Want to Vote: Older Immigrants Find It's Never Too Late for Citizenship," *Asian Week*, March 26, 1998, 13.

63. Ibid. The statistical data were provided by the San Francisco–based organization Chinese American Voters Education Committee (CAVEC).

64. Jeffrey S. Passel, "Election 2004: The Latino and Asian Vote," Urban Institute Immigration Studies Program (Washington, D.C.: Urban Institute, July 27, 2004).

65. Patrick J. McDonnell and Ken Ellingwood, "What a Difference Four Years Makes," *Los Angeles Times*, October 23, 1998, A3.

66. Mirta Ojito, "The 1998 Campaign: Immigration, Once Divisive Issue, Is Muted," *New York Times*, November 3, 1998, 33.

67. Frank Wu, "Push for Citizenship: Anti-immigrant Sentiment Has Spurred Many Groups to Naturalize Their Members—The First Step in Political Involvement," *Asian Week*, June 21–27, 1996, http://www.asianweek.com/062196/Citizenship.html.

5. On Not Making Ends Meet

1. The experience of Borey's mom presented in the epigraph of this chapter depicts the compounding factors that led to elevated sanctions among immigrant TANF recipients, and is from *Eating Welfare*, produced and directed in 2000 by the Youth Leadership Project of the Committee against Anti-Asian Violence (CAAAV), Bronx, New York. According to Gwendolyn Mink, although the Personal Responsibility Act of 1996 does terminate a sixty-year-old program, the guarantee it rescinds

has been available to poor mothers and children for only thirty years. For a more detailed discussion see Gwendolyn Mink, *Welfare's End* (Ithaca, N.Y.: Cornell University Press, 1998).

2. Leo R. Chavez, *Covering Immigration: Popular Images and the Politics of the Nation* (Berkeley and Los Angeles: University of California Press, 2001), 250.

3. Syd Lindsley, "The Gendered Assault on Immigrants," *Policing the National Body: Race, Gender, and Criminalization,* ed. Jael Silliman and Anannya Bhattacharjee (Cambridge, Mass.: South End Press, 2002), 184.

4. Chavez, *Covering Immigration,* 250.

5. P.L. 104–193, section 402(a)(ii).

6. P.L. 104–208, section 531(a)(B).

7. Ibid., section 551(a)(A).

8. See the *San Francisco Profile of Immigrants and Refugees: A Research Tool for Welfare Reform, Job Readiness, and Self-Sufficiency,* a manual produced by the Newcomer Information Clearinghouse, International Institute of the East Bay, for the San Francisco Foundation, San Francisco, California, March 1997.

9. See Michael Fix and Wendy Zimmermann, "All Under One Roof: Mixed-Status Families in an Era of Reform," *International Migration Review* 35, no. 134 (Summer 2001).

10. We do see some advocacy measures, particularly in relation to women experiencing domestic violence and subject to abuse through stringent sponsorship requirements. I discuss this in greater detail later in the chapter and in chapter 6.

11. Veronica Geronimo, "The Impact of Welfare Reform on Asians and Pacific Islanders," Asian Pacific American Legal Center of Southern California, Los Angeles, California, September 2001.

12. The welfare law defines work activities as: unsubsidized employment; subsidized private and public sector employment; work experience; on-the-job training; job search and job readiness assistance; community service programs; vocational educational training (not to exceed twelve months for any individual); job skills training directly related to employment; education directly related to employment; satisfactory attendance at secondary school or in a course of study leading to a certificate of general equivalence, for those who have not yet completed secondary school or received secondary certification; the provision of child care services to an individual participating in a community service program. See P.L. 104–193, Title I, section 407(d)(1)–(12).

13. In general, solo caretakers must work a minimum of twenty hours per week if mandatory work requirement began in 1998, twenty-five hours per week if work requirement began in 1999, and thirty hours per week if work requirement began in the year 2000 or thereafter.

14. Early reports on Wisconsin's welfare-to-work program, by the Women and Poverty Public Education Initiative, tell of traumatic and in some cases fatal consequences because women had to leave their children in the supervision of irrespon-

sible adults or had to leave their children, especially those over six years of age, alone. See "Welfare: 'Reform' in Wisconsin," May 29, 1998, newsgroups: misc.activism. progressive.

15. Kenneth J. Neubeck and Noel A. Cazenave, *Welfare Racism: Playing the Race Card against America's Poor* (New York: Routledge, 2001), 182.

16. P.L. 104–193, Title I, section 408(a)(7).

17. However, immigrants with new affidavits of support are subject to the new federal deeming rules, with exceptions for immigrants who would go hungry or homeless without assistance, and for victims of domestic violence.

18. California Department of Social Services, State Implementation Guidelines, "California Work Opportunity and Responsibility to Kids (CalWORKs), Implementation of the Welfare-to-Work Provisions."

19. In San Francisco, the ethnic immigrant breakdown of 1996 AFDC recipients revealed that 30.9 percent immigrated from China and 33.9 percent from Southeast Asia. Of immigrant households receiving AFDC in 1996, 45.9 percent were single-parent families, and 54.5 percent were female-headed. In December 1997, in Santa Clara County, 36.6 percent of AFDC recipients were Asian/Pacific Islander, primarily from Southeast Asia (28.2 percent Vietnamese, 3.8 percent Cambodian, 1.2 percent Chinese, 1.1 percent Filipino, 1.3 percent Pacific Islander, 0.6 percent Laotian, 0.6 percent Korean, 0.1 percent Japanese). Of single-parent families enrolled in CalWORKs in Santa Clara County, 20 percent are A/PI recipients.

20. These sixteen countries from which immigrants to California were identified as the largest and neediest in relation to CalWORKs were Bosnia-Herzegovina, Cambodia, El Salvador, Ethiopia, India, Iran, Laos, Mexico, Nicaragua, People's Republic of China, Philippines, Russia, Somalia, South Korea, Taiwan, and Vietnam. According to the 2000 census, Santa Clara County was a *majority minority* county with more of the populace being Asian and Latina/o immigrants than belonging to any other group: 44 percent are non-Hispanic white, 26 percent are Asian, 24 percent are Latino, 3 percent are African American, and 3 percent are of two or more races. This data is from *KIN: Knowledge of Immigrant Nationalities in Santa Clara County,* a publication of the Immigrant Action Network, Office of Human Relations of Santa Clara County, September 12, 2001.

21. Response from SSA staff presented at the June 24, 1998, CalWORKs Implementation Advisory Committee Meeting, San Jose, California.

22. Field notes: report from the Santa Clara CalWORKs Implementation Committee, June 24, 1998.

23. Field notes: report from BOSS at the roundtable on the state of "welfare reform" and its effects on the Asian-Pacific Islander community, San Francisco, California, July 7, 1998.

24. Field notes: Immigration Task Force, input on draft of CalWORKs Plan, November 6, 1997.

25. Statement from Bridging Borders in Silicon Valley, Summit on Immigrant

Needs and Contributions: An Action Plan for Immigrants in Santa Clara County, December 6, 2000.

26. Number of AFDC households with adults likely to face time limits, 656,126; number of unemployed persons not receiving public assistance, 1,002,318; employable general assistance recipients, 89,101; college graduates, 105,226; public high school graduates, 272,854; underemployed but not unemployed individuals, 1,009,329. See California Budget Project, "Are There Enough Jobs for All Those Who Must Work?" budget brief, May 1997.

27. California Budget Project, "Are There Enough Jobs?"

28. Ibid.

29. Ibid.

30. Ibid.

31. Shawn Fremstad, "Immigrants and Welfare Reauthorization" (Washington, D.C.: Center on Budget and Policy Priorities, February 4, 2002), 11.

32. Pseudonyms are used for all client profiles.

33. Jason B. Johnson and Edward Epstein, "Anger over S.F. Welfare Cuts," *San Francisco Chronicle,* Tuesday, April 21, 1998, A1.

34. Randy Capps, "Hardship among Children of Immigrants: Findings from the 1999 National Survey of America's Families," *New Federalism,* Series B, no. B-29 (Washington, D.C.: Urban Institute, February 2001), 3.

35. Ibid., 4.

36. Field notes: Immigration Task Force, Input November 6, 1997.

37. Doris Y. Ng, *From War on Poverty to War on Welfare: The Impact of Welfare Reform on the Lives of Immigrant Women* (San Francisco, Calif.: Equal Rights Advocates, 1999). Equal Rights Advocates was founded in 1974 as an organization dedicated to "ending discrimination against women and girls through litigation, legislative advocacy, public education, and advice and counseling."

38. Ibid., 18.

39. Ibid., 19

40. Interview with Gloria Tan, executive director of the Asian Women's Resource Center, San Francisco, California, October 1997.

6. The Devaluation of Immigrant Families

1. Shawn Fremstad, "Immigrants and Welfare Reauthorization" (Washington, D.C.: Center on Budget and Policy Priorities, February 4, 2002).

2. Randy Capps, "Hardship among Children of Immigrants: Findings from the 1999 National Survey of America's Families," *New Federalism,* Series B, No. B-29 (Washington, D.C.: Urban Institute, February 2001).

3. Janice Peterson, "Feminist Perspectives on TANF Reauthorization: An Introduction to Key Issues for the Future of Welfare Reform," briefing paper no. E511 (Washington, D.C.: Institute for Women's Policy Research, February 2002).

4. Deeana Jang and Luella J. Penserga, "Beyond the Safety Net: The Effect of Welfare Reform on the Self-Sufficiency of Asian and Pacific Islander Women

in California" (San Francisco, Calif.: Asian and Pacific Islander American Health Forum, June 1999), 1–8.

5. P.L. 104–193, Section 407(2)(A,B,C).

6. Interview, Gloria Tan, Asian Women's Resource Center, San Francisco, California, October 1997.

7. Peterson, "Feminist Perspectives on TANF Reauthorization," 9.

8. Deeana Jang, Asian Pacific American Health Forum, presentation at the San Francisco conference "Impact of Welfare Reform on Immigrants' Training," April 22, 1998.

9. Jang and Penserga, "Beyond the Safety Net," 4.

10. Leni Marin, "Identifying Battered Immigrant Women," in *Domestic Violence in Immigrant and Refugee Communities: Asserting the Rights of Battered Women,* ed. Deeana Jang, Leni Marin, and Gail Pendleton (San Francisco, Calif.: Family Violence Prevention Fund, 1997).

11. Telephone interview with Meising of the Asian Women's Shelter in San Francisco, California, October 21, 1996.

12. Interview with Grace Nakamura, Legal Aid Society of San Mateo County, California, October 24, 1996.

13. P.L. 104–208, Section 552(f)(1).

14. Field notes: Jang presentation, April 22, 1998.

15. Demie Kurz, "Women, Welfare, and Domestic Violence," *Social Justice* 25, no. 1 (Spring 1998).

16. Dong Suh, MPP, and Luella Penserga, "Riding the Waves of Change: Improving the Health of Asian and Pacific Islander Women under Medi-Cal Managed Care Expansion," policy report, Asian and Pacific Islander American Health Forum, San Francisco, California, December 1996.

17. Field notes: CalWORKs Community Health Alliance, presentation at the CalWORKs Implementation Advisory Committee, June 24, 1998; final draft of the report, July 7, 1998.

18. Ibid., presentation.

19. Rex S. Green, Lynn Fujiwara, et al., "Alameda County CalWORKs Needs Assessment: Barriers to Working and Summaries of Baseline Status," submitted to Social Services Agency and Department of Behavioral Health Care Services, County of Alameda, February 10, 2000, p. 8. Research conducted through the Public Health Institute, Berkeley, California.

20. Ibid., 6.

21. The Balanced Budget Act of 1997 reversed $11.4 billion of immigrant benefits stripped away by the 1996 welfare reform law. The 1997 bill restored SSI to individuals receiving SSI benefits on August 22, 1996; immigrants lawfully residing in the United States as of that date who were then or should later become disabled would be eligible for Medicaid and SSI benefits.

22. Under the Balanced Budget Act of 1997, Congress allocated $24 billion (over a period of five years) to the states to provide health care to low-income uninsured

children whose families did not qualify for Medicaid. States could elect to expand their Medicaid programs, create new programs, or both. California created the Healthy Families Program.

23. Suh and Penserga, "Riding the Waves of Change," 3.

24. Interview with Luella Penserga, October 28, 1997.

25. Suh and Penserga, "Riding the Waves of Change," 5.

26. Ibid., 2.

27. Ibid., 8.

28. Dong Suh, "The End of Health Care for Immigrants?" report, Asian Pacific Islander American Health Forum, San Francisco, California, June 1996.

29. Ibid., 6.

30. Ibid., 6.

31. Mae M. Cheng, "Immigrants Avoiding Health Care," *Newsday*, New York, May 9, 1997.

32. Ibid.

33. Suh, "End of Health Care for Immigrants?"

34. Capps, "Hardship among Children of Immigrants," 4.

35. Ibid., 4–5.

36. Fremstad, "Immigrants and Welfare Reauthorization."

37. See Lynn Fujiwara, "Mothers without Citizenship: Asian Immigrants and Refugees Negotiate Poverty and Hunger in Post–Welfare Reform," *Race, Gender, and Class* 12, no. 2, for a more detailed examination of hunger and food stamp cuts among Asian immigrant families.

38. "Healthy Solutions for America's Hardworking Families," briefing paper, National Immigration Law Center, Washington, D.C., March 20, 2001.

39. M. E. Fix and J. Passel, *The Scope and Impact of Welfare Reform's Immigrant Provisions*, New Federalism Series, Discussion Papers (Washington, D.C.: Urban Institute, 2002).

40. A household is food insecure if it reports cutting back on the size of meals or skipping meals due to lack of income, or reducing food intake to such an extent that members experience hunger.

41. J. L. Tujague and L. True, "The Impact of Legal Immigrant Food Stamp Cuts in Los Angeles and San Francisco," preliminary summary, by the California Food Security Monitoring Project (San Francisco, Calif.: California Food Policy Advocates, 1998).

42. Ibid.

43. Capps. "Hardship among Children of Immigrants," 3.

44. Capps et al., "How Are Immigrants Fairing after Welfare Reform? Preliminary Evidence from Los Angeles and New York City," final report (Washington, D.C.: Urban Institute 2002), 34.

45. Doris Ng, *From War on Poverty to War on Welfare*, 13.

46. *San Jose Mercury News*, "Making Welfare Work," special series, April 6, 1997–December 7, 1997.

47. Joanne Jacobs et al., "Update: How They're Doing," *San Jose Mercury News*, July 27, 1997, 11.

48. Bert Elijera, "Food Banks Attempt to Fill Gap," *Asian Week*, December 11–17, 1997, 14.

49. Field notes: Food Pantry visit, February 27, 1998.

50. J. T. Cook, "The Food Stamp Program and Low-Income Legal Immigrants," *Nutrition Reviews* 56, no. 7, 1995: 219.

51. Food Stamps Act of 1977, as amended. SEC. 2. (7U.S.C. 2011). Available at http://www.fns.usda.gov/fsp/LEGISLATION/fsa77.pdf.

52. Cook, "Food Stamp Program and Low-Income Legal Immigrants," 220.

53. Fremstad, "Immigrants and Welfare Reauthorization."

Conclusion

1. Avery Gordon, *Ghostly Matters: Haunting and the Sociological Imagination* (Minneapolis: University of Minnesota Press, 1997).

2. Gwendolyn Mink, "Aren't Poor Single Mothers Women? Feminists, Welfare Reform, and Welfare Justice," in *Whose Welfare?* (Ithaca, N.Y.: Cornell University Press, 1999).

3. Jason DeParle, "What Welfare-to-Work Really Means," *New York Times Magazine*, December 20, 1998.

4. Statement made by then-president Ronald Reagan, http://www.brainyquote.com/quotes/authors/r/ronald_reagan.html.

5. Nira Yuval-Davis, "The 'Multi-Layered Citizen' Citizenship in the Age of 'Globalization,'" *International Feminist Journal of Politics* 1, no. 1 (June 1999): 122.

6. Pnina Werbner and Nira Yuval-Davis, "Women and the New Discourse of Citizenship," in *Women, Citizenship, and Difference*, ed. Nira Yuval-Davis and Pnina Werbner (London: Zed Books, 1999), 10.

7. Ibid.

8. Mai Ngai, *Impossible Subjects: Illegal Aliens and the Making of Modern America* (Princeton, N.J.: Princeton University Press, 2004).

9. George Lipsitz, *The Possessive Investment in Whiteness: How White People Profit from Identity Politics* (Philadelphia: Temple University Press, 1998), 74.

10. Ibid., 80.

11. Ibid., 70; here, Lipsitz is citing Mark Potter, "San Diego: City of Shame," in *San Diego Reader* 25, no. 32 (August 8, 1996): 96.

12. Book by Minuteman founder and "Unfit for Command" author to target illegal immigration, February 22, 2006, http://www.minutemanproject.com/.

13. Ibid.

14. "1 Million March for Immigrants across U.S.," MSNBC.com, http://www.msnbc.msn.com/id/12573992/, retrieved September 25, 2006.

15. George W. Bush, television address to the nation on immigration reform, May 15, 2006.

Index

Lynn Fujiwara is assistant professor in the Program of Women's and Gender Studies and the Department of Sociology at the University of Oregon.

Made in the USA
San Bernardino, CA
02 February 2020